Making a go of it

Making a go of it

A study of stepfamilies in Sheffield

Jacqueline Burgoyne
Sheffield City Polytechnic

David Clark
MRC Medical Sociology Unit
Aberdeen

Routledge & Kegan Paul
London, Boston, Melbourne and Henley

First published in 1984
by Routledge & Kegan Paul plc

14 Leicester Square, London WC2H 7PH, England

9 Park Street, Boston, Mass. 02108, USA

464 St Kilda Road, Melbourne,
Victoria 3004, Australia and

Broadway House, Newtown Road,
Henley-on-Thames, Oxon RG9 1EN, England

Photoset in 10 on 11 Times Roman
by Kelly Typesetting Ltd, Bradford-on-Avon, Wiltshire
and printed in Great Britain
by St Edmundsbury Press Ltd
Bury St Edmunds, Suffolk

Library of Congress Cataloging in Publication Data

Burgoyne, Jacqueline L. (Jacqueline Lesley), 1944–

Making a go of it.
Bibliography: p.
Includes index.
1. Remarriage—England—Sheffield (South Yorkshire)—
Case studies. 2. Stepparents—England—Sheffield
(South Yorkshire)—Case studies. 3. Parents—England—
Sheffield (South Yorkshire)—Case studies. 4. Children
—England—Sheffield (South Yorkshire)—Case studies.
I. Clark, David, 1953–   . II. Title.
HQ616.B87   1984   306.8'4   84–6801

British Library CIP data also available

ISBN 0–7102–0318–7

Contents

Preface

In this book we present the principal findings from a study of forty remarried couples carried out in Sheffield between 1976 and 1979. As we have been writing we have had a number of different audiences in mind, so that the chapters which follow include not only a description of how the project evolved and a detailed presentation of our findings, but also a more general discussion of remarriage as a social institution and some of the main theoretical and methodological issues which bear upon the study of family and domestic life.

The couples in our study gave up a great deal of time to talk to David Clark and to answer his questions. On occasion some of them admitted to having benefited from the opportunity to talk freely about the particular circumstances of their family lives, but for the most part their principal reason for taking part in the study was a desire to help others in a similar position. We have tried to honour that commitment by writing a book which we hope will be interesting and accessible to remarried couples themselves as well as to members of those occupations who have a 'professional' interest in families of all kinds, and to present our findings in a way which allows those who took part to 'speak for themselves'. As a result the first versions of this book were, from a publisher's point of view, impossibly long; several edits later we trust their voices can still be heard. In the meantime several articles on specific aspects of the study have been published in various books and journals and JB has also written a short 'self-help' book on the problems of separation and divorce entitled *Breaking Even: Divorce, Your Children and You* (Penguin, April 1984) which draws upon this study in several places.

As we hope to demonstrate, the beliefs and professional decisions of judges, magistrates and lawyers, social workers, counsellors and doctors and, on occasion, teachers and clergymen greatly affected the couples in our study, both through their specific determination of some aspect of their domestic life and family identity as well as through their influential contributions to the climate of public opinion about remarriage and steprelationships generally. As we suggest in the first chapter the findings of social scientists are frequently referred to in the training of members of such occupations and must, therefore, have some sort of effect on their understanding of family relationships, including those created by a remarriage. We hope that this book will be widely read by such practitioners.

The first two chapters, which deal with the frameworks and perspectives on remarriage which informed our work and a description of how the research itself was carried out, offer a background to our findings so that some readers may prefer to go straight to chapters 3 to 6 in which our findings are presented. Discussion of the study couples as a 'sample' and their likeness to the remarried population as a whole may be found in chapter 2 (pp. 28–53). Appendix 1 contains a life history for each of the couples who took part in the study. These were compiled after the interviews were completed; each couple chose a pseudonym and checked and approved the content of their life history. Wherever we have used quotations from interviews in the text we have tried to present them in a way which makes them immediately intelligible but because of the complications endemic to remarriage, readers may find it helpful to refer to these for further details about the individual involved. An impression of the diversity of history, circumstances and experiences of the couples in the study may be gained simply by reading straight through these life histories. The difficulties we have had in analysing and presenting our material, and which have made the inclusion of the life histories so important, point very clearly to the paradox at the heart of any personal, professional or academic understanding of contemporary family life. Our appreciation of an individual's sense of their home, family and intimate relationships as unique must be matched with an ability to perceive similarities and trends in patterns of family life, and to recognise the institutions and structures of power in industrial societies which shape what we designate as our 'personal' life.

There are two groups of people without whom this study would, literally, not have taken place. First we would like to take this opportunity of placing on record our thanks to all those who took part in the study. We have no adequate way of expressing our gratitude to them for their generosity and trust; in a very real sense this book is *for* them and for the unnumbered others who find themselves in similar circumstances. We would also like to thank

Sheffield City Polytechnic, especially the former Deputy Principal, Mr Douglas Thacker, for considering this project worth supporting in the first place, as well as the Social Science Research Council whose grant facilitated its completion.

We are particularly grateful to a number of colleagues with whom we have discussed our work over the years. Robert Chester of Hull University gave us a good deal of advice and encouragement in its early stages and throughout we have benefited from the comments and criticisms of contributers to the Chelsea College Seminar on divorce and remarriage and the National Marriage Guidance Council's Research Seminars.

Diana Cosham and Barbara Cleaver, who typed the interviews for us, deserve recognition as an indispensable part of the research team. This was, at times, a very difficult and trying task and we realised that they made our work infinitely easier because of the very high standards they set themselves. We should also like to thank Diana, Barbara, Mies Rule, Lorraine Gibb and Brenda Chatterton for typing various parts of this manuscript. Mrs Margaret Foster, who looked after inter-library loans at the Collegiate Crescent Library of Sheffield City Polytechnic, dealt with our requests for obscure material tolerantly and successfully.

In a different sphere we would both like to thank Diane Clark for sharing so fully in our preoccupations as we worked together on this study and, in particular, for her support to David whilst he was interviewing. JB would also like to thank David Hills for encouraging her to undertake this research in the first place; her sister, Alison Jefferson, and her colleagues, Eileen Green and Rob Sykes, for their supportive friendship over many years.

What we fervently hope will be the final version of this book has been prepared in the months immediately following the launching of a British Stepfamily Association. For reasons which will become obvious as you read this book, we wish it well.

Chapter 1

The theory and practice of remarriage

'The triumph of hope over experience' was how Dr Johnson described the swift remarriage of a widower who had been unhappy with his first wife. The judgment may be less than charitable, yet it is one which touches on the experience of that increasing number of women and men who encounter more than one marriage in a lifetime, for recent high rates of divorce have by no means dampened enthusiasm for matrimony, though they may have profound effects upon what we understand by both the personal relationships and the institution of marriage. The experience of remarriage, seen not only at an individual level but also within the context of the broader structures which shape it, forms the subject matter of this book. Through it we seek to go beyond divorce and remarriage as a public issue in order to say something about modern family life in general. For remarriage constitutes a *sociological* as well as a *social* problem and accordingly its study elicits questions of both theory and practice.

Examination of the relationship between personal experience and the public, institutional structures of contemporary societies is an essential concern for sociology. C. Wright Mills (1967) makes the point abundantly clear in his famous distinction between the 'personal troubles of milieu' and 'the public issues of social structure'. For Mills such a dichotomy is at the heart of the sociological imagination, based as it is upon the contention that troubles are transformed into issues when 'some value cherished by publics is felt to be threatened' and when the private trouble is reformulated in terms of its consequences for the political and decision-making sphere. Public issues, then, have no reality *sui generis*, but become such as a result of redefinition of the situation whereby the problem is designated a matter of public, political concern. Mills includes marriage and divorce as one of his examples of how this transformation takes place:

> Consider marriage. Inside a marriage a man and a woman may experience personal troubles, but when the divorce rate during the first four years of marriage is 250 out of every 1,000 attempts, this is an indication of a structural issue having to do with the institutions of marriage and the family and other institutions that bear upon them. (op. cit., p. 9)

Thus marriage breakdown and divorce become public issues partly because large numbers of individuals are involved and also because the numbers involved imply a threat to the 'cherished values' associated with life-long marriage and monogamy. Recognising that remarriage also has both personal and public dimensions, Mills's distinction represents for us a way of structuring our preliminary discussion of remarriage and its social consequences.[1] Such discussion must, however, also include consideration of the changes taking place in patterns of marriage, family and personal life generally, for as Bernard has argued in her own study of remarriage in the United States,

> although the marriages here described are remarriages and the families involved are the families of *re*marriage, almost every problem that the family of the first marriage has to meet must also be met by these families. . . . All that we know about marriage and the family in general, therefore, is pertinent to an understanding of the men and women and children (in stepfamilies). (Bernard, 1971, p. 3)

By the same token, 'the study of remarriage illuminates both substantively and theoretically the nature of marriage and family life in general' (ibid.).

Family life as a private matter

In contemporary industrial societies such as our own we take for granted that family troubles are essentially personal matters for which individuals must accept responsibility, and, on occasion, take the blame. By the same token domestic life based upon membership of a family/household is widely regarded as one of the most important sources of individual satisfaction and fulfilment whose benefits are sharply contrasted with the public worlds of politics, work and bureaucratically organised urban life.

If the external, public world of work necessarily involves the strain and conflict of obeying orders, acting out roles and few opportunities for autonomy and self-expression, the fiercely protected privacy of domestic life provides, by contrast, a haven or retreat in which the 'real self' is renewed and strengthened. Thus the family life of others, even that of kin and neighbours who live in close proximity, frequently remains largely unknown and mysterious to outsiders unless its privacy and autonomy is threatened by some internal or external crisis. The fact that the everyday occurrences of family life remain largely inaccessible to curious outsiders has important implications for the researcher, which will be discussed in chapter 2, but it is also important to consider both the origins of beliefs about the family as a private sphere and the extent to which family life, in fact, enjoys such autonomy and insulation from public intervention and control.

Writers of many different views and perspectives all tend to agree that contemporary conceptions of the family and domestic life as 'an emotional refuge in a cold and competitive society' (Lasch, 1977, p. 6) have their origins in the social and economic changes of the Industrial Revolution, particularly the separation of home and work and thus private and public life.

Such changes in patterns of family life in the nineteenth century have been widely documented (for example, Anderson, 1971; Sennett, 1977; Laslett, 1977; Banks, 1956 and Hobsbawm, 1977). The distinctive characteristics of Victorian upper-middle-class family life, with its emphasis on the privacy and separation of family life, are best understood in the wider context of Victorian bourgeois perceptions of their new industrial world. To be sure set pieces like the Great Exhibition of 1851 demonstrated pride in industry and its achievements, but this was matched by a fear of some of the consequences of such a creation. The great cities, with their poverty, crime and political unrest, were stark reminders of the dark side of the industrial world so that, for the bourgeoisie at least, home and family life came to provide a refuge and escape. This retreat into domesticity particularly affected women and children as changes in dominant ideologies dictated that because of their innocence and vulnerability they should be increasingly closely protected and shielded from potential danger. Men, by contrast, had to take their chance amidst the dangers and temptations of the world beyond the family which offered many opportunities for the infringement of the strict sexual codes of morality which buttressed a family unit based on life-long monogamy. As the privacy of family life increased, those public appearances in which the social rank and respectability of the family as whole could be confirmed and displayed became more significant. Banks's study of Victorian middle-class lifestyles and patterns of expenditure demonstrates clearly how the expansion of the middle classes in the nineteenth century was accompanied by the development of characteristically bourgeois patterns of domestic expenditure and consumption (Banks, 1956). The ownership and display of appropriate symbols of prosperity, achieved through dedication to a work ethic which emphasised diligence, thrift and self-denial were important ways of demonstrating respectability. Because of adherence to such values of thrift and self-denial, the problem for the middle classes became one of how to spend their wealth in socially approved ways. This was resolved by concentrating consumption within the home and family circle, so that whilst gambling and 'riotous living' were frowned upon, domestic expenditure on the home itself, servants, entertainment and clothing was an important source of prestige and a legitimate area of public display. As Hobsbawm has suggested (Hobsbawm, 1977, p. 271) material goods and commodities provided the cues necessary to 'place' a man and his family in an age of unprecedented social change, social mobility and alterations in patterns of consumption. The material objects of this bourgeois world were used to confer prestige and social approval, so that public status and identity became entwined with certain approved patterns of domestic consumption and the exemplary performance of prescribed family roles. As a result beliefs in the importance of particular patterns of family life gained increased currency and became an integral part of the dominant ideas of the age. On a limited scale, members of the lower middle class consciously attempted to emulate the domestic ambience and family commitments of their superiors. Furthermore, aspects of bourgeois family morality were also pressed upon the working class and the poor through school and church teaching as well as the activities of both private philanthropists and the growing army of officials who began to be involved in the organisation and control of the family life of the masses. By the beginning of the twentieth century a distinctive public morality had established itself which emphasised the importance of a stable family life for both personal welfare and the public good. Yet whilst the personal and individual benefits of family membership accrued from the apparent privacy and autonomy of the domestic unit, at the same time an increasing range of 'experts' and practitioners began to stake their claim in this allegedly private sphere, especially in relation to the well-being of children.

Writers of widely divergent theoretical and political perspectives have described contemporary family life in terms of its increased *privatisation*. Whilst their assumptions and explanations differ, they point to a decline in the significance of wider kin and neighbourhood networks and an apparent retreat into home-based domesticity. Three versions of this process of privatisation are summarised below with the intention of highlighting those features which cast most light on the way in which the boundary between the 'public' and 'private' spheres should be defined and understood in our present and more specific consideration of contemporary patterns of remarriage.

Changes in structure and function and the emergence of the isolated nuclear family

One of the most well-known theoretical contributions to sociological discussion of the changing structure and function of the family was made by Talcott Parsons and, as both Morgan and Rosenbaum have pointed out, his writing has continued to exercise a profound influence on the study of the family, even though his more general works have been widely and justly criticised (Morgan, 1975, pp. 25 ff; Rosenbaum, 1978, pp. 74 ff.). Functionalist perspectives based on Parsons's work are still presented as self-evident propositions in much family sociology and continue to provide a framework for the kind of public and political discussions of family life which emphasise the benefits to society as a whole of conventional family beliefs and structures.

Writing in response to a variety of analyses suggesting that industrialisation had brought about a decline in the significance of the family, Parsons argued that changes in family structure, particularly the isolation of the conjugal family from the wider kin network, were an important concomitant of the process of modernisation. The structural differentiation of contemporary society thus removed some of the family's functions to more specialised agencies, for example, education to schools and health care to specialised medicine. But at the same time the family itself became '*a more specialised agency than before*, probably more specialised than it has been in any previously known society' (Parsons and Bales, 1955, p. 9). As a result, Parsons argues, society becomes *more* dependent on the family for the performance of those specialised functions designated to it. These are:

> first, the primary socialisation of children so that they can truly become members of the society into which they are born; second, the stabilisation of the adult personalities of the population of the society. (ibid., p. 16)

Thus, as changes in structure make the nuclear family an increasingly specialised agency, families become ' "factories" which produce human personalities' (ibid, p. 16). Furthermore, a decline in family size, the increasing normality of households limited to two generations, and a relative lack of contact with the wider kin network each contribute to the efficiency of such family production. The small, isolated family group is also able to concentrate its energies and resources upon its children. For its adult members, on the other hand, it is a source of personality stabilisation through the creation of a 'sharp discrimination in status . . . between family members and non-members' (ibid., p. 20).

As a result writers and researchers who employ, albeit implicitly, a Parsonian view of the family make a clear distinction between functional and dysfunctional family structures. Conventional family units which act as an effective socialising agency for children as well as emotional fulfilment and stability for its adult members appear to enjoy considerable privacy and autonomy in order to get on with their job effectively. By contrast 'problem' families of all kinds, as well as other deviant groups or individuals, elicit much greater public curiosity and scrutiny from policy-makers, welfare practitioners and even, on occasion, researchers like ourselves.

Privatisation and changes in class structure: the family and the embourgeoisement thesis

Discussion of post-war changes in the British and American class structure has focused in the main on the political consequences of transformations in working-class lifestyles. References to the increasing affluence, instrumental work orientations and altered political consciousness of the 'new working class' of affluent workers have therefore been accompanied by descriptions of considerable changes in family life and in patterns of domestic consumption (Klein, 1965). In an important paper which stimulated a number of empirical studies Lockwood described the 'privatised worker' as one who derives little or no satisfaction from his work and for whom work 'is socially isolating, and to a large extent socially meaningless; a situation in which the dominant relationship is the cash nexus' (Lockwood, 1975, p. 22). He argues that post-war experiences of housing and residential mobility reinforced certain aspects of the work experience of this group. In their later, classic study of affluent workers in Luton, Goldthorpe *et al.* found that the men in their sample who had dependent children and thus bore heavy financial burdens as husbands and fathers were most likely to have instrumental attitudes to work. Work was therefore perceived primarily in terms of a set of goals external to it but whose attainment was only economically possible through the form of labour they had adopted (Goldthorpe *et al.*, 1969, p. 147). By contrast, family life was regarded as 'a major source of expressive and affective satisfactions' contrasting sharply with the world of work (ibid.,

p. 149). The authors concluded that in the future there would be 'mounting inducements to relegate work to the level of merely instrumental activity and to seek employment which offers a high economic return' (ibid., p. 174). Moreover, as the manual worker became more 'family-centred' expectations of him as husband, father and bread-winner were intensified:

> To the extent that his out-of-work life becomes dominated by home and family concerns, the link between this and the worker's occupational life is likely to be narrowed to one of a largely economic kind. In other words, a privatised social life and an instrumental orientation to work may in this way be seen as mutually supportive aspects of a particular life-style. (ibid., p. 175).

This particular version of the privatisation thesis stresses critical connections between economic structures of both production and consumption and the retreat of the working class, led by its most affluent members, into a private family-based domestic life, which despite certain innovatory and prototypical characteristics was hitherto more typical of the middle class.

Marriage, personal life and the growth of modern consciousness

The problem of the personal and social consequences of industrialisation has been a major preoccupation of sociology from its earliest beginnings and many writers have included a specific consideration of its effects upon patterns of family life. As part of a much broader concern with the forms of consciousness which are associated with modernisation, Berger and Kellner argue that marriage has become the relationship in which *par excellence* adults learn to make sense of the social worlds they inhabit. Their well-known argument, based on an earlier theoretical treatise by Berger and Luckmann (1971) is that modernisation, defined as 'the institutional concomitants of technologically produced growth' (Berger and Kellner, 1974, p. 15) has been accompanied by fundamental changes in consciousness, affecting the individual's experience of everyday life. For example, they point to the web of meanings attached to every detail and aspect of everyday life through which men and women make sense of and negotiate their daily routines. Where such meanings are shared by a group of individuals they can be said to occupy the same 'life-world'. The highly developed division of labour within modern society, however, makes for not one, but a plurality of life-worlds; each has its own routines, patterns and symbols of interaction. Consequently, life may be experienced as atomised and segmented. Perhaps the most significant aspect of this is the division between public and private spheres. Thus urban consciousness, which, because of mass media, education and so on, is not confined to those who actually live in large cities, is essentially pluralistic. The individual is thereby presented with a range of options – in beliefs, values, lifestyles – from which he or she may choose according to preference. Such a wide variety of possible identities and careers encourages the individual to expect, or possibly fear, personal changes in the future which will necessitate coming to terms with new life-worlds. Within this tapestry of past and anticipated change, individual identity and biography run as a constant, integrating thread. In consequence, Berger and Kellner argue, identity in the modern world is peculiarly 'open' or 'unfinished'.

> Biography is . . . apprehended both as a migration through different social worlds and as the successive realisation of a number of possible identities. . . . This open ended quality of modern identity engenders psychological strains and makes the individual peculiarly vulnerable to shifting definitions of himself by others. (Ibid., p. 73)

A 'permanent identity crisis' (ibid., p. 74) thus pervades modern consciousness wherein considerable emphasis is placed upon the notion of the individual as the author of his or her own destiny.

Berger and Kellner argue that much of this process of identity creation takes place within the private sphere, which is 'more and more segregated from the immediate control of public institutions (especially the economic and political ones) and yet defined and utilised as the main social area for the individual's self-realisation' (ibid., p. 31). Most central of all is the married partnership, which has become the vital context within which individual identity can be understood and negotiated. They illustrate this through the examples of courtship and the period of early marriage, where, in conversations, accounts of past biographies, exchanges of opinions and – especially – planning for the future, the new couple arrived at shared distinctions and understandings. A joint life-world is thereby created which will enable them to make sense of everyday life, both within and beyond the private sphere itself.

For Berger and Kellner the privatisation of family life, which is the focus of so much emotional and psychological investment for the individual, is the result of a process of modernisation in which, 'Public institutions now confront the individual as an immensely powerful and alien world, incomprehensible in its inner workings, anonymous in its human character' (ibid., p. 32). By contrast, the private sphere of the family and personal relationships offers the individual 'power, intelligibility, and, literally, a name, the apparent power to fashion a world . . . that will reflect his own being'. Accordingly, when the stakes are so high, individuals have 'no tolerance for a less than completely successful marital arrangement' (ibid., p. 46).

All three accounts focus on the apparent separation of domestic, family and personal life from the public sphere of the economy, politics and the state. Whilst the functionalist version implies that this privacy and autonomy is both functionally desirable and has some basis in reality, the other two versions, although primarily concerned with the personal and public effects of such beliefs, treat the notion of an independent, autonomous 'private sphere' as inherently problematic. This issue is of considerable contemporary political significance. The more persuasively it is argued that 'the family' is different from other areas of life and should, wherever possible, be protected from state intervention of any kind, the more the economic leader, or 'head', of the family, stereotypically the husband/father, is encouraged to care and provide for 'his own' by making individual arrangements for housing, health care, education, insurance and pensions for his family within the significantly named 'private sector'. Thus the belief that the family is, or ought to be protected as a private arena insulated where possible from state intervention has political as well as personal implications. Consequently descriptions and analyses of the family in the literature of the social sciences which consciously stress, or even tacitly imply, the autonomy of the family unit in contemporary society may serve, through their subsequent popularisation, to legitimate further a particular ideological view of family life. In addition, as Brittan (1977) has suggested, where there is a strong commitment to the view that the family is the basic, central institution of modern society and that problems in other spheres, e.g. juvenile delinquency, school achievement, attitudes to work and employment, have their origins in the family, then solutions to social problems will be limited to intervention in the lives of those families who are obviously at fault or in trouble (Brittan, 1977, p. 71). Thus 'the family' or, more specifically, particular kinds of families, are frequently designated as a source of widespread problems for political and ideological reasons and an association is made between the state of 'the family' and the nation's moral and economic health.

Clearly those writers who have associated the growth in privatised lifestyles with changes in class structure and orientations towards work recognise the critical interdependence between public and private spheres. The construction and daily organisation of a private domestic family life in which the worker can 'be himself' depends upon his income and position in the housing market and is much affected by both the context and timetable of his working life. Thus, as Goldthorpe and Lockwood's analysis shows, in subtle and complex ways, the privatised lifestyles of affluent workers remain clearly distinguishable from their non-manual counterparts. Such analyses draw our attention, therefore, to the continuing effects of class inequalities on family and personal life.

By contrast, although Berger and Kellner acknowledge the interrelationship between the public world of institutions and the private sphere of personal life, referring to a 'dialectical relationship between . . . what is experienced as outside reality (the world of institutions etc.) and what is experienced as being within the consciousness of the individual' (op. cit., p. 32), most of their analysis seems to be focused on subjective meanings and Brittan's criticisms of their general propositions apply equally well to their specific discussion of marriage. Their construction of an ideal-typical married relationship based on the American middle classes therefore precludes consideration of how social inequalities based on either social classes or gender differences affect opportunities, expectations and the subjective meanings which individuals attach to their own lives and futures. If a sense of individuality, autonomy and freedom is based upon being able to choose and negotiate alternative biographies, then white Anglo-Saxon, male college graduates clearly have many more alternatives outside the realms of pure fantasy than black, female educational failures. The most obvious defects in their analysis of marriage occur where they entirely ignore the effects which macro-structures have on everyday experiences of married life, and more specifically, the ways in which structural factors determine how the expectations and experiences of men and women will differ in marriage. Everyday talk in which married couples make sense of the past and plan for a joint future takes place in given historical circumstances, structural contexts and particular sets of constraints. Such constraints are both economic, affecting life chances and standards of living, and ideological, in that individuals are not entirely free to define their own life-worlds. They therefore draw on socially available meanings and moralities which structure and limit the range of alternatives open to them. For example, Berger and Kellner emphasise the increasingly egalitarian nature of married partnership and yet their article in which, incidentally, individuals are always referred to as 'he', ignores the ways in which the new joint biography to be created after marriage and especially after parenthood, varies in relation to the differing experience of the male and female partners before marriage. As Bernard has argued, there is a wealth of evidence to show that marriage both means different things to men and women and also has very different consequences for the two sexes

(Bernard, 1973, pp. 19–41). This omission on Berger and Kellner's part appears to be linked with their failure to consider more than superficially the extent to which the characterisations and scripts of married life are already written as part of much broader structural configurations. Their overall problem, therefore, lies in an over-emphasis on the autonomy of the private sphere (see Morgan, 1981). Although this book is principally concerned with a specific aspect of family life, remarriage, and a particular family structure, the stepfamily, the issues created by the research we describe may only be adequately understood by reference to much broader questions about the significance of family life and the extent of public influence and control over the family as an apparently private sphere. In some respects remarried couples and their children provide a particularly useful 'case study' from which to consider and evaluate these broader theoretical issues because, as we intend to show in chapter 4, the experience of divorce and remarriage is likely to bring such couples in contact with a number of experts and public agencies and thus under greater public scrutiny and control than their first married counterparts.

Remarriage as a private trouble

Most of the private troubles of the remarried stem from an earlier stage in their biography and remarriage is frequently seen as a solution to the individual and social problems associated with widowhood, marital separation and lone parenthood. As a result, as we hope to demonstrate from the results of our own study, whilst individual expectations are high, couples bring to their new partnerships an emotional and material inheritance from the past which inevitably complicates their married and domestic life, at least during the early years of their new partnership, and sometimes for very much longer periods.

Whether to remarry at all and whom to choose pose problems not shared in the same way by those marrying for the first time. At first sight a second marriage may offer solutions to the material, practical and emotional problems of widowhood, separation or single parenthood. Women left on their own to bring up children might find in a new partner a degree of economic security and relief from the ambiguity of their formerly married status whilst at the same time offer their male counterparts the comforts of a shared domestic life and the restoration of married 'normality'. At one level the advantages of remarriage are overwhelming but studies of the widowed and divorced show that some, at least, feel ambivalent about the prospect.

Whether male or female, widowed parents tend to wait longer than their divorced counterparts before remarrying. This is demonstrated in the National Children's Bureau study of one-parent families; a larger proportion of the divorced mothers had remarried (25 per cent) or set up home with a man in the years between when the study child was seven and eleven than either the widowed mothers (15 per cent) or those with illegitimate children (9 per cent) (Ferri, 1976).

The National Children's Bureau study also investigated parents' attitudes to remarriage, showing more widespread negative attitudes to remarriage among the divorced and separated than the widowed (Table 1.1).

Table 1.1 *Parents' attitude to remarriage*

Percentage	Widowed	Separated/divorced
Positive	18	18
Negative	40	59
Uncertain/other	41	22

(Ferri, 1976, Supplementary Table)

Goode argues from his American data that divorced women experience strong pressure upon them to remarry. He describes their situation as one of institutional ambiguity where conflicts stem both from the social disapproval they experience and from their own status confusion. Such conflicts are resolved through remarriage:

> The greater clarity of role definition that results is easily seen. So far as strangers are concerned there is no particular reason to question the new marriage, there is a father for the children and a common domicile. The mother is once more wife-mother and the lesser events, problems and solutions of daily life are very similar to those in families where there has been no history of divorce. (Goode, 1956, p. 211)

In a more recent British study Geoffrey Gorer also asked his divorced respondents about their attitudes to remarriage; half expected to marry again, one-third already had a second partner in mind, whilst a quarter did not expect to remarry and a quarter were uncertain (Gorer, 1973, p. 226). These relatively high levels of uncertainty and even antipathy to remarriage suggest that Goode's conclusions might need to be modified in the light of British evidence. In the case of the bereaved, however, it is likely that feelings of loyalty to a dead partner and the desire to conform to social convention will deter widowed parents from seeking a rapid remarriage. More especially they may be inhibited from expressing such intentions to the researcher; with some justification we might see Goode's concept of 'status confusion' as a more typical characteristic of the widow or widower than of the divorced person. Some of Marsden's informants discussed the significance of continuing to wear wedding rings:

> taking the ring off signalised a definitive resolve in these circumstances and usually indicated that a woman was once again seeking marriage or had definitely ended her marriage. All the widows and almost all the separated women wore rings but only two-thirds of the divorced or unmarried mothers did. (Marsden, 1969, p. 160)

Marris, in his study of *Widows and their Families* found that

> the greatest objection to remarriage . . . was the belief that they could never love another as much as the husband they had lost, and hence they would not sacrifice their independence to a stranger, whom they could not help comparing unfavourably with the man whose place he had taken. (1958, p. 58)

The legal formality of divorce proceedings, even when they are not simply making marriage to a previously selected partner possible, seem to set people free to look for someone else in a way which is not shared by bereaved parents who can see no formal end to their period of mourning. For Marsden's widows this was most often signified by the advice of kin and friends to *begin to forget* and think of finding someone new.

Although the percentage of widows and widowers is about the same, widowers left to care for dependent children are probably more likely to remarry than widows with dependent children. George and Wilding's study of motherless families demonstrates that, in addition to the domestic and economic difficulties encountered by fathers bringing up their children on their own, they face considerable misunderstanding and social disapproval. Whilst mothers are expected to be able to cope on their own, and are admired for doing so, fathers are frequently seen to be somehow less than men for attempting it (George and Wilding, 1972, p. 39).

Those who consciously decide that they do wish to remarry face a number of practical problems when it comes to meeting a new partner in a social world where it seems that all leisure and informal social interaction is based on couples. In addition, the sense of guilt and recrimination over the failure of a first marriage which continues to haunt many divorcees may undermine confidence to the extent that they are unsure about being able to choose more wisely next time. Indeed, some may question whether or not they are capable of sustaining a successful new partnership at all.

Conventional wisdom characterises early married life as a period of personal change and adjustment to each other and to the married state and although remarried partners are used to 'being married' itself, their early married life may have other complications. By definition couples are older than their first-time counterparts and have thus already established day-to-day personal and domestic routines stemming from their first marriage and, possibly, a period spent on their own. Everyday domestic life, which is constituted from accustomed preferences surrounding, for example, food, the timing of meals, styles of eating; whether and what to watch on television; leisure activities; patterns of friendship, neighbouring and contact with kin may all have very different meanings for each partner as they begin a joint domestic life together. In addition, the material and economic constraints of income, maintenance arrangements, position in the housing market and so on which determine standards of living and influence domestic lifestyles may pose particular problems for those remarried partners who continue to pay or receive maintenance for the children of their first marriage.

Conventional wisdom, supported by much of the social science literature on steprelationships, also suggests that the most significant problems of the remarried arise when one or both of the partners brings children of their first marriage into the new household. The negative stereotypes attached to stepparents, particularly stepmothers, in a wide variety of cultures and historical periods, suggest that conflict between stepkin is regarded as both endemic and inevitable. A number of British and American women journalists have written personal accounts of their experiences of remarriage (Maddox, 1975; Simon, 1964; Thomson, 1967; Rooseveldt and Lofas, 1976). These writers demonstrate considerable agreement about the common problems of steprelationships many of which, with those of the remarrying couples themselves, may have their origins in the earlier experiences of the children involved. For many of these children a custodial parent's remarriage represents yet another domestic and personal change in the sequence of events which started when they were first made aware of their parents' intention to part, bringing in train a variety of new relationships and potential anxieties. In such circumstances differing experiences and expectations about the web of everyday family life cause conflict and uncertainty. As there appear to be few norms structuring the stepparent role in our own society many men and women may find themselves trying to construct a new role *de novo*. Hampered by their unfamiliarity with their newly acquired children, and in some cases with parenthood itself, they feel uncertain about their own legitimacy as a parent to the child or children of their new partner. In addition they may experience considerable jealousy and frustration, perhaps shared by their partner, at the way instant parenthood impinges on the private pleasures of a new relationship.

There seems to be general agreement that stepmothers have a much more difficult time than stepfathers. The impressions of investigative journalists (Maddox, 1975; Thomson, 1967) are partially confirmed by survey data from Bowerman and Irish (1962), Duberman (1975) and Chester (1977). A number of explanations have been advanced for this, which may be summarised under two main headings. First, the previous family experiences of children who acquire full-time stepmothers are likely to have been the more unsettling and distressing. Second, it is widely agreed in our own culture that the mother's role as parent is the more demanding and diffuse, so that much more is expected of the stepmother who must try to become substitute parent to children whose childhood histories, tastes and idiosyncracies are virtually unknown to her.

It is safe to assume that in general, children left with their father after the death or departure of their mother will probably have experienced a period of relatively greater emotional change and domestic upheaval than children left with their mother. A period of prolonged illness or the crisis of an unexpected death may affect the bereaved mother or father equally, but, as George and Wilding (1972) demonstrate, the emergency care and support offered to fathers who for one reason or another are left to cope on their own, is likely to be gradually withdrawn as the crisis is felt to have passed. If the children are still young their father must either find substitute care for them from amongst their female kin, pay a housekeeper or give up work himself in order to care for them. George and Wilding found that such arrangements tended to be unsatisfactory and precarious, so that children were subjected to further periods of change. Whilst the father's remarriage may end this period of domestic uncertainty and solve many of his problems, it is not surprising that his children may remain unconvinced. If they have formerly been looked after by elderly relatives they may also have been spoiled and indulged to compensate for the loss of their mother, so that the arrival of their new stepmother may, in their minds, be related to the withdrawal of this indulgence. Children of divorced parents still normally remain with their mothers; if contested, custody of younger children will usually only be given to a father if he is able to demonstrate some significant fault or inadequacy in his ex-wife's behaviour towards the children, so that it may be assumed that the children in the custody of divorced fathers will generally have experienced some additional sufferings and uncertainties during the time when their parents' marriage was breaking up. For these reasons, therefore, a child's previous experiences may create more difficulties for intending stepmothers than stepfathers.

The sexual division of labour within the nuclear family ensures that the greatest responsibility for the care and upbringing of children rests with the female, so that stepmothers are expected to take the much wider range of responsibilities which are attached to the role of mother. The Rapoports, summarising a wide range of evidence of parenting, conclude that prevailing conceptions of father's role in the family tend to place him on the periphery (Rapoport, Rapoport and Strelitz, 1977, p. 237).

By contrast mothers are not only expected to do the work involved (Oakley, 1974) but also to take public responsibility for how the children 'turn out'. The Newsons claim that:

> even in this age of vastly increased involvement of fathers, where young children are concerned, mothers remain more vulnerable to social criticism. This is because of social expectations: in the end, criticism of the upbringing of a young child is still primarily aimed at the mothers. Fathers are not expected to take public responsibility for either the behaviour or the appearance of very young children, and blame will be transferred to the mother even where the father has voluntarily accepted the major involvement. (Newson and Newson, 1972, p. 30)

If this accountability is transferred to the newly acquired stepmother of children who have still to come to terms with a period of great change and uncertainty, she, and those who judge her, may be bound to feel that she is failing. It is also significant that when she begins to take over household responsibilities from her new husband, she has to create an identity for herself within the domestic sphere by her cooking and household management as well as the routine issues of dress, cleanliness and so on, which are a taken for granted part of child care. This is precisely where she is most likely to find herself compared with the children's mother, whose influence inevitably persists in matters of discipline and routine, and, above all, food. Maddox found that 'stepparents talk a lot about food and mealtimes. . . . In many stepfamilies, meals are excruciating, the time when the expectation of happy family life comes up against the reality' (Maddox, 1975, p. 136). Even if the dead parent is not idealised, as some psychologists have suggested happens (Fast and Cain, 1966) or the mother without custody complicates life as a significant 'third force' (Duberman, 1975, p.

82), it may be difficult for the stepmother to succeed when so much is expected of her.

Chester's data suggest another factor which accentuates the difficulties of stepmothers; they are more likely to have been single before their marriage than stepfathers, and they therefore lack previous experience of parenting or even of the married state itself. Chester received 760 replies to a questionnaire published in the magazine *Woman's Own* (1977), 296 related to stepmother families, and 464 to stepfather families. Seventy-four per cent of the stepmothers had been single before their present marriage, whilst only 53 per cent of the stepfathers had previously been single. Chester's results show generally that stepmothers were more likely to be finding their new role difficult; one third of the stepmothers said that they found their family situations more difficult than they had expected. Thus the range of potential private troubles following from remarriage, especially where children are involved, seems extensive and somewhat forbidding and for the individuals involved they are usually perceived as essentially personal matters for which they alone must find solutions. However, the recent and widely discussed rise in divorce and remarriage rates has, as Mills suggested, made it increasingly difficult to explain such trends entirely in terms of the private troubles of individuals; in some respects remarriage has also become a public issue.

Remarriage as a public issue

The proportion of all marriages which are remarriages for one or both parties has increased steadily since the 1969 Divorce Reform Act came into effect in 1971. In 1981 over 33 per cent of all marriages included at least one remarried partner. In his discussion of official statistics demonstrating changing patterns of marriage, Leete argues that this rapid increase in remarriage rates 'is almost entirely attributable to marriage of two divorced people and of divorced people marrying previously unmarried people' (Leete, 1979, p. 41). There has been little change in the number of marriages involving the widowed so that, in so far as the rapid increase in the number of remarriages constitutes a public issue in Mills's term, it is inextricably linked to a much more widely acknowledged concern about the social consequences of rising divorce rates. Not only has the substantial increase in the number of younger divorced people created a much larger pool of potentially available marriage partners but, as Leete notes, 'prospective remarriage for one or both parties is frequently a reason for divorce' (op. cit., p. 41). Thus, whilst many commentators have used high and rising divorce rates as evidence of a decline in the importance of marriage as an institution or even the breakdown of family life itself, paradoxically marriage remains an almost universal experience, entered into at some time by over 90 per cent of the population.

It is clear from Mills that public issues frequently arise from, and generate conflict between, groups or publics with widely differing interests (Mills, 1967, p. 8). Sometimes such conflicts are clearly and directly political but in our own society, family issues and debates are not always polarised along traditional party lines. However, it is clear from examination of public discussions of, for example, social and legal policy as it affects marriage and divorce, that considerable differences in attitudes, beliefs and perspectives underpin such discussions. On the one hand many 'experts', senior practitioners in personal service occupations and social policy-makers share experiences of training and daily practice and certain common ideologies which are based upon the relativistic assumptions and perspectives of the social sciences. As such they tend to accept the inevitability of those social changes which have radically altered patterns of marriage and family life and are concerned to provide the kinds of social analysis and policy which will minimise the distressing personal and social consequences of such changes.

This kind of thinking is illustrated in Ronald Fletcher's influential essay on changes in family life, *The Family and Marriage in Britain*, first published in 1962. In it Fletcher took issue with church leaders, moralists and other commentators who, even then, used rising divorce rates to predict the eclipse of the family. Instead, he argued that high rates of divorce were inevitable and essentially unalarming:

> we must consider the possibility that if the conceptions, status and expectations of marriage and family life in our society are high . . . then it may be that *we must expect* a greater degree of resort to divorce. . . . May it not be that high standards and expectations of marriage and family life actually *entail* a high rate of resort to divorce . . . it is at least possible that a higher rate of divorce might well be indicative of a higher conception, a healthier condition of marriage in society, rather than a worsening of it. (Fletcher, 1975, p. 77)

Summarising a variety of studies of contemporary patterns of family life which illustrate the high levels of personal investment made in married partnership and family life, Fletcher went on to suggest that an individual decision to divorce and remarry either immediately or some time later shows that:

> though some people find it desirable to terminate *one* marriage it is not marriage and family life from which they are wishing to escape since so many of them choose it again within so short a time. (op. cit. p. 168)

Trends in remarriage were also regarded optimistically by the Finer Committee in its public discussion of the problems of one-parent families, noting that 'the high proportion of divorced persons who marry again . . . thus reduce the population of one-parent families' and that 'the prevailing social attitude requires that the breakdown of marriages should not impose shameful disabilities on the unsuccessful spouses and they should no longer be stigmatised if they marry again' (Finer, 1974, paras 3.52 and 2.6). Similarly the Home Office Working Party on Marriage Guidance, whose membership included senior members of the various marriage counselling agencies, historically very much concerned with the preservation of marriage, having reviewed recent changes in patterns of marriage, recognised that: 'Men and women are now free, to marry, to manage their relationships within marriage, to determine the size and spacing of their family, to terminate their marriage *and increasingly to try again*' (Home Office, 1979, p. 23, our italics).

There are, however, 'other publics' whose 'cherished values' are deeply threatened by the increasing normality and acceptability of remarriage. For these groups and individuals the prevalence of divorce constitutes a disturbing public issue. Specifically this results from the fact that the desire to remarry is frequently a reason for divorce and, more generally, the growth in the number of divorcees in the marriage market has itself increased the chances of finding another partner. It is therefore argued that unhappily married couples are no longer deterred from ending a marriage by the prospect of a gloomy future spent alone. Thus increases in the number of divorces which are followed by rapid remarriage are seen to threaten valued and widely held commitments to life-long marriage and to undermine the stability of the family unit within which it is felt children should be brought up.

Such 'publics' include, most obviously, church leaders and lay members for whom the remarriage of divorced persons poses theological, moral and practical problems. Their numbers are further swollen by members of certain ruling elites, such as some Members of Parliament, senior members of the civil service, and the legal and medical professions, many of whose beliefs about family life and attitudes towards divorce are based on the moral framework of church doctrine and teaching. Rex has suggested that, as a result of changes which took place in the social composition and power structure of the upper class in the nineteenth century, the 'old' landed aristocracy, based on membership of the House of Lords, have continued to play a special part in public life as guardians of moral issues and moral education. This has been maintained at a local level through involvement with both church and magistrates' courts and nationally by a continuing exercise of 'considerable influence over the content of law, legal education and the actual personnel of the legal profession' (Rex, 1974, p. 215).

Much public discussion of remarriage of the kind to which 'experts' and Rex's 'moral guardians' contribute is focused, albeit often implicitly, first on its challenge to beliefs, policies and practices based on the normality of life-long marriage and, second, upon its effects on children. Although it is impossible to generalise with any confidence about contemporary public attitudes towards marriage and divorce it is clear that the majority of young people still expect to marry themselves (McCann-Erikson, 1977; Rauta and Hunt, 1975) despite their awareness of current high divorce rates. Public attitudes towards divorce are much harder to isolate. Certainly the couples in our own study held a very wide range of beliefs about the permanence of marriage and had varying ideas on the subject of divorce. They also showed that they were aware that other people held very different views. It is, therefore, impossible to refute or confirm the claims of particular interest groups or 'publics' when they say that they are presenting the views of 'the majority' or of 'most ordinary' or decent families. Whilst specific publics may have a particular interest in supporting life-long marriage organised around a traditional domestic division of labour for religious, policy or political reasons, they may find implicit and articulate support for their views amongst 'ordinary people' who would generally prefer their own, and other members of their family's, marriages to be lasting rather than temporary.

Images of stepfamilies

Although there is relatively little satisfactory or reliable data on the effects that divorce and remarriage can have on children, it is frequently referred to in discussions about the public issues of divorce. Most of this material may be used in a way which confirms the potential damage wrought by high rates of family 'breakdown' and the negative public stereotypes of family and household arrangements which do not conform to the norm of the unbroken nuclear family. Table 1.2 is offered as a summary of the principal studies of relevant aspects of remarriage and steprelationships, collected during the course of a literature search for our present study. It is organised to show the contradictory images of stepfamilies which are projected by such material.

We use the term here in the same way as Tufte and Myerhoff:

> an image is a particular kind of symbol . . . that refers to and makes present something absent. . . . Images have an immediacy, a natural ability to be convincing because they appeal to us through our senses, circumventing (at least at first) our critical faculties. Images are fundamentally and inevitably rhetorical, then, persuading us of the validity of the information they carry. (Tufte and Myerhoff, 1979, p. 9)

Thus, if images have the power to 'convince and manipulate' (ibid., p. 9) then we wish to understand images of the stepfamily as normative models. To do this it is important to be aware of the relationship existing between different perceptions of stepfamily life – lay, academic and professional – and their portrayal to different publics. For the social scientist, as we shall try to show, conflicting images might also be a product of differing theoretical presuppositions and methodological strategies.

In many ways it is the *negative* images of stepfamilies which are the most pervasive; indeed the number and range of problems presented in Column 1 produces a familiar, if joyless picture. The difficulties which we have catalogued there affect not only the stepparent and the stepchild but extend to the natural parent and, more generally and diffusely, to the quality of family life itself. Yet this gloomy impression contrasts strongly with the more optimistic claims and statements of stepparents themselves as they are represented in Column 3. Most of the material included in Column 1 is derived from two kinds of study; first, clinical case material (for example, Fast and Cain, 1966; Schulman, 1972 and Pfleger, 1947) and second, from large-scale questionnaire surveys of children and adolescents (Bowerman and Irish, 1962; Wilson *et al.*, 1975). Each presents particular difficulties of interpretation. The evidence from clinical psychology raises two important problems. First, its practitioners see only those members of stepfamilies who are referred to them because something has 'gone wrong' in their family lives, so that little, if anything can be inferred from their findings about steprelationships generally.

Second, while some studies which contribute to the stepfamily's negative image successfully avoid the methodological problems which arise from the use of the samples based on social and psychiatric referrals by sampling from an entire age group or school population, they do tend to make causal inferences from statistical relationships in a way which ignores the subtleties and complexities

Table 1.2 *Images of stepfamilies*

Column 1 Negative	Column 2 Mixed	Column 3 Positive
Affecting stepparent 1.1 It may be difficult *either* to substitute for 'idealised' dead parent *or* compete with departed live parent (Bowerman and Irish; Wolff; GAP) 1.2 Third, non-residential parent may still be a significant figure; access creates complications (Duberman; Fast and Cain; Maddox; GAP)	1 *Mortality – versus divorce-generated stepfamilies* After divorce they may mark the end of a period of conflict . . . BUT (Simon; Bowerman and Irish)	1 *Stepfamily is an improvement on:* – an earlier unhappy marriage (Chester; Bowerman and Irish Goode; Schlesinger; Bernard) – a period of being a one-parent family (Ferri)
2 Both stepparent and stepchild experience *jealousy* as they compete for the time, attention and affection of the individual who has brought them together (Wolff; Bernard; Pfleger; Maddox) 3 *Stereotypes* of 'wicked stepparent' are still prevalent (Smith; Pfleger; Heilpern) and continue to affect stepparents (Maddox)	2 *Sex of stepparent* Greater difficulties experienced by stepmothers (Chester; Bowerman and Irish) Male parental role obligations are less specific, taxing (Rapoport)	2 *An 'obvious' solution* to domestic, financial problems, especially for fathers left with dependent children . . . BUT (Wilding and George)
4 *Ambiguities* and *uncertainties* inherent in the stepparent role lead to: 4.1 Lack of legitimacy as a parent figure, particularly in matters of discipline (Bernard; Fast and Cain; Maddox) 4.2 Lack of incest taboo and problems of sexuality (Mead; Maddox; Heilpern; Fast and Cain; Bernard; GAP) 4.3 Lack of spontaneity leads to 'conscious parenthood' (Maddox; Fast and Cain)		

Affecting natural parent 1 Close relationship with child(ren) which developed during one-parent family period is disrupted. (Langner and Michael; Bowerman and Irish) 2 Mothers feel that their children will be hostile to the idea of their remarrying (Marsden; Ferri) 3 Bereaved/disturbed parents who have not yet come to terms with the grief surrounding the end of their first marriage may encourage their child(ren)s negative attitudes towards the new stepparent. (Wolff)	3 *Length of time between break and remarriage* Rapid remarriage is better for the children (Smith)	3 *A remarriage is regarded as socially desirable*, recreating an outwardly normal family situation (Goode)
Affecting the children 1 School achievements adversely affected (Wilson; Douglas) 2 Undermines their self-esteem (Rosenburg) 3 Creates worry about their own capacity to sustain a happy marriage (Langner and Michael)	4 *Age of children at time of family breakdown* Effects are greatest if children are under the age of seven (Langner and Michael)	4 *Stepparents themselves feel that they are getting on all right* (Duberman; Chester; Schlesinger)
Affecting family life 1 Stepfamilies are not as happy as unbroken families (Langner and Michael; Bowerman and Irish; Maddox) 2 They experience additional financial worries and complications (Maddox; Duberman) 3 Sibling rivalry is heightened in stepfamilies (Pfleger; Podolsky; Maddox; Duberman) 4 Complicates extended family relationships (Firth; Maddox)	5 *Social class of stepfamily* The lower the social class of the stepfamily, the poorer the adjustment of the stepchild (Langner and Michael) Financial problems more acute, the lower the social class of stepfamily	5 *A stepfamily can provide a more diverse, flexible family unit*, in contacts with a larger number of adults (Thomson; Duberman)

of family relationships which, we would argue, should be the real focus of our attention.

The middle column of Table 1.2 contains a number of mixed and inconclusive images of the quality of stepfamily life. Some of the material is drawn from the studies described above, so our earlier methodological criticisms should apply. More significant however are the important differences, and sources of confusion, which spring from the distinction between mortality- versus divorce-generated stepfamilies. Other factors, which may bear on either case, concern the age at which children lose a parent, the age at which they acquire a stepparent and the sex of the stepparent.

The most positive images of stepfamilies are presented in three studies in which stepparents were asked to make their own judgments about the success of their family life. Whilst Duberman's American study (Duberman, 1975) includes a great deal of evidence of stepparents' insistence on their generally 'excellent' family relationships, Bohannan and Erikson found that in a comparative study of 106 stepchildren and 84 children from unbroken homes 'the stepchildren were . . . just as happy and just as successful socially and academicaly as the children from natural families' (Bohannan and Erikson, 1978). The preliminary results of Chester's questionnaire enquiry also indicate that three-quarters of the stepparents reported reasonable or considerable satisfaction with their family situations. Nine out of ten stepparents claimed that their children had adjusted well to the second marriage, and more than half said that they felt that their family situation had improved over time. Thus the main findings were reported in *Woman's Own* with the comment that 'one of the surprising results of our own survey is . . . that men and women are making a far better job of building a new family than was ever supposed'.

Bohannan's results also demonstrate some of the contradictions inherent in the stepparent role:

> The stepchildren's own reports were the most dramatic testimony to the quality of fathering they had received. But when we asked the stepfathers for their opinions, we received some unexpected responses. In general, they saw their youngsters as less happy than the natural fathers rated theirs. They also tended to view themselves as less effective than the natural fathers saw themselves. In other words, the mothers and children thought the stepfathers were just as good as the natural fathers, but the stepfathers didn't believe it themselves. (Bohannan and Erikson, 1978)

Such studies are important because they illustrate the paradox which lies at the core of investigations into the nature of steprelationships. In societies where the nuclear family is regarded as an ideal – the natural, healthy and desirable type of domestic arrangement – family structures which cannot entirely conform to that norm will be regarded and their members may regard themselves, as deviant. In discussions of the public issues involved the attention of researchers, policy-makers and other 'experts' will be focused on the structural ambiguities and aspects of family relationships which distinguish such families most clearly from 'normal' nuclear families. However, when asked, stepparents themselves seem to be at pains to point out their conformity and commitment to nuclear family norms.

It is possible that there may be as yet unexamined parallels between stepfamilies and other anomalous families, for example, families in which adoption has taken place or which contain recognisably sick or handicapped members. Margaret Voysey's study of families with a mentally or physically handicapped child, *A Constant Burden*, has helped us considerably in assessing the positive images projected by stepparents in these studies (Voysey, 1975). Her book, subtitled 'the reconstitution of family life', examines the way in which parents have to come to terms with the discovery that their child is handicapped and the way their family life is changed. From the outset she asked two important questions:

> Firstly why do parents say what they say and, secondly, what if anything does it tell us about what it is like to have a disabled child? Any answer to the second question depends on that given to the first. (Voysey, 1975, p. 1)

Her evidence, taken from a series of interviews with parents of handicapped children, showed that they claimed that having a handicapped child affected their family life very little. Since the results of other research, indirect evidence from parents' accounts of their experiences and her own observations led her to believe that having a handicapped child *must* inevitably create problems, she tried to establish how and why parents construct such claims in the face of all evidence to the contrary. Voysey suggests therefore that the parents' insistence that they 'managed' and that the experience of having a disabled child had not greatly altered their lives, should be seen as their attempt, when interviewed, to give an account of their lives which used the images available to them of a normal family life. She argues that: 'in a certain sense, parents' responses tell us nothing about what it is like to have a disabled child in the family, but a lot about people's ideas of what it ought to be like' (op. cit., p. 2). This prompts two questions; why do families with handicapped children feel that they must deny, ignore or underplay difficulties created by the child in order to present themselves as normal and, second, from where do these images of the 'normal' family come?

For Voysey a partial answer to the first is given through recognising the significance of research interview itself to the parents involved.

> In situations where it is known that they have a disabled child, its effects on family life are potentially evident, and parents' good character is at stake. The research interview was one such situation. . . . In effect they [the parents] were being asked to evaluate their own performance of the constituent activities of parenthood. (Op. cit., p. 39)

From careful examination of her data she suggests that the parents whom she interviewed presented their lives and experiences in terms of their concepts of the normal family because they had been encouraged to do so as a result of their contacts with members of professions and agencies officially responsible for their child.

It was therefore important for all the parents concerned to 'discover what was wrong with their child, to see in his appearance and behaviour an underlying condition that could account for observed discrepancies between his behaviour and that of a normal child' (op. cit., p. 95). Typically, their conversations with other parents, doctors and, later, health visitors tended to focus on explanations of their child's condition and encouraged them to consider their own performance as parents. Such judgments tended to be based on how closely parents felt themselves to conform to an idealised notion of the 'good parent'.

> This ideal is based on a conception of normal family life in which childrearing is a central activity. In general, parents are supposed to subjugate their own interests to those of their children, and moreover to enjoy any sacrifices thus incurred. This conception bears a questionable relationship to the experience of *any* parents and is even less likely to reflect that of those who have had a disabled child. However, because it is widely legitimated and, further, actively implemented by agents accredited with official responsibility for the care and control of children, parents of the disabled are constrained to present their experience in such a way that they appear to be fulfilling the demands of normal parenthood. (Op. cit., p. 2)

Thus, in the public setting of the research interview, as well as in their contacts with members of helping professions, such families try to present themselves as normal families by stressing those aspects of their feelings and experiences which approximate most closely to their image of the normal family and by defining as unimportant or irrelevant those aspects of their family life which they believe distinguishes them from ordinary families.

Such an analysis sheds a good deal of light on the paradoxical nature of both formal research findings and more general public discussions of remarriage and steprelationships. Whilst moral guardians, 'experts' and many social scientists have tended to focus on the problems, stressing the way in which stepfamilies deviate from the idealised norm of the unbroken nuclear family, when questioned themselves members of such families point to their commitment and conformity to dominant family norms. Thus remarried couples, when they consider their own family lives, try to believe that, despite complications of various kinds, they are 'making a go of it'.

Chapter 2

A natural history of the research project

Why a natural history?

In recent years there has been a growing and healthy tendency for more detailed and explicit accounts of research procedures and strategies to find their way into the published outcomes of sociological research. Whereas studies written up in the 1950s and 1960s, in an era when publicly at least, the scientific paradigm of sociology went unquestioned, made little reference to the experience of actually *doing* research, a decade or so later, fundamental changes have occurred, affecting the intellectual nature of the discipline itself, its practitioners and the political and organisational contexts in which research is carried out. In the same way that we now speak of different sociologies, so the consumers of the results of research must be aware of the diversity of possible research strategies and, more importantly, the variety of methodological assumptions determining them. As a result it has become common for researchers to accompany their findings and conclusions with more detailed accounts of their research work, so that the reader may be more aware of the organisational, political and, sometimes, interpersonal context of the research process itself. It is our intention in this 'natural history' to describe as clearly as we can, first, how the methodological presuppositions guiding our work evolved and how they affected decisions about data collection and analysis and, second, how the final 'shape' of the research was affected by the inevitable constraints and frustrations of the real world beyond the methods textbooks. Such an account is not, however, intended to follow the 'we know our sample is inadequate but we did not have the time/money/resources . . .' tradition. Throughout the book we have made explicit the specific limitations of our study where we see them, but we hope that this account will enable our readers to draw their own conclusions where necessary.

At a very early stage of our work careful reading of Voysey's (1975) study of the process of family reconstitution following the birth of a handicapped child confirmed some of our existing doubts and criticisms concerning the taken-for-granted positivism of much work on family life. Voysey's work raises important questions about the relationship between the public accounts of family life given by informants in the context of a sociological research interview and their other, more private, experiences and evaluations. It is, therefore, crucial to us that the accounts of remarriage and family life presented in this book should be read and interpreted in the light of information provided about the general context of the project and, specifically, the nature of the personal contacts and relationship between the investigators and the study families.

Finally, as the research has progressed our interest in 'the family' as an area of study has grown so that we would hope that such an account and consideration of some of the specific methodological problems encountered in studies of family life may make some contribution to the development of a stronger, more theoretically based tradition of research on the family in the future.

Our account, therefore, includes certain autobiographical events and specific incidents which seemed to us to illustrate the nature of our project or which may have materially affected its outcome. The first person singular is used referring to JB in the description of the earliest stages of the work before DC was appointed to work full-time on the project in May 1977. Otherwise the account is written jointly and is, thus, a negotiated version of what happened. As yet we have not disagreed sufficiently to necessitate separate accounts.

The early stages

In some senses at least this research project was born out of the merger of Sheffield City College of Education, where JB had been working for the previous five years, and the local Polytechnic. The 'merger', anticipated with dread by many college staff, seemed bound to be an improvement for me; as a part of a much larger group of sociologists with specialist teaching interests and experience, I suddenly found myself with fewer hours of more manageable, more specialised teaching. As an undergraduate I had particularly enjoyed a course I had followed on the sociology of the family and I was also doing a good deal of teaching on sociology of deviance courses. Indirect personal involvement in the breakdown of a marriage and a new partnership, coupled with the growing realisation that by 1975 there was 'a lot of it about' set me thinking about divorce, remarriage and steprelationships, as it seemed both interesting and a sensible topic to embark on in the context of a new department with its heavy commitment to the training of teachers, social workers and members of the paramedical occupations. For a short time as a teenager I had been a stepchild myself as my father had remarried some years after my mother's death. However, I was away at boarding school at the time and spent my holidays with relatives so that, despite being presented on occasion by journalists looking for a 'human interest angle' I still do not regard it as a significant factor in my choice of research topic.

The entries in my research diary at that time emphasise two related themes arising from my reading of the available literature, including Maddox's recently published book: stepfamilies and remarriage generally as a source of social problems, and the apparently greater difficulties experienced by stepmothers. Thus my first writing for personal consumption was based implicitly on a social problems perspective. I was, of course, already aware that the rhetoric of research applications must inevitably include reference to 'an important (and preferably, growing) problem which we need to know more about . . .' and it was possible to illustrate such statements by registration statistics showing considerable increases in divorce and remarriage rates. It seemed important to me then, as it does to us now, that the results of any research I did should be accessible to at least some of those directly involved, so that they might be helped to see that, in part at least, their personal circumstances are part of a wider set of experiences shared by many others. Thus the publication of a description or ethnography of life in a stepfamily should be of benefit to stepparents themselves as well as to those like teachers, lawyers, social workers and others who encounter problems of remarriage and steprelationships professionally. This conviction has constantly been strengthened by the arrival of large numbers of unsolicited letters from stepparents whenever reports of our research appear in national newspapers. Many of these letter-writers seem pleased that public attention is being directed to the private, individual problems which they are facing.

This emphasis on the problems of stepparents became part of the research proposal which I submitted to the Polytechnic in the summer of 1975 when I discovered, quite unexpectedly, that one of the LEA research assistantships was vacant. I intended to locate a group of stepmothers, as they seemed to experience most acutely the problems of stepparenthood, and to use the study as a way of formulating the issues and sociological problems more clearly before making an application for a research grant to finance a large-scale social survey of stepfamilies. My request for a Polytechnic research assistant was agreed to and within a year of the merger and my first tentative explorations of the subject as a possible area of research I found myself with a full-time co-worker on a project which, in retrospect, seemed still very ill-defined in terms of either objectives or research strategies. However, one of the unintended but highly advantageous consequences of this state of affairs was that from an early stage I was able to share decisions about both the aims and methods of the research with David Clark which might otherwise have been already made. Within a very short time of his arrival in June 1977 we had, I felt, already become co-workers, sharing responsibility for the direction of the work. This eased some of the potential for the conflicts which so often seem to occur between research assistants and their supervisors.

Thus the 'birth' of this particular research has been both a direct and indirect result of the Polytechnic's support. The first two years of the study were made possible through the provision of a research assistant and associated clerical expenses. The Polytechnic's support of our research has been unstinted and has only been marred on occasion by the experience, shared by all who work in unwieldy self-important bureaucracies, of vainly expecting speedy answers to requests for anything as trivial as a replacement desk key or as important as the necessary 'management' signature on a research application which must be posted by the end of the week.

Gaining a sample

When DC took up his post in June 1977 our most pressing task was that of gathering together a sample of stepmothers. Whilst our subsequent method of sample collection was to prove eclectic in the extreme, we sought throughout to impose two major constraints upon the procedure.

First, as far as possible we attempted to avoid gathering together a sample of volunteers; we therefore tried to eschew all forms of advertising the project in order to get individuals to come forward as participants. Of course, in so far as no one is obliged to take part in such studies, the men and women who eventually agreed to involve themselves in ours were volunteers, especially when set against the far greater number who later refused to participate or simply did not reply to our letters. However, in every case except one, those couples who agreed to be interviewed had been approached directly by us in the first instance. They did not, therefore, become involved as a result of any initiative which they themselves had taken in response to a general appeal for volunteers.[1]

Second, given the early existence of a social problems orientation to the project, we steadfastly avoided drawing a sample via the offices of local social services departments. Whilst we later interviewed men and women who had had dealings with social workers of various kinds, we were anxious that this should not in itself be a defining characteristic of the sample. To have interviewed a group of people already exposed to social work ideology and practice would, we felt, have precluded the chance of researching what we referred to as 'normal' stepfamilies.

Gathering together a sample of stepmothers and their husbands for the purpose of participating in a study of their family lives was a task which presented a number of difficulties. A principal one was posed by the social invisibility of such individuals. Stepparents were, at that time, unrepresented by any organisation or pressure group designed to draw public attention to their family situation. As a result, there was no apparent and accessible entrée to the universe of stepfamilies. Naturally, as for other groups,[2] it would have been possible to extract a sample from such a universe by homing in on them from a general survey based on a stratified random sample of the national population. This, however, was a methodological luxury beyond our financial means. We had to settle, therefore, for a more direct approach, or perhaps several approaches, centring on those aspects of stepparenthood which would cause that fact to show up in some more public and identifiable manner. Accordingly, it was decided to contact stepmothers through the office of the local Registrar of Births, Marriages and Deaths at the point when they publicly (though not *qua* stepmother) notified their intention to marry. The Sheffield Registrar was approached and generously allowed us to take down each week the names and addresses listed in his office. It is appropriate that we register here our gratitude towards him, for without his co-operation, the development of the research would have been considerably hampered.

The business of collecting the names began with DC's arrival in June 1977 and continued henceforth, each week, until March 1978. During this period we sent out a total of 535 letters, describing the project and inviting participation. One fear which we had about drawing a sample in this manner was that it would lead to a group of stepmothers who were newly embarking upon the task of stepparenthood and that our findings would lack a perspective built up over accumulated time and experience. In fact, twenty-eight of the thirty couples which we subsequently contacted in this way had been living together before their marriage. As our intention at that stage was to contact and interview stepmothers and their husbands, letters were sent only to remarrying men (divorced or widowed) since, should they have custody of any children from a previous marriage, their new wives would be about to become stepmothers. There was, of course, the risk that many of these men would be childless, or non-custodial parents, but this was unavoidable and since there was no way of telling which individuals fell into our chosen category, it was necessary to send out letters to everyone.[3] The letter outlined the nature and purpose of our study and invited those interested in participating to fill in their name and address on the reply slip and return it to us in the prepaid envelope provided. Of the 535 letters which were sent out during the ten-month period, 204 negative replies were received, many from couples who did not have any children or whose children were not living with them but who nevertheless were thoughtful enough to indicate this in their reply.[4] Some of these replies were accompanied by letters outlining individual circumstances and occasionally included good wishes for the success of the study. In addition, we received a further eight replies from people eager to participate in the study but who subsequently did not take part in the full interviews. Three of these came from men who had erroneously conceived of their new family situation as a stepfamily (i.e. neither of the new spouses' children by previous marriage were resident in the family of remarriage). Two other couples, having agreed to be interviewed, persistently refused or failed to keep their appointments, whilst another couple moved out of the area before the interviews began. One man telephoned to say that his future wife was living in Scotland, where he would be moving after his remarriage. He was nevertheless interviewed in what proved to be a useful pilot. Another man, clearly anxious to talk about his experience of losing custody of his child after the break-up of his first marriage, was also interviewed.

There were some hostile replies to our letter and the 'invasion of privacy' which some recipients felt it constituted. One man, who would not leave his name, harangued the hapless Polytechnic switchboard operator for several minutes whilst she struggled unsuccessfully to contact us on our extension. We also received a strongly-worded letter of protest from a senior figure in the Local Education Authority who had received one of our letters. Another man replied, stating that 'such correspondence should be "under private cover" ' and requested that his name be struck off our records. Thereafter we stamped all envelopes 'confidential'. Yet the noise created by such reactions was as nought in comparison to the deafening silence which accompanied the 291 letters we sent out which received no reply whatsoever.[5] The poor response rate, coupled with a changing interest based on preliminary interviews with a variety of individuals[6] as well as initial conversations with the study families, did in fact, have a fundamental influence on our thinking concerning the project as a whole.

We found that of those thirty-two couples who finally agreed to take part, the majority were stepfather rather than stepmother families. Initially, with unrealistic optimism, we thought that these stepfather families could be gathered into a separate sub-sample and the data used for comparative purposes. It soon became clear however, that we would not, in the time allowed, be able to make contact with an adequate number of stepmothers. Yet within a comparatively short space of time, this apparent loss seemed capable of being turned to advantage. As each interested reply was received, the family in question was visited by DC who explained to them some of the aims of the study and the general ideas which inspired it, along with the number and type of interviews which we had in mind. Frequently this led on to conversations concerning the experience of divorce and remarriage, custody, access, maintenance and so on. In the course of these preliminary visits it became apparent that whilst some of these families did not conform to the original prerequisite of containing a stepmother, there were many aspects of their experience worthy of sociological study. A crucial turning-point was therefore arrived at during the autumn of 1977 when we resolved to conduct a study of a group of *stepfamilies*, of varying types, rather than simply a study of stepmothers. The subsequent nature of the study was, then, a product of practical constraint and a developing awareness of a sociological research problem.

Henceforth we redoubled our efforts at contacting a suitable number of families. We had in mind the figure of forty – a reasonable interview load in the time available, but large enough to account for a variety of aspects of the experience of second marriage. Other possible methods of contacting stepfamilies were discussed and we decided to seek the co-operation of primary school headteachers and general practitioners in passing on a letter to any stepfamilies known to them. We then wrote to headteachers and doctors requesting them to contact us for copies of such a letter, which, along with reply slips and stamped addressed envelopes, could be passed on to individual families. The reaction of headteachers to our letter varied from outrage on ethical grounds, through mild annoyance at the imposition of yet another routine, bureaucratic demand, to genuine interest and support for our project. In all we distributed sixty packages during September 1977 but have no way of telling how many of these actually found their way to individual families, since when, for example, a headteacher asked for 'a half dozen letters', it was impossible to tell how many of these, or indeed whether any at all, were subsequently forwarded. We were, however, brought into contact with two more families who were prepared to take part in the study.

Our letter to the doctors was distributed under the signature of Professor Eric Wilkes of the Department of Community Medicine at Sheffield University, a fact which we hoped would draw attention to the letter and distinguish it from the large number of importunate missives regularly received by general practitioners. Yet despite our efforts, the response to our circular, which was sent out in October 1977, was not great. One doctor, herself a stepparent, contacted us and expressed a desire to take part in the study. In another case a receptionist in a surgery passed on the letter to her daughter who was about to remarry and she and her intended husband entered the project. Thus far we had a sample of thirty-six.

A further means of reaching stepparents suggested itself to us in the form of a discussion group where men and women could meet to talk informally about their family experiences and in particular the question of being a parent to someone else's child. Our idea was that such a group, whilst not intended to create a source of potential interviewees, could provide a valuable sounding-board for our developing ideas as well as a means of isolating issues for treatment in the interviews. The discussion groups were to be chaired by another member of the department; we were to sit in and learn from them. At about the same time that the schools letters were sent out, therefore, we distributed a number of posters, drawing attention to the proposed group and inviting interested parties to contact us for further details. Once again the reality of the response fell far below our aspirations. Largely, we suspected, as a result of inadequate publicity, though perhaps also for intrinsic reasons, only two couples contacted us. When no more enquiries were received we decided to invite these to take part in the study itself. One family were American and were only resident in the area for a short period. Nevertheless, they were interviewed in a 'dry run' for the first interview, the other family agreed to take part and participated throughout. A sample of thirty-seven.

As time went on, colleagues expressed increasing concern with our plight and one was able to pass on a letter to a stepfamily whom he knew. Another local general practitioner, herself a stepparent, and with whom we had had discussions at the beginning of the project, was able to put us in touch with a stepfamily among her patients. Contacts with the remaining three families were even more unorthodox. Another Sheffield stepmother and her husband joined the sample following a letter which she had written to Jacqueline Burgoyne in reply to the item in the *Sunday Times*. In another case, an article appeared in a local evening newspaper concerning an alsatian dog which had befriended a kitten; the dog's owner, it transpired, was a stepmother. DC duly wrote to the woman and her husband, and she readily agreed to take part in the study. Finally, on one occasion, DC gave a talk to an evening class in sociology at a local college of further education. The session concluded with a discussion of research methods in family sociology, which included an outline of our own research problems. The following day a member of the group telephoned to say that she had a friend who was a stepmother to four children and who, as a part-time sociology student herself, was interested in taking part. By such diverse avenues we obtained a sample of forty families.

Characteristics of the study families

What were the major characteristics of these forty families? The information included in this section is intended to give a collective picture of the families we studied but it must be emphasised that neither the size of our sample, nor the research strategies used, were intended to yield reliable quantitative data. The material which we present in chapters 3 to 6 is essentially descriptive; our results are intended to provide some preliminary answers to questions about the experience of remarriage and stepparenthood and in particular to demonstrate how remarried people themselves describe and make sense of their own family lives. Consequently the 'background information' which underpins our analysis is of two kinds; detailed description of the history and present circumstances of each couple as well as sufficient quantitative data about all the study couples and, where possible, remarried people generally, to locate individuals in terms of the background characteristics of the sample generally. Summaries of both kinds of information are available to the reader first from the life histories in appendix 1 and, second, from the description of the sample presented below.

Previous marital status and custody of the children

As we have explained, the initial focus of our planned research was steprelationships, so that we recruited into our sample couples where remarriage had either followed the death of, or the divorce from, a first partner. Although our attention shifted and we have subsequently tended to concentrate more on remarriage after divorce, comparison between the divorce- and mortality-generated stepfamilies has on occasion been very useful. We were, of course, also interested in remarried people as parents, both with and without custody of their children.

The three possible previous marital statuses yield a variety of permutations when one or both partners remarry. The distribution of these within our sample is shown in Table 2.1, along with arrangements for custody of children.

Table 2.1 *Previous marital status and custody of children*

Women				
Previous marital status	None	Non-custodial	Custodial	All
Divorced	1	0	31[1]	32
Widowed	1	0	2	3
Single	4	0	1	5
All	6	0	34	40

Men				
Previous marital status	None	Non-custodial	Custodial	All
Divorced	8	11	14	33
Widowed			4	4
Single	3	0	0	3
All	11	11	18	40

[1] In two cases (Mrs Elliot and Mrs Pelham) custody of their children is split between them and their ex-husbands.

The final column of Table 2.2 is derived from registration statistics and indicates the percentage of *all* remarriages, i.e. those in which either one or both partners are remarrying, according to the various combinations of marital status.

There are, therefore, too high a portion of two-divorcee couples in our sample and we believe that this may be related to another vital factor in which our study couples differ from the remarried population as a whole, i.e. the relatively large number of custodian fathers found amongst them. From Eekelaar and Clive's (1977) data, we would expect only between 10 and 15 per cent of divorced fathers to retain or gain custody of their children. However, almost half of the divorced fathers in our sample had custody of children. As we have already suggested, all our sample members were, in a sense, volunteers, because they chose to respond to our initial contact. We might speculate therefore that for many of the custodian fathers, recognition of their unusual position and particular difficulties may have encouraged them to consider taking

Table 2.2 *Combined marital statuses*

Divorced man – single woman	3	Heathcote; Parker; Stanley	26[1]
Divorced man – widow	2	Dyson; Walker	4
Widowed – spinster	2	Kennedy; Prior	3
Both widowed	1	Shannon	7
Widower – divorcee	1	Chapman	4
Bachelor – divorcee	3	Elliott; Farmer; Spencer/Deam	24
Both divorced	28		30
Bachelor – widow	0		2
Total	40		100

[1] Source: *Marriage and Divorce Statistics* 1977, Population Series FM2 no. 4. Derived from Table 2.1.

part in the study. Nine of these fourteen men had married divorcees, and it may be that although registration statistics show divorced men frequently marry spinsters, they are less likely to do so if they have custody of children.

Age at and duration of first marriage

The individuals in our study conform to a pattern observed in a number of studies of those who divorce; the mean age at which they had married was younger than for first marriages generally. This was 22.8 years for the men and 19.1 years for the women in the sample. It is clear from official statistics that marriages where the bride is under twenty are much more likely to end in divorce than those of couples over twenty (see, for example, Leete, 1979, p. 72 ff). This is confirmed in other studies (Thornes and Collard, 1979; Dunnell, 1979). Dunnell's data from the OPCS Family Formation survey also confirms the association between youthful marriages and pre-marital pregnancy. In our sample, 15 of the 35 women who had been married before had been pregnant at the time of their first marriage and the brides of 8 of the 37 remarried men were pregnant when they married.

Official statistics on the duration of marriage are notoriously difficult to interpret (see Chester, 1976). They raise, for example, important questions about defining 'separation' and the point at which a marriage can be said to have ended. It was clear that, on occasion, informants themselves found it hard to point to a specific event or period which marked the end of their marriage. For our own calculations we have relied upon our informants' definitions. These are subjective and not necessarily consistent, so that whilst for some the transition was clearly marked in the change to living apart, whether one or other moved out, or both moved to new, separate accommodation, in retrospect, others described their marriage as 'over' as soon as they had first become aware of the changes which were to bring about their eventual separation. The mean length of their first marriage for the divorced men in our study was 8.5 years and 8.2 years for the divorced women.

Relative ages of the remarried partners

The ages of the men and women in our study were recorded at the time of their first interview. The men's ages ranged from Mr Shannon (55) to Mr Deam (24). Their mean age was 37.4 years. The women's ages ranged from Mrs Brown and Mrs Dyson (55) to Mrs Browning (24), with a mean age of 34.9 years (see Table 2.3).

Table 2.3 *Relative ages of partners*

Husband 1 to 2 years older than wife		3
Husband 3 to 5 years older than wife		5
Husband 5 to 6 years older than wife		5
Husband 7 to 8 years older than wife		1
Husband 9 or more years older than wife		8
Husband older than wife	TOTAL	22
Husband and wife same age		6
Wife 1 to 2 years older than husband		4
Wife 3 to 4 years older than husband		4
Wife 5 to 6 years older than husband		3
Wife 7 to 8 years older than husband		0
Wife 9 or more years older than husband		1
Wife older than husband	TOTAL	12
		40

Most first marriages take place within a relatively narrow age band and in the majority of cases the husband is about two years older than his wife. However, the pattern is not so clear in the case of remarriages. Not only is the age difference likely to be greater, but there are also important differences which are related to previous marital status. In his review of changing patterns of marriage and divorce, Leete concludes that in 1976:

> about 90% of divorced males who married spinsters were older than their wives, and only seven per cent were younger. In remarriages of two previously divorced people the distribution is less skewed with slightly more than one quarter of husbands marrying older wives.
>
> By contrast for more than half the bachelors who married divorcees the wife was older – the reverse of the pattern for all marriages. (Leete, 1979, p. 49)

Thus, the pattern for remarriage is complex because second marriages take place at a number of different stages in the life cycle and involve couples with different and diverse previous marital histories.

Even so, the norm of men marrying women younger than themselves persists and, in the case of divorced men, many marry women *much* younger than themselves. For example, in 1977, 55 per cent of the divorced men aged between 30–34 who married spinsters married girls ten or more years younger than themselves, whilst 70 per cent of men aged between 35–39 marrying spinsters chose brides ten or more years younger. This type of union is perhaps one of the most popular stereotypes of remarriage following divorce. However, where *both* partners are divorced they are likely to be closer in age.

In addition, a larger number of remarriages than first marriages involve the untypical pattern of a younger groom and older bride. However, 30 per cent of the women in our sample were older than their husbands, a much higher proportion than for the remarried generally. For example, in only 10 per cent of those remarriages for one or both parties in 1977 was the bride older than the groom (OPCS: FM2 no. 4: 1977).

Length of time the couples had been together when the study took place

As a consequence of the method used to contact the majority of our sample, over half of the couples had been married for about a year at the midpoint of the study. However, all but seven of the forty couples had lived together for a period before their marriage so that their *de facto* partnerships were of a longer duration. The differences in *de facto* and *de jure* durations are set out in Table 2.4.

Table 2.4 *Length of partnership: period of cohabitation, marriage and length of* de facto *partnership*

	No. of couples who had cohabited for a given period	No. of couples who had been married for a given period	No. of couples with *de facto* partnership of given length
1	19	25	2
2	4	5	12
3	3	0	8
4	1	1	2
5	2	1	3
6	1	0	1
7	1	4	4
8	1	0	3
9	0	2	2
10	1	0	1
11	0	0	0
12	0	1	2
Totals	33[1]	39[2]	40

[1] The following couples did not cohabit: Graham; Heathcote; Kennedy; Morgan; Parker; Prior and Shannon.
[2] Mr Deam and Mrs Spencer did not marry during the study period.
For the sample as a whole:
The mean period of co habitation = 2.5 years.
The mean length of marriage = 2.6 years.
The mean length of *de facto* partnership = 4.6 years.

It is evident, therefore, that much of the material discussed in subsequent chapters focuses on the early stages of our couples' lives together as families. Therefore, the comments we have made, for example, on the effects of the legacy of the past and the amount of change they have experienced, relate in the most part to a group of families who have only been together for about five years and we are able to infer very little from our sample about stepfamilies of longer duration.

Until recently relatively little was known about the extent of cohabitation as either a preliminary or alternative to legal marriage. Data from the 1976 OPCS Family Formation survey suggests that, 'two per cent of all women aged 16–49 were living in unions which they regarded as being like a marriage.' Significantly, 'Second or later "marriages" were much more likely than first "marriages" to have non-legal unions; 30% compared with one per cent' (Dunnell, 1979, p. 8).

From her analysis of these later 'marriages' Dunnell suggests that there has been a general trend towards earlier 'marriage' after separation and that women are now more likely to cohabit in the early years after separation. Four years after separation, however, a higher proportion of women had actually remarried (op cit., p. 39). The experiences of our sample may shed some light on this. When the divorced meet new partners shortly after separation, or indeed where their new relationship has been the 'cause' of their separation, they are in any case unable to marry immediately. Like a number of couples in our sample they await the finalisation of one or both divorces and then remarry at once.

However, as we indicate in chapter 3, other couples who were free to remarry did not do so immediately, but instead delayed their decision until they felt 'more sure of each other' or until, after some years of living together, they decided to marry for financial or legal reasons.

Children and the family structure

Our sample only included couples where at least one of the remarrying partner(s) had custody of children from their first marriage. The mean number of children currently living at home with a parent and stepparent was 3.2. The families in our sample were, therefore, larger than average, since in over half of the households in Britain made up of mother, father and dependent children, there are two children (*Social Trends* 1981, Table 2.2). For some of the families their size was increased because both partners had custody of the children whom they brought into their new family. In addition, since they had been together, eighteen of the couples had already had children of their own within their new partnership (see Table 2.5).

Social class

It has become a necessary matter of tradition amongst social scientists that class be included as a key variable in survey investigations. It was clear to us from a very early stage that the personal and family life of the remarried couples we studied was greatly affected by their position in the housing market, their economic circumstances and the kind of involvement they had with their work. Accordingly, the data presented in chapters 5 to 7 bears witness to the centrality of those economic and material factors which shape domestic life in our own society. It has, however, proved very difficult to find a satisfactory method of categorising our couples in class terms. Mindful of the debate and criticism surrounding the use of

Table 2.5 *Types of stepfamily and children of the new partnership*

	Custodian father	Custodian mother	Both custodian parents
Children of new partnership	4	11	3
No children of new partnership	1	11	10
Total	5	22	13

occupational classifications generally (Young and Wilmott, 1956; Goldthorpe and Hope, 1972; Westergaard and Resler, 1975, p. 29, 287) as well as the specific objections of feminist writers to stratification classifications based solely on the occupation of the male husband/father (see Acker, 1973; Garnsey, 1978), we decided to use a broader, more general classification, which took into account the background, history and present circumstances of *both* partners. When we tried to do this it became obvious that some couples were clearly working-class both in origins and present circumstances; other couples were obviously now middle-class, but an 'intermediate' group remained who were much harder to place. In some cases the partners' jobs were designated 'intermediate' (Registrar General's IIIN or IIIM), for example, firemen or policemen. For other couples the actual circumstances of divorce and remarriage had influenced the working lives and economic circumstances of one or both partners, resulting in considerable social mobility (see, for example, the Grahams's life history). We eventually decided, therefore to present our sample in terms of the three categories shown in Table 2.6. At the time of the study 20 of the wives were working, 14 full-time and 6 part-time.

Housing

Twenty-two of the forty couples lived in homes of their own, whilst eighteen were in rented accommodation. Of the middle-class couples, only the Gilmours lived in rented accommodation; all of those whom we designated to the intermediate group owned their own homes; three 'working-class' couples, the Priors, Thornleighs and the Turners, were owner-occupiers.

As we suggest later the circumstances in which remarrying couples begin their partnership are very significant and differ considerably from those marrying for the first time. At the time of the study:

Table 2.6

Middle-class	13
Intermediate	7[1]
Working-class	20
Total	40

[1] The following couples were included in this category: Baker; Brown; Bingham; Graham; Smithson; Snow; Worthing.

8 couples were living in *his* former home;
10 couples were living in *her* former home;
22 couples were living in a house/flat which was *new to both of them*.

However, of those living in a home new to both of them:

11 had begun their partnership in *her* home;
3 had begun their partnership in *his* home;
8 had found a *new home* at the time they started to live together.

Thus, 21 of the couples had started their partnership in the wife's former home, and 11 in the husband's former home.

The data presented in subsequent chapters provides an ethnography or 'thick description' of remarried couples with families, which focuses particularly on the experiences of finding a new partner, setting up home and reconstituting family life together. Whilst there is insufficient demographic data available on remarried households to describe the remarried population accurately, we do know that our sample differs from that population in a number of significant respects. Our sample contains too great a number of couples in which both were previously divorced; too many women married to men younger than themselves, and too high a proportion of custodial fathers to reflect the remarried population generally. In addition, the majority of the families had only been living together for a relatively short time, so that they are bunched at what might be termed the 'family reconstitution' phase of the remarried family life cycle. Although it is impossible to draw any conclusions about the class distribution of the *remarried* population as such, our own sample contains a higher proportion of middle-class couples than would be found amongst either the population of Sheffield or Great Britain as a whole.

In addition, we should emphasise the local character of our sample. Fourteen of the men and eleven of the women were born outside Sheffield and in only five cases did both partners come from outside Sheffield. Whilst the Johnsons, Kennedy, Parkers and

Shannons have 'cosmopolitan' work and kinship networks which give them connections throughout the country (see Stacey, 1960 and 1975) the majority of couples in the study were born and brought up in a city of about half a million people which has the reputation of being the 'largest village in England', and which is in many respects both culturally and geographically distant from those places where the public issues surrounding divorce and remarriage are most frequently debated. As we have carried out this study, we have, as observers, bridged these two worlds and it has become increasingly important for us to recognise the deep and entrenched differences of attitude, experience and material circumstances between the families in our study and those of the moral guardians, 'experts' and policy-makers referred to in the previous chapter who have a public, professional interest in remarriage and steprelationships. For this reason the subtitle of this book – a study of remarried couples in Sheffield – is important.

The interviews

It will be clear from our description of the difficulties encountered in gaining a sample that to conduct research into aspects of what most men and women in our society consider to be their 'private' lives creates certain difficulties. Divorce and remarriage may have become widespread and prevalent social phenomena, but for some of the reasons referred to at the end of the last chapter we quickly found that any attempt to study them sociologically would require caution, sensitivity and, above all, tact. From the beginning therefore we approached the interviews with care born of the desire to obtain uninhibited and candid statements from our respondents. We believe that we have been in some measure successful in this but are only too aware of the problems of interpretation which semi-structured interviews and the accounts which result from them can produce. We therefore wish to outline the interviewing strategy we adopted, before concluding the chapter with a brief discussion of our methods of interpretation.

As we have mentioned, the interviews proper did not begin with the first meeting which DC had with each family; this initial contact was used as an opportunity to elaborate upon the aims and purposes of the study as expressed in the letter and where necessary to answer questions and clarify any difficulties or misunderstandings. It was also an opportunity to gather salient details about family size and structure as a preliminary to the first full interview. Needless to say, many of these encounters, which were often quite lengthy, yielded interesting data in themselves and were invaluable in helping us to frame questions and hypotheses. Many of the questions put to us by the couples were perceptive and presented DC with the tricky but profitable task of explaining sociological objectives to a lay audience. It was apparent that several couples had agreed to participate in order to demonstrate the 'ordinariness' and 'normality' of their lives, despite divorce and remarriage. The interest which they showed in our initial contacts and, as time went on, the growing commitment which many of them displayed towards the project as a whole, has guided us throughout our work, wherein we have attempted to present our findings and draw conclusions in a way which will be of interest to 'ordinary people' as well as family and sociology specialists.

It was decided to devote the first interview to the collection of detailed life history data for each respondent. No formal interview schedule was used for this. Instead, the interview began with an introduction from DC which took the following form:

> As you can see, for this first interview I haven't got any specific list of questions to go through – What we're trying to do first of all is put together what we might call a 'life history' for each person taking part in the study. So I'm interested in finding out a little about where you were born and brought up, something about your family, where you went to school, what you did after you left school, where you met your first husband/wife . . . and taking it on from there, right up to the present. . . .

This proved to be a remarkably successful method of initiating the interview and many individuals appeared to find it relatively easy to take up their narrative with only minimal prompting. In other instances, a more structured question–answer routine was found to be preferable, but again the questions followed no set pattern other than an attempt to follow through, in chronological order, the major life-cycle transitions and events. Almost all the men and women were quite uninhibited by the use of the tape recorder, which was used to record all the interviews.

One minor difficulty in conducting the first interview arose out of our insistence upon seeing each individual separately. Whilst our initial approach had emphasised a study of *couples*, we believed that to collect adequate life histories it would be important to interview each individual alone. Some of the couples found this disconcerting at first and in several cases there was clearly a desire to know what a partner had 'said' in his or her interview. It was therefore found throughout the study that the 'best' interviews were conducted when the interviewee's spouse was out of the house altogether and the interview could proceed uninhibited by constraints of time or convenience. For some families this was not possible. None the less *every* interview was conducted with the respondent alone, save in some cases the presence of a small infant, and in the 'privacy' of a separate room. For some of the larger families living in relatively cramped accommodation, this posed difficulties in itself and it is a testimony to their co-operation and patience that we were able to adopt the practice so extensively. After the first visit, the idea of the separate interview had usually been accepted and few subsequent logistical difficulties arose.[7]

The main immediate problem arising out of these first interviews was emotional and personal. DC found, for instance, that even after just one preliminary discussion, many men and women were prepared to give frank and open accounts of their experience of marriage and divorce or bereavement. In some cases these accounts were moving to an extent that was difficult to come to terms with and which rendered the interviews psychologically draining. As time went on, however, the emotional impact of the interviews diminished in the face of a growing desire to understand the issues which underlay the accounts. By the second round of interviews many of the respondents also appeared to have altered slightly in their orientation. Certainly DC found that in several cases the first interview had provoked further discussion between partners and even, in some cases, new attempts at understanding personal difficulties and circumstances. By the third interview this manifested itself most strongly in those couples who appeared to have developed a genuine commitment to the study and its aims, and who in some cases appeared to look forward to and enjoy the interviews.

Throughout the study period we attempted to foster this commitment in various ways. Letters were sent out, for example, containing details of a radio broadcast in which we appeared talking about stepfamilies. Christmas cards were sent to all families and in some cases DC made informal visits to couples' homes; others were met by chance in banks, pubs and at sporting events. Not all sample members enjoyed the experience of taking part in the study, however, and in two cases couples withdrew after the first interview, which they had found to be a painful reminder of past experiences. A third couple persistently put off their second interview and were eventually considered as a withdrawal. Others clearly found the interviews disturbing at times, but persevered with them through altruism and a belief in the study's value.

By the time of the second interview we felt able to organise our questions and hypotheses in a more formalised way. Accordingly, an *aide mémoire* was used as a basis for semi-structured interviewing in which we asked questions on a variety of specific themes. Each of these second interviews was tailored to suit the appropriate circumstances and past experiences of the individual concerned, so that certain questions were put only to previously unmarried men or women, custodial parents, non-custodial parents, those who had had childless first marriages, the divorced, the widowed, and so on.

In the first interview we had attempted to facilitate the free flow of a narrative account and had found that this typically took the form of a story, told in the first person, with the individual concerned as one of the central characters. Our aim in the second interview was to collect further data on others who had appeared in the narrative and, where possible, examine the relationships between the individual's personal troubles and the wider material, legal and economic structures which shaped them. Accordingly, we began by asking respondents to compare first and second marriages in a variety of contexts, or in the case of the previously unmarried, to describe their feelings on marrying someone who had been divorced or widowed. Specific questions were asked about the impact of marital break-up on health and personal well-being before going on to discuss experiences with various professionals, such as doctors, lawyers, social workers, and so forth. Custody, maintenance and access arrangements were also explored and variations between custodial and non-custodial parents examined. Finally, we looked at family and social networks, as well as work and leisure, in an attempt to see how these had been affected by remarriage.

In general, each set of interviews was of diminishing duration. Whilst first interviews averaged one and a half to two hours, the second interviews usually lasted only about an hour and the third slightly less. In every case there were individuals who proved to be loquacious exceptions. It was the third interview, which was concerned with parenting in the stepfamily, which couples seemed to enjoy most. Our typist, for example, pointed out to us the lighter tone which pervaded these interviews and the way in which our respondents 'sounded happier'. A variety of factors might be used to explain this. Certainly, by the time of the third interview each of the couples and their respective families were well known to DC and a familiar interviewing pattern had emerged. He too felt more relaxed about the interviews. As the textbooks put it, some measure of 'rapport' had been established.[8] Furthermore, we had been able once again to refine our questions to the point where they could be stated more clearly and directly and, in some cases, it was possible to use variations on similar questions asked by researchers in other projects. For example, we found the work of the Newsons especially helpful. The very subject matter of the third session, child care, may have made it an easier interview experience than its antecedents. It was apparent that several couples had been expecting the interviews to be of this type from the outset and in describing their feelings and concerns about children were able to give expression, more generally, to their experience of remarriage. This was not *always* easy, of course; fears and underlying uncertainties concerning such things as the effect of divorce or bereavement upon children were clearly a source of tension in the interview. Continuing guilt or doubt might easily manifest itself on these occasions, as also might a preoccupation with the relative merits of 'step' and 'natural' parenthood.

DC's final contact with the couples came towards the end of the study period, in the summer of 1979, when the life histories, which appear in appendix 1, were being prepared. After the third interview each couple had been asked to nominate a pseudonym for use throughout the book. Many chose old family names and thereby, we feel, have helped to retain an important though indefinable authenticity within the text. These names are, of course, used in the life histories which each couple had the opportunity to read, and, where they felt it necessary, to amend. Some, for example, were concerned that details of occupation or origin might make them recognisable (usually to a former partner) and therefore suggested alterations where appropriate. Others would happily have used their actual names and in casting aside DC's explanation of our concern to disguise identities, showed little apparent concern for anonymity. All names used in the text are pseudonymous, however, and all occupations and other relevant details have been appropriately altered in each case.

In another, albeit oblique, sense the couples also remained anonymous to one half of the research team. All of the interviews were conducted by DC and on no occasion did JB come into contact with the families. This provided an interesting situation in which DC, in addition to the data collected in the interviews, also had a useful and increasingly extensive background knowledge of the families in terms of the physical and material circumstances of their home lives, their appearance, manner and even the colour of their wallpaper. JB, by contrast, could get to know them only through the transcripts, which were made from each tape-recorded interview. A healthy disparity in our knowledge and understanding thus developed and we both found it possible to learn and develop insights from the particular basis of the other's position *vis-à-vis* the families. Nevertheless, we had considerable problems when it came to making sense of the material we had collected.

Methods of interpretation

It would be contrary to the spirit of sociological enquiry to which we subscribe to spell out in scientistic terms the methods we have used to analyse our data. Rather, we hope that in making sense of our findings, the reader will be sharing with us in a process of interpretation, both on the level of methodology and of data analysis. No study of this type could hope to present the data it has collected in *un*edited form, however, and, indeed, much of our material remains unused. It would therefore be pointless to suggest that we have not been selective in presenting our findings. We hope none the less that, in the tradition of the best ethnography, our editorial role does not entirely pre-empt further interpretation and evaluation.

It will be apparent from our discussion of the interviews that in talking with the couples in our sample we were progressively able to refine the types of questions which we wanted to ask. Initially, however, our desire was to cast our net as widely as possible and to collect detailed accounts of the experience of remarriage. In order to do this we have used as our starting point the life history. The collection of a life history for each individual taking part in the study was the object of the first interviews. By the term life history we refer to a detailed account or testimony, given by the individual, with suitable prompting, probing and questioning by the interviewer and covering the major life historical events relating to that person. The life histories which we have collected are, of course, focused, and concentrate on the substantive field of our interest, namely marriage, the family and interpersonal relations. The method might equally well be employed, however, to study work experience, religious belief and practice, leisure, etc. It has several important advantages.

The undoubted claim of the life history over other methods, we believe, is the richness of the data which it yields up. As we hope our findings reveal, the technique can produce vivid and detailed descriptive accounts arising out of lengthy, loosely-structured and open-ended interviews. Indeed, in many ways the life history approach can make the conventional interviewer/interviewee distinction redundant. DC certainly found that for several sessions 'monologue', rather than interview, best described the encounter. We might speculate that this arises out of a situation in which individuals, typically, have little opportunity wherein they may speak openly and at length about their private lives. The great advantage which any interviewer has in this situation is that of being there as a person who wants to *listen* to a personal 'story'. This, then, forms the raw material of our analysis. We might view this type of account in one of two ways; it may be considered to have either an objective or a subjective status. Consider it at first as an *objective* account. Becker, who has championed the use of the life history, suggests the following:

> The image of the mosaic is useful in thinking about such a scientific enterprise. Each piece added to a mosaic adds a little to our understanding of the total picture. When many pieces have been placed we can see, more or less clearly, the objects and the people in the picture and their relation to one another. (Becker, 1970, p. 421)

Similarly, the life history might be deployed, as Denzin suggests, to complement data collected from other sources and using other methods, which can then be verified by means of 'triangulation' (Denzin, 1972, p. 26). Such a method is, of course, commonly employed by historians in 'piecing together the past'. However, as some historians who have concentrated on the use of *oral* testimonies have pointed out, the technique will necessarily produce discrepancies; yet as the oral historians have demonstrated so profitably, the discrepant may well be an appropriate area of enquiry in itself (Ennew, 1979). Accounts might then be viewed as having a *subjective* status. This is particularly relevant in our own case where we interviewed husbands and wives separately and gathered independent accounts of their 'common' experience, i.e. meeting, courtship, the decision to cohabit/remarry and their subsequent life together. Our purpose in this was not, as some perhaps imagined, to 'catch them out', nor was it an attempt to discover what 'actually' happened, instead the method was used in order to understand how different emphases, beliefs and ultimately, personal theories and ideologies about family life might emerge in the context of the interview.

The approach which accords a subjective status to the data may therefore be considered as an alternative. We might, indeed, argue that the 'objectivity' of the account(s) will in any case always be open to refutation, whereupon it seems preferable to adopt an approach to the life history such as that advocated by Denzin, when he argues that

> The sensitive observer employing the life history will be concerned with relating the perspectives elicited to definitions and meanings that are lodged in social relationships and social groups. Additionally, the variable nature of these definitions across situations will be examined. (Denzin, 1970, p. 221)

Yet whilst this strategy may be appropriate within symbolic interactionism, we shall argue that it cannot stand alone as an adequate explanation of a particular social phenomenon. Denzin's belief that 'the subject's definition of the situation takes precedence over the objective situation' (ibid., p. 221) begs the question of how the 'objective situation' is compounded. We would wish to argue that it arises out of the interpenetration of a variety of structural constraints – legal, material, economic – which combine to shape the subject's own definition. Situations, then, are not merely *defined* as real: sometimes they are real.

This is not the place to enter into a discussion of the relative merits of symbolic interactionist, ethnomethodological and phenomenological positions. In the remainder of this chapter however, and indeed throughout this book, we hope our position will become clear. Following C. Wright Mills, we hope to address not only biography, but also history, and, most crucially of all, the relations between them (1967). The life history method is, of course, our primary tool for understanding biography and the more detailed questions which we put in the second and third interviews respresent an attempt to isolate the important macro constraints which shape it.

The life history accounts we have collected are, of course, even in their verbatim transcript form, substantially edited. They arise, as we have suggested, out of a negotiated encounter between interviewer and interviewee. This should not deter us, however, since the process of editing, selecting and reinterpreting is itself an important one, whereby each individual in our study arrived at a public account of a, seemingly, private experience. It is important that we acknowledge the public nature of these accounts; as Voysey (1975) has indicated, they may be heavily coloured by the professional ideologies and rhetorics of doctors, lawyers, social workers and more diffusely labelled 'experts' on family life. We should in reading them, therefore, be attuned to these possible undertones as representations of more broadly-based attitudes to family life. The tension which frequently exists between these private beliefs and their accompanying public rhetorics, however, is clearly evidenced in many of the interview passages which follow.

The life history method allows us to see the development of these relationships within the field of our interest – second marriage. Each of the first interviews therefore constituted in itself an account of a social *process*; the men and women we spoke to were, however indirectly, being called upon to 'explain', 'rationalise' and 'defend' their circumstances. In this context the interview was conducive to the creation of a moral career or personal biography in which events, situations and outcomes could be given meaning and presented as internally logical. Like Goffman (1968a; 1968b) we found both 'success stories' and 'sad tales'. Likewise we heard of breakthroughs, turning-points, impasses and watersheds. The interview therefore provided a (semi-) public setting in which to rewrite biography. As we shall see, this is a process which is central to the whole experience of family reconstitution.

Two problems should therefore be borne in mind in turning to the data itself. Both concern the tension between public and private spheres. First, we must try to make some assessment of the extent to which private testimonies given in research interviews are themselves publicly scripted. Second, we must assess how the *events* portrayed in the accounts have been shaped and constrained by more broadly-based structural factors.

Chapter 3

The private troubles of the remarried

We begin the task of exploring our respondents' accounts by looking at the extent to which divorce and remarriage can be looked upon as a private trouble, a personal, traumatic upheaval in the life of the individual. Consequently, we are immediately drawn into that web of social relations which makes up the so-called private sphere and which is so frequently the object of deeply-held beliefs and commitments. In handling accounts of marital breakdown and family reconstitution, therefore, we are confronting aspects of human experience which in certain respects are bound up with a sense of identity and personal worth. Our object is to understand how beliefs and attitudes of this nature may be reshaped in the process of divorce and remarriage, giving rise to new expectations and aspirations as well as new family and living arrangements. In other words, the accounts must be read for the implicit ideologies of family life which they contain, as well as their detailed description of marital break-up and remarriage. We begin with a specific exploration of two sub-groups within the sample, whose experiences of marital breakdown contrast most sharply, before moving on to a more general examination of the process of family reconstitution.

Two case studies

Even in a sample of forty couples we have been faced with a variety of accounts illustrating contrasting aspects of second marriage. In trying to make representative illustrations from our data we were therefore confronted by considerable problems of interpretation and evaluation. Much of our discussion arises from a detailed examination of small sub-groups within the sample and on occasions we quote passages from the interviews at some length.

Here, where our concern is with laying bare the processual aspects of divorce and family reconstitution, we shall begin by concentrating on two groups with contrasting experiences of marital break-up.

In her study of a Midlands club for the divorced and separated, Nicky Hart distinguishes between differing experiences of divorce and separation on the basis of the degree of involvement which the individual might be said to have had in the relevant events and circumstances of the break-up. Hart therefore contrasts 'active' and 'passive' roles in the process of separation (1976, p. 112) and argues that those who portray themselves as 'acted against', just over one half of her respondents (ibid., p. 115), were less likely to be prepared for the state of demarriage which followed than their more active counterparts. Hart's method of distinguishing the two responses creates certain problems however. For example, ego is 'active' when he or she deserts spouse or forces spouse to leave; alternatively, ego is 'passive' when his or her spouse deserts or when spouse forces ego to leave (ibid., p. 112). However, whilst such a classification may be advantageous in so far as it is simple to impose, it may frequently belie the complexities of a particular case. Consider, for example, the situation of a faithful husband who leaves his wife because of her continual infidelity over a long period of time. Using Hart's system, such an individual would belong to the category 'active', whereas the man's account of events might reveal considerable and prolonged passivity in the form of a desire to maintain the marriage, followed by a reluctant decision to leave. The lesson in this is that any assignment of 'active' or 'passive' status must be based on one's interpretation of the individual's account rather than any *apparently* objective criteria. Again we would reiterate the point made earlier, that it is not the 'truth' of any set of events which concerns us, especially in a context where apportionment of 'guilt' and 'blame' may be readily offered by the actors themselves, so much as what is *perceived* to be true, as this will have important consequences for subsequent behaviour and attitudes.

In the following case studies we attempt to distinguish between 'active' and 'passive' in terms of how the situation is defined by the individual concerned and we are therefore seeking to explore the manner in which individual actions, needs, motivations and aspirations are assessed in relation to the factors which precipitated the break-up. Our purpose in this book is not merely to discuss the circumstances which result in divorce however; what concerns us far more are the factors which lead the separated or divorced person into new relationships, including cohabitation and remarriage. 'Active' or 'passive' involvement is therefore relevant to us only in so far as it may shape entry into the state of demarriage and determine the nature of future matrimonial outcomes. Furthermore, by definition our sample is made up of those who have already remarried and so a variety of possible combinations might be found to exist between, for example, 'active' men marrying 'passive' women, or *vice versa*.

One category which we have not mentioned so far but which naturally interposes itself between the extremes of 'active' and 'passive' consists in those marriages which are ended following mutual agreement to separate. Hart found that these 'joint decision' separations made up only 5 per cent of her total sample (ibid., p. 112). In our case, only 6 of the 64 divorced men and women accounted for the break-up of their first marriage in such terms and it was clear that, even in retrospect, many of them found it hard to construct anything like a conciliatory account of what had taken place. It would appear from our findings that it is the rhetoric, rather than the realisation, of 'civilised' divorce which has pervaded recent experience of marital dissolution.

In view of this relatively low incidence of mutually agreed marital dissolutions we have decided to concentrate in the case studies on the 'active'–'passive' distinction. Whilst this concerned Hart purely in terms of its implications for the subsequent period of separation, we are interested in following it a stage further, to the point where the individual meets a new partner and makes a decision to cohabit or remarry. For this reason we have singled out those couples in the sample where both partners gave 'active' accounts in order to compare them with those where both gave 'passive' accounts. There are seven couples in each category. The 'active/active' couples, whom henceforth we shall refer to as the *initiators* are: Snow, Dunwell, Thornleigh, Parkes, Pelham, Johnson and Roberts. The 'passive/passive' couples, whom we shall term the *recipients* are: Brown, Vickers, Browning, Baker, Hurst, Hutchinson and Wickham. Their statements are examined below in a section which might profitably be considered as an ethnography of contrasting experiences of marital breakdown and remarriage.

'Initiators'

Ennui

Perhaps the most characteristic feature of this first group is the extent to which they portray the break-up of first marriages in terms of *ennui*. Marriage for them the first time around had become boring, unstimulating, unchallenging and, ultimately, devoid of meaning. Despite, in some cases, relative material affluence and well-being and all the outward appurtenances of a 'successful' marriage, they found themselves 'growing apart' from their partners and drifting aimlessly. As Mrs Pelham puts it:[1]

> . . . we weren't rolling in money but on the other hand we weren't hand to mouth or anything, you know. There was no sort of financial problem, we had our own, you know, home that we were buying but no, oh yes, we'd bought a car and we were all right [but] I was bored basically, er . . . I think, looking back, er . . . it was . . . you see, it . . . it . . . it's all sort of self-analysis, isn't it?

Similarly, Mrs Dunwell:

> I'd made my mind up that it wasn't working. I couldn't see a way out and in fact it had been . . . the marriage had been stale for probably four or five years, although I'd not realised what was wrong with it. I just thought it was me being funny, until I realised that in fact there was a lot of things that weren't in the marriage that I really wanted.

Mrs Parkes expresses the dilemma graphically:

> I wanted something out of life, as it was I was getting nothing out of life at all except the kids and that was it . . . that was it . . . there was nothing else, I didn't go out anywhere . . . ( ). You read about people that are prisoners in their home and I was, and I were lonely, even though I'd got the kids. OK, it's great having your kids. . . . I love them, but you *need* adult conversation as well, you need something else, everybody does. And now you see, I've got me work and I drive . . . and that's something that I ought to have been doing years and years ago . . . ( ). I am a person in me own right now, whereas before I wasn't. . . . I was just a wife and a mother and that was it . . . ( ). You've got to have something else in life or you just go simply round the twist, and I think this is what *did* break up our marriage, it was like, as I say, living in a prison . . . constantly.

Although the men, by contrast, were not trapped in the home in the same way, they too speak of boredom and frustration. Mr Benson:

> . . . round about 1964 it started to come apart at the seams and when I look back at it now, and I can look back on it from the perspective of this marriage, er . . . it wasn't a question of . . . infidelity or any of that rubbish, even in those days and of course society's attitude to these things has changed a lot since then, but even in those days it wasn't that, it was . . . it was to do with the fact that er . . . that . . . this woman was no challenge, there was

> no way you had to keep pace with that woman, she wasn't generating pace at all, all the pace generation was being done by me . . .

Even now Mr Parkes finds it difficult to identify definite problems in his first marriage, but tries nevertheless to articulate a general discontent:

> . . . when you sit . . . and you look back on it, and you think . . . you know, 'what went wrong like?' . . . and I can't put nowt into focus . . . there's just nothing . . . it's like a big void period . . . I can remember . . . various little small things . . . so many small things happened . . . nothing significant, except moving to a new house, but . . . you know . . . with her . . . it were . . . a dead end, nowt to look forward to . . .

Mr Dunwell's comments on his first marriage are perhaps still more muted:

> Er . . . I don't know, it was amiable enough, er . . . I don't think there's anything particularly outstanding about it . . . there's not really much I can say, there . . . there wasn't . . . there were no big fights or anything like that . . . contented I would say, fairly contented, er . . . I think that's the way to put it, yes . . . yes . . .

These feelings and sentiments seem to reveal a certain amount of difficulty in legitimating the break-up of a marriage. We might expect 'initiators' to develop more overt 'theories' or rationalisations of marital breakdown as a means of self-justification but it does seem that this is peculiarly problematic for some men and women whose marriages appeared outwardly and materially successful. It was clear that they had no desire to cast themselves, or be cast, simply in the role of adulterer – the person who 'ran off with someone else' – and to this end their statements did at times take on the characteristics of a folk theory of divorce. Mr Pelham is undoubtedly the best example of this. Here are the very first words which he spoke in the first interview.

> I suppose that nine out of ten marriages that are still going now are like mine was, people are existing, you know, they're not living. They've got married and things are swinging along, the job's progressing nicely, the financial situation is progressing nicely, but there's just no . . . no interest between the two. Now as I say, I would think that nine out of ten present marriages are like that, you know, just two people living together for convenience and obviously, because they've got the kids and it's easier to do that than it is to break away and form a new life,

because for most people I think that that is quite adequate. I think they're quite happy as long as they've got a job that they enjoy, they've got enough money to go out for a pint or whatever their hobby is and they've got a nice house and they don't row too much. I think that's enough for most people. It's not for me and it's certainly not for Ann [second wife].

Meeting a new partner

Of the fourteen men and women in this group, at least nine might be said to have recognised such problems in their marriage and acted upon the realisation without however going so far as to separate from their spouse. Some therefore consciously began to move in social circles where opportunities for meeting new partners might arise; others, less consciously, began to behave towards members of the opposite sex in ways which resulted in new relationships being formed. Yet even when actively sought for, opportunities of meeting someone new might be difficult to find, especially where a person was still living with his or her spouse. Inevitably, several of the couples met at work – a context where contact between men and women could lead to new liaisons, without necessarily arousing suspicion or opprobrium.

For the women a variety of factors coincided. Going back to work was often seen as the solution to problems stemming from isolation and boredom in the home. At the same time this apparent release from domestic tyranny brought both financial independence and a heightened sense of personal worth and self esteem, which in turn facilitated the forming of new relationships. Mrs Thornleigh's experience is a clear illustration of the inter-meshing of these factors, operating on a number of levels.

> . . . I started going out with the girls from work, and I suppose it's the same old story . . . (   ) . . . out with the girls, only dancing, you know, once or twice a week. I'd got my own money 'cos I was working, I'd found my independence and that was the end. We just had nothing at all in common.

Eventually she met Keith, her second husband, whilst at work, but until then she had had no extra-marital sexual relationships.

> We went out on a date, it was strictly platonic and we met on a . . . on a platonic basis for quite a while.
> Q. What made you decide to go out with him, when you'd never been out with any other men?
> I don't know, I don't know er . . . quite honestly David, er . . . at first, probably er . . . the mystery at first er . . . we . . . he . . . I just don't know, you know, he says 'shall we go dancing?' so I

> says, 'OK' and I'd refused loads of people, well I say refused loads of people, you know, when we . . . you know . . . what it is when you go dancing and 'can I see you again?' and 'can I do this and this?' and it was 'no, no', and I strictly went home with the girls and everything, so it's difficult to say why I chose to go out with Keith. I shall probably never know, I just did.
> Q. How did your relationship develop then?
> Er . . . it was strictly platonic and then it wasn't until I'd been going out with him, oh, I don't know, probably six/seven months that anything happened.

Mrs Thornleigh's statements underline the uncertainties and fears which surround the break-up of a marriage and perhaps reveal a reluctance to end a marital relationship, even when it is felt to be itself beyond repair.

Mrs Parkes too, as we have seen, was 'desperate to get out of the house' and had been taking a variety of sedatives over a long period of time. Eventually she took a job as a barmaid, which was how she met her second husband. As she puts it, the relationship gave her 'the opportunity I'd been looking for to leave my husband'. Similarly Mrs Snow took a job driving in order to overcome her bouts of depression and quickly found that she enjoyed the attention of the men she met during the course of the day. She went out with several of these before meeting Mr Snow and eventually separating from her husband. Mrs Pelham had also begun going out regularly with a girlfriend during her first marriage but eventually met Mr Pelham through a part-time job which she had taken.

Many of the men and women pointed to the uncertainties felt in meeting someone new. Likewise even when this was an intended outcome of a particular set of actions it was often difficult to admit as much in the interview. For some it was apparently as difficult to acknowledge to themselves. To a certain extent this might be a problem of the interpretive categories available in giving accounts and on several occasions the desire to avoid words and phrases which were redolent of unwelcome and morally suspect stereotypes was all too obvious. Similarly, some continued to carry a burden of guilt which lurked just below the surface in their circumlocutory statements and which they found it difficult to slough off, even after remarriage.

Splitting up

For the initiators, the actual circumstances of marriage break-up took various forms and the interviews often revealed the continuing difficulties which many had in giving some meaningful account of the events which had taken place. Above all, the descriptions showed extensive uncertainty, fear and hesitation on the part of those who had sought to terminate their first marriage. As we shall see later, the emotional consequences of such experiences frequently intruded upon new relationships and definitions of self in second marriage.

Four of the women (Mrs Dunwell, Mrs Parkes, Mrs Thornleigh and Mrs Roberts) had clearly been plagued with indecision about whether or not to leave their respective husbands and in each case long periods of procrastination preceded the eventual separation. Mrs Dunwell:

> I'd made the decision earlier, sort of in a flash, rather than thinking ever so carefully about it, about six months before and he'd sort of said, 'well right, I'll buy you a house and you can move out' . . . this was a in a big argument . . . and we did in fact get as far as looking round property, er, then . . . but I chickened out, thinking, you know, it's . . . I . . . I . . . it just won't work, I just can't manage on my own, I don't know how . . . how I could do it . . . and thought it was just a . . . such a big row that had occasioned it and then six months later it happened again, you know, I knew that I should have stuck to my guns then.

Her husband bought a small terraced house for her to move into. As she explains:

> . . . neither he nor I knew at that time that I was going to live with anybody else, so I think . . . I think he'd . . . probably even got it in his mind that eventually when he'd finished University [he had gone to study law as a mature student] and the tension wasn't there, or he thought it may not be there, that we . . . we would get back together. He even said that he ought to have a key for the house, you see, which I utterly forbade, he said that he ought to have access to the house as and when he wanted to come and see the children. I said, 'well the door's there to knock on', you know, 'I don't want you . . . coming in and out, just as if I'm sort of . . . I'm . . . I'm just taking time off from the marriage, because that's not what it is!

As Mrs Dunwell intimates, things turned out rather differently than had been expected; for whilst on holiday in Germany, Mr Dunwell's first wife had discovered her husband's relationship with her in the form of a poem which Mrs Dunwell had written. Mr Dunwell's account of subsequent events demonstrates how the confusion was further compounded. On returning from Germany he and his wife discussed their problem with two friends:

> We more or less agreed that, er . . . we'd stay apart for some

> days, which was probably the fatal thing as far as the marriage was concerned ( ) [because] I went straight to Jenny, to visit Jenny and er . . . I suppose I started living with her from that moment on ( ). Whilst we were away in Germany Jenny had moved into a little terraced house which her husband had provided for her. I think her husband perhaps thought that er . . . if she was left on her own with the children for some time, she'd eventually come back to him, because . . . er . . . well, as I say, she'd more or less decided she was going to leave her husband before the relationship with me built up.

For Mrs Parkes the problems of separation centred around finding suitable accommodation. Eventually she found herself leaving her seven children with their father in order to go to live with Mr Parkes. After two months, however, she returned to her family. Before long she left again and went to live with Mr Parkes and his mother. Twice more she returned to her husband only to leave again within a short space of time. By now the children had been taken into care. Eventually she and Mr Parkes found a small house to rent and were able to establish a home together, gradually obtaining custody of each of the children. Not surprisingly the physical and emotional effects which these events had on them both were deep and long-lasting. As Mrs Parkes puts it:

> I lost a terrific amount of weight for a start and couldn't sleep for two years . . . made me nerves very bad . . . and I think that it affected Stephen (second husband) in the same way . . . his hair didn't fall out or anything like that . . . like mine did . . . but it made him ill when his marriage broke up as well, you know . . . it affected us both very, very similar and I think that it took me about what . . . four or five years to get over it, which we did . . . slowly, by working together . . .

Mrs Thornleigh's separation was set in train by her husband's discovery of her lover. Again we see the indecision:

> [My husband] told me it was a case of either me or him er . . . I couldn't stop, I'd got to go, I'd got to leave the children, leave everything. And that's when I suddenly stopped dead in me tracks, I thought, 'No, I can't leave the children.' So I told Keith that it was all over, no way could I leave my children.

Her passage through this private trauma was, however, signposted by the advice of two 'experts' – a solicitor and a doctor:

> I went to the solicitor and told the solicitor exactly what had happened, that I'd, you know . . . he was very good, being . . . you know, it was a case of either stop at home with the children

and my ex-husband or leave and go with Keith, and then the solicitor, you know, more or less gave me the facts that he couldn't throw you out, he could make life very unbearable but he couldn't throw you out and sooner or later he would go, if I carried on my relationship. Er . . . I did see Keith, er . . . and that's when, you know, the knocking about really started. I lost weight, er . . . I knew I shouldn't have seen him but I just wanted to see him, I just wanted to. [Then I] went to the doctor's and the doctor told me that I'd got to get away from it all, so I told him that no way could I leave my children, so he says, 'Yes you can, your children will be all right,' he says, 'I know your husband, he's a good father.' He says, 'He might not be a good husband but he's a good father.' So he says, 'You'll just have to' . . . I says, 'Well, you know, how do I do it?' He says, 'Well you just go home,' he says, 'have you got somewhere to go?' I says, 'Oh yes, I've got somewhere to go,' so he says, 'Well go home, decide when you're going, leave a note and just go.'

She took the advice and went to stay with some friends; after a few weeks she and Keith found a flat together but within a month she had returned to her family. Two months later, quite suddenly, on New Year's Day 1975, her husband left.

Q. Did you expect that your husband would leave like that?
No. No, I didn't. I was . . . life was very unbearable by that stage, I mean this . . . he . . . he'd started drinking, which is a thing he hadn't done and he was coming home and he was vomiting, he was coming home at three/four o'clock in the morning, and you know, he was most out of character . . . and then, as I say, we came back from me mum's and he'd gone, lock, stock and barrel, he'd taken every single thing that was his. And it . . . may sound cruel, but to me it was then such a relief, everything the doctor told me had happened, everything the doctor had said had happened, it had just fallen into the pattern, er . . . even when he left, he left a cheque for housekeeping . . .

The men place different emphases in giving their accounts of separation. As a result of the circumstances of their work Mr Johnson and Mr Roberts were both able to separate from their wives in a way which secured maximum public discretion. Mr Roberts:

I went to see me boss and we had a southern office . . . so I talked it over with me wife, I says 'well, what do you think we should do?' (   ) So I made a decision then, I was lucky, I had a good boss and he sent me down to London for about nine months . . . although we separated officially between us selves, if she hadn't told anybody, as far as anybody knew . . . I'd just gone down south to work . . . and, er . . . I came home, when I came home at weekends and slept in the back room and that was it . . . ( ) We got a legal separation right at the beginning. The day I went to London my wife went straight down to the court and got a legal separation.

Neither Mr Thornleigh nor Mr Johnson had met new partners at the time of their respective separations, but in the cases of the five other men the decision to split had been brought about as a result of relationships with other women – in each case the person they subsequently went on to remarry. Mr Pelham was asked if he had decided that he wanted to live with Ann before he made the decision to leave his wife:

Yes, yes, oh yes, yes, because up until meeting Ann . . . that was what sort of precipitated it, up until then it was what I thought was a normal marriage ( ) . . . it was just sort of drifting along . . . not unpleasantly. I mean it wasn't a ball all the time, but it wasn't unpleasant . . . ( ) . . . and then Ann came along and then, er . . . bang!

In fact the *two* couples got together to try to resolve their problems; in both cases the 'passive' partners wanted reconciliations, but he and Ann were adamant:

. . . there was one time when all four of us met in a pub and . . . obviously it was very strained and, er . . . not at all relaxed, er . . . but Ann and I decided that we did want to break . . .

Mr Roberts too, had been equally sure of his motivations, even though he had gone to live with his father after the separation:

I'd every intention of getting married, yes, every intention and, er . . . it's hard to say . . . if I hadn't thought I were going to get married to her [second wife] I wouldn't have taken the steps I took ( ) . . . I don't think I would ever have left if I wasn't . . . had at the back of me mind the intentions of getting married . . .

A consideration of the experiences of a group of men and women who depict themselves in an initiating role in the break-up of their first marriage leads us to ask about the implications which this might have for future relationships. It is clear that most of this group had already met and formed a relationship with someone else before actually separating from their spouses. Indeed it seems to be the case that the explicit or tacit 'search' for a new partner had marked the formal recognition of marital difficulties and formed the basis of an attempt to resolve them. With the exception of Mr Thornleigh,

Mr Benson and Dr Benson, new relationships had been entered into before separation was initiated and it is apparent from many of the quotations we have examined so far that an intention to live with or remarry someone else was the *raison d'être* for the split. These men and women were, in other words, seeking to exchange an unhappy and unsuccessful relationship for the promise of a happy and successful one. The transition between the two was therefore often extremely rapid, with very little opportunity for what, in the context of bereavement, would be termed 'grief work'. For these people personal and psychological readjustment, reassessment of hopes, motivations and needs and reflections on past and future relationships were carried out at a run. There was little or no opportunity for serious reflection; decisions requiring evaluation and consideration were often made in pressing circumstances and the accounts tend to emphasise contingency and preterition.

'Recipients'

The second group, whom we have labelled 'recipients' can be contrasted with their more active counterparts in various ways and their careers from first to second marriage tend to be differently signposted. These men and women often portrayed themselves as ill-prepared for the break-up and poorly equipped to rebuild their family and emotional lives. Shock and surprise followed by isolation and loneliness predominate in their experiences and periods spent living alone seem to have produced different expectations in second marriage. Marrying the 'wrong' person might be the fullest explanation offered for the break-up of a first marriage and care in finding the 'right' one perceived as sufficient basis for a successful remarriage.

Infidelity

In contrast to the preoccupation with 'drifting' or 'growing apart' which so strongly characterised the accounts of the men and women in the previous group, the dominant theme among those who had been relatively *passive* in the events and circumstances surrounding the break-up of their marriages was that of infidelity. Six of the women and five of the men spoke of the unfaithfulness of their first partner. Once again, however, responses varied; in some cases infidelity was given as the sole reason for marital breakdown, whilst in others it was merely one in a series of apparent causes. It is clear from the statements made by the men and women in our sample, though, that whatever the legal definition of 'irretrievable breakdown' and despite attempts to attenuate the language of blame, acts of adultery are still usually perceived as sufficient, if not always necessary, grounds for ending a marriage. As we might expect, no philosophy of sexually 'open' marriage emerges from this particular set of accounts. But as we have already seen, neither did it appear among those more actively involved in extra-marital relationships.

In several cases the discovery of a partner's infidelity had come as a complete surprise. Most graphic of all is Mrs Baker's description of her experience:

> What's the saying? 'Ignorance is bliss'. Well that was perfectly true . . . to my understanding he worked damned hard for us. We were in a nice comfortable position, in a nice house. He was working all the hours God sends and I thought he was entitled to his days off, on his own if he wanted them that way. He used to go off and play golf when he was on the night shift . . . other times I used to think he'd gone out, er . . . working, when he used to go out in plain clothes . . . well all the time he was off, out gallivanting with other women.

The discovery came after over nine years of marriage:

> I said, er . . . 'I couldn't understand.' I thought, 'Well you know, all right, some fellas have a fling and then, that's all it is, don't want their marriage to. . . .' I asked him if this is what it was, you know – but a year! I said, 'Didn't it occur to you to break it up? Was it serious all that time?' He said, 'No, 'course not,' it was just somebody he was sort of . . . knocking off, for want of a better word, er . . . I said well why didn't you pack in and think to yourself, 'Well I know Janice loves me, I know the kids are smashing kids, we've got a nice carry on, I'd be a fool to. . . .' And he said, 'Well I didn't,' and I realised then why he didn't, because it'd become such a habit to him it never occurred to him. He just thought he could get away with it for years . . . (   ) I think he played around and got away with it for so long he just thought it'd never happen.

Mr Brown had had some kind of intimation of what was happening but this did not serve as any kind of emotional preparation for learning that his wife had a lover. For him the marriage could not continue:

> It was in May actually, when I found out, you know. I'd sensed something previous . . . it must be like a sixth sense, you know (   ) I couldn't forget, you know, obviously you know and, er . . . I gave it while August and things got bad to worse, you know, she never stopped crying and, er . . . she wouldn't do it any more. Well she didn't like, you know, but er . . . I left in August on, I

think it was a Saturday, the next Sunday I went down to get some things – she'd got the bloke in the house again.

In each of these cases, both for the women and for the men, the discovery of infidelity seems to have produced an inevitable feeling that the marriage must end. Reconciliations were rarely considered seriously and certainly did not figure large in the accounts. For the other men and women, though, marriage continued for varying periods after the discovery. Indeed some respondents gave the impression of almost having come to terms with a partner's unfaithfulness, which they had come to view as an accepted, if unfortunate, aspect of married life.

Living alone

These perceptions of the self as the 'wronged' party must undoubtedly be borne in mind when we come to examine the experiences of the men and women in this group from the time when their first marriages had ended. Significantly, and in contrast to the 'initiators', all but one of the fourteen (Mr Brown) lived alone or as single parents for some time after their separation. In some cases (Mrs Hutchinson, Mr Hutchinson and Mrs Vickers) the period lasted for up to five years. Most of the men and women, however, as in the sample as a whole, did remarry or begin cohabiting within a short period of the marriage break-up. Another distinguishing feature of the group is that it contains the three couples in the sample of forty who met through what might be described as semi-formalised means. In two cases (Wickham and Vickers) these took the form of items placed in the personal column of a local newspaper. The Bakers, on the other hand, met through mutual membership of a club for the divorced and separated. All the cases, however, reveal a distinct stage of demarriage rather than an unbroken passage from first marriage to second.

Some of the men and women relied on parents for help during the period of separation, others encountered problems associated with living alone, factors which in both cases produced a pronounced and conscious attempt to start again, to rebuild a social life and meet new partners. In contrast to the 'initiators', only one of the 'recipients' (Mr Browning) had begun a new relationship whilst still married to and living with his first partner. Accordingly they were faced with the prospect of living alone or as single parents. For some, as we have seen, this brought loneliness, isolation and depression. It is important therefore to look in some detail at the circumstances which eventually led these men and women to meet new partners.

Starting again

Almost everyone in this group spoke of the difficulties of breaking out into new social circles, especially in situations where domestic obligations weighed heavily. Custody of children created special problems of this kind, as Mr Vickers describes:

> . . . you're working all day and you're dashing home to . . . run the house and look after two children . . . you're just sort of stuck in a rut at home, not seeing anybody and not going anywhere.

Mrs Browning found that her situation seemed to intimidate new partners.

> . . . When I'd had any dates, er . . . once you'd said that you'd got a little boy or that you'd been married they just didn't want to know (   ). Well, I suppose it was taking responsibility on of somebody else's child, not so much that you'd been married before, but when you've got a boy or girl, I suppose it's that that scared 'em off.

Mr Hurst saw the problem on a more interpersonal level:

> I've always been a hard mixer, er . . . I would never, you know, just go out and, er, chat women up . . . er, you know, the ideal place really is dance halls, to go and meet people, and, er . . . I've never ever been a dancer so, of course, I never bothered going there much. Er . . . I never used to go anywhere apart from this club up here anyway, if I went out, so chances [of meeting somebody] were pretty remote.

Mrs Wickham and Mrs Vickers, out of apparent frustration and loneliness, both placed personal column advertisements in a local newspaper in the hope of meeting someone new.

The sense of isolation, which the state of demarriage is so likely to foster and which led Mrs Wickham and Mrs Vickers to advertise for friendship, was overcome by Mr and Mrs Baker through membership of a local club for the divorced and separated, which was where they first met. Mr Baker had been living alone with his two sons for almost eighteen months and after some initial problems felt he was coping rather well.

> . . . to start with, the loneliness . . . at first, you know, I mean they were in bed for eight o'clock, half past eight and, er . . . that was it, once they'd gone to bed it was just a case of watching the television or just sitting there, you know, sometimes just sitting, looking at the 'phone, just wishing it would ring.

His ex-mother-in-law had also introduced him to a society for the divorced and separated:

> . . . there's all different functions, but the only time I used to go was on a Wednesday night (   ) Just after Christmas, the first Wednesday after Christmas I went down, I was just stood at the bar and Janice was stood next to me and we just got talking.

For him the society was no more than an ordinary pub, 'you just go to socialise . . . the only difference is everybody's in the same boat', but for Mrs Baker the place clearly had a different significance. She began going as soon as she separated from her husband and had moved back to Sheffield with her children:

> I needed to get out of myself and to do something different and yet it's something I've never done . . . gone out on my own . . . I couldn't, even though I'd got a lot of confidence . . . walk in a pub and stand there, I felt as if I were there to be picked up. The Divorced and Separated Club gave me that somewhere to go where there were women on their own and they weren't there to be picked up. Everybody sort of chats together and somebody joins in or some inclu . . . somebody comes . . . I included him. Er, then I saw him again after the New Year . . . 'cos that began to be my night out.

It appears from our evidence that the manner in which a marriage is ended and the type of role played in the break-up by each of the partners will have long-term consequences for any subsequent relationships which they may go on to develop. The two most typical forms of explanation of marital breakdown which our respondents in these two groups gave were, as we have seen, on the one hand, explanations emphasising the initiating role of the individual in searching for alternatives to a relationship which had apparently become unsatisfying, in contrast to those where individuals portrayed themselves as acted against, often quite unexpectedly, by their partner's infidelity. Clearly, the initiators had been motivated to act in certain ways through a combination of perceived goals and variations in individual circumstance. It would be wrong, however, to over-emphasise their actions as an entirely calculated and rational response to a diagnosed personal dilemma; nevertheless, they do cast themselves as being in control of their destiny in a far greater way than do the recipients. However circumspectly the initiators might describe their actions, therefore, and however much they may be sensitive to allusions deriving from unwelcome stereotypes, they do nevertheless display a more overtly theoretical approach than do the recipients to the idea of remarriage. The paradox of this is that the initiators, unlike the recipients, appear to have had little opportunity, in the form of a period living alone, in which to reassess their hopes, motivations and priorities. Instead their expeditious cohabitation and remarriage tended to create a situation in which the end of one relationship overlapped with the beginning of another. We might suggest that such a situation calls for still greater self-conscious application to the problem of reconstructing family and personal life. For those who define the state of marriage as 'normal' and any alternatives to it as likely to attract unwanted public scrutiny, then clearly a high priority is likely to be placed upon family reconstitution as a project calling for considerable personal and affective investment. By contrast, recipients may be more likely to assess the situation in terms of the fortuitous choice of a second partner, so that strategies concerning remarriage may amount to no more than the prudent choice of a second partner in order that the 'mistakes' of the past may not be repeated. As we shall see, however, a variety of other consequences which stem from the emotional legacies of the past will continue to affect the lives of the remarried.

Family reconstitution

In considering the forty families as a whole, the theme of emotional and material reconstruction is continually in evidence. The passage from marriage through separation and divorce to remarriage is punctuated by numerous experiences in which past and future lives are re-negotiated, boundaries are drawn anew and expectations and priorities are reordered. Meeting a new partner, second courtship, making the decision to cohabit and eventually remarry are events which are all influenced in turn by earlier circumstances and experiences. So too in second marriage, stepfamily life may stand as a constant testimony to the past. Regular opportunities may arise in which first and second marriages can be contrasted and compared and in which past and present can be used to illuminate and make sense of one another. Whether the outcomes are evaluated positively or negatively by the individuals concerned, they cannot be ignored if we are to build up an adequate ethnography of divorce and remarriage.

Accounting for marriage break-up

Considerable variation existed in the forms of explanation which our respondents proffered when asked to give some personal account of marriage break-up. For some, as we have seen already, the preferred explanations were particularistic and individualistic; marriages had failed because of 'incompatibility', personality clashes, or the unacceptable behaviour of a partner. For these people, the problem lay in having 'chosen the wrong person'. Others identified changes in self, personal maturation and altered ideals and values as important factors. For some, despite considerable efforts, no explanation at all seemed satisfying or meaningful. Explanations and rationalisations therefore varied considerably in their degree of theoretical sophistication but were important in each case for the thread of continuity which they might provide in linking diverse aspects of the experience of marital breakdown and family reconstitution.

Three of the men (Morgan, Hobson and Turner) and three of the women (Fox, Worthing and Elliot) opted for strongly particularistic explanations of the failure of their first marriage and saw individual, psychological and personality problems as playing a central part in marriage breakdown. Mr Morgan, for example, simply blamed himself:

> . . . it were me own fault, I know that, well [I'm] saying my own fault – 99 per cent my fault, just one of them things.

Conversely, Mrs Elliot blamed her first husband. He was, however, a previously unmarried stepfather to her two illegitimate children.

> . . . it was a complete wash-out my marriage, first marriage anyway.
> Q. Why do you think it broke up then?
> Because of the children, him not liking . . . not . . . he . . . he was jealous of the children. He was jealous . . . he was very jealous of me and I couldn't go out, I couldn't do nothing, and er . . . I was . . . it was horrible to live with him.

Two of the men spoke of the sexual problems they had encountered in their first marriages. Mr Hobson:

> . . . well I think it, er . . . she were never very affectionate, er . . . er . . . sexual-wise, you know, she's very . . . what shall I say . . . straight, you know, er . . . she'd been brought up in a . . . the . . . in a funny way . . . anyway she never let herself go, you know, sort of thing (   ) . . . we didn't have a great whizz in bed, you know or anything like that, it were . . . a poor sort of marriage as far as sex were concerned.

Mr Turner found that his former wife's sexual recriminations stayed with him for a long time and created problems later.

> I'd lost interest, lack of confidence shall we say, rather than losing interest, it was the confidence side of it that was the problem.

Several women in the sample described the violence and beatings which they had suffered in their first marriages. Perhaps surprisingly, however, marital violence was rarely given as the primary reason for marriage breakdown, indeed many women seem almost to have accepted it as an unpleasant but normal aspect of married life. Mrs Fox and Mrs Worthing, however, depict their former husbands' violence towards them as a major factor in the break-up of their first marriages. Mrs Fox:

> I've gone to work with thick lips, I've got busted teeth, what he's done . . . er. I've had two cracked jaws, I've had cracked ribs, he's pushed me downstairs, I've had cracked ribs, er . . . he's brayed me before I've gone to work and he's brayed me when I've come home (   ) . . . many a time I've thought about it, it were just, he were sick, he'd got summat wrong, I don't know why but all of a sudden it were like a trigger, somebody would pull a trigger and it'd flare up, but it got worse and worse.

Similarly, Mrs Worthing's first husband had been violent, even before they were married.

> . . . even when I were courting, he'd lashed out at me and butt me . . . I suppose, even in anger, but it got worse as he got . . . got married, 'cos he hit me when I were first carrying Sarah, that's the first one, and I knew then . . . I mean a few months pregnant and he was hitting me and I knew . . . I sort of had it in t'back of me mind all the time that . . . one day I would have to leave him . . .

It is clear from statements such as these, along with many others, describing such things as a former partner's unfaithfulness, inability to stay in regular employment, selfishness, financial incompetence or whatever, that for many people it is the particularistic and individualised explanations of marriage breakdown which are the most readily available. A broken marriage in these terms becomes a 'mistake', as Mr Stanley put it:

> I mean it works for some people and some formulas it don't work . . . er . . . it's one of them things . . . but some marriages will just work on their own accord without anybody trying, it's just a natural . . . you know . . . chemical reaction, if you like.

Remarriage, likewise, is seen as a natural and logical course of action, whose success is simply dependent upon finding the right partner.

Several of the men and women saw the situation in a slightly more complex manner, however, and felt that personal maturity and growth had played a significant part in the break-up of their first marriage. For some, for example Mr Graham, youth and inexperience had taken their toll. He describes his reaction to the news of his fiancée's pregnancy:

> . . . that obviously came as a bit of a shock, er . . . and her . . . I didn't say anything to my parents and I . . . I sort of thought about it, I, I thought, 'Well, the only thing I can do really is to get married to give the child a name,' you know, but, er . . . if I'd got my time to come again, I wouldn't have done, obviously, because I didn't really know what I was doing really . . . I was sort of immature really.

Mr Bingham also had to get married for the first time when his girlfriend became pregnant. He too felt that he had been insufficiently experienced to cope with marriage. Mr Thompson attributed his former immaturity to life in the Air Force:

> I think our marriage was sort of buggered from the start really . . . the fact that we were both immature, er . . . in the forces you don't tend to mature y'know, until you leave.

In some other cases the accounts pointed to more than immaturity and contained a sense of awakening, personal transformation and growing dissatisfaction based on changing attitudes and values. Mrs Dunwell, whom we have already considered as one of the initiators, put this very strongly.

> I'd grown up, yes. Well, I think it's . . . I mean it's ridiculous, I'd been going out with him from seventeen. I know when you're seventeen you think seventeen is being quite mature and eighteen is extremely mature but I . . . I honestly wouldn't recommend anyone that I know to get married now before they're about twenty-three or twenty-four and even then to think hard, because you do alter and obviously, living with somebody, the effect that their character has on yours is . . . is quite marked, you start off as one person and after eight years of an early marriage you come out a totally different person, well . . . not totally different, the basic part of you may not have altered but your . . . your ideas and what you want out of life has. I must have been very immature when I got married, I mean that's the only thing I can think of.

Whilst for Mrs Dunwell the realisation of her feelings had been slowly developing, for Mrs Smithson a need for change had come more dramatically during a spell in hospital following a miscarriage.

> I were in hospital, oh, a few weeks and, er . . . just layed there, er . . . it were like . . . thinking all about me life, you know, and I just thought that, er . . . there must be something better . . .

(   ) I just thought I'd wasted it, I still think I wasted ten year, I just did nothing in that ten years as I lived with him, but sit in t'house I didn't do anything, I didn't go anywhere, you know, I just brought three children up . . . which I don't regret that, you know, I wouldn't be without 'em, but, er . . . when I think about it . . . and you know, you think, 'Oh, I'd have me life again', no I wouldn't do that.

Q. So you made your decision quite quickly then to leave your husband?

Yes, yes, yes, it were because I hadn't thought about it . . . er . . . before then, you know, I'd just, er . . . sat back and relaxed sort of thing and, you've . . . you've got to . . . they inject you for this, you're like on a . . . dream world and I just . . . it were just like . . . flashes, you know, in fact me mum just can't get over it, she says how . . . I altered . . . but I did alter, as I say, I altered right . . . right sharp.

Along with some of the initiators, women like Mrs Smithson clearly felt trapped in the home, in a position which was made intolerable by the very lack of esteem in which their domestic duties appeared to be held. It was apparent that these duties *were* seen as potentially capable of providing personal reward and fulfilment, witness for example the guarded and qualificatory remarks where child rearing is concerned, but that some reordering of priorities and relationships was felt to be necessary in order to make this possible. By contrast some of the men were able to speak of over-involvement in their job or career, resulting in neglect of wives and families, as a factor in marriage breakdown. Mr Heathcote describes the events which followed him taking a part-time job selling life insurance:

. . . that I suppose was the beginning of the end, as far as my marriage was concerned, because I spent so much time . . . I started at that point in time to get my priorities in the wrong order . . . a part-time job took priority over my wife and kids. Not intentionally – I were doing it for their benefit, she wanted to be able to spend money, I'd got to go out and earn it.

Mr Gilmour's account is similar

. . . work was sort of having to take precedence, er . . . i.e. it paid the bills, er . . . it kept her in the manner to which she had become accustomed er . . . so I'm afraid work's first priority er . . . as much as I would have liked it to have been otherwise, er . . . that was the job, that was the type of person I was, er . . . she basically always knew this. That was it, it put a great strain on things, er . . . really, er . . . she liked to go out, she liked a lot of

> bright lights etc., I don't particularly, er . . . I mean, I see enough people during the day, I get enough excitement during the day to solve my problems, but my wife used to like to go out at night, well you can't go out penniless, put it that way.

Such accounts had the advantage over those of the 'frustrated housewife' in so far as they seemed, to the men at least, almost warrantable, given a particular set of assumptions about the role of husband and father as bread-winner. Nevertheless, a second dilemma later presented itself to these men in second marriages, where they were faced with the conscious choice of continuing as before, or of attenuating their work-life in order to invest greater amounts of time and energy in the private, domestic sphere.

For some of the men and women we spoke to, despite much thought and reflection, no explanation of why their marriage had ended seemed plausible. Even when, several years later, Mr Hammond looked back on what had happened he was unable to visit upon it any satisfactory rationalisation.

> . . . personally myself I don't know all what I'd done wrong and that's what I'm more interested in . I mean where had I gone wrong for it to happen like this? Because they say love is blind and, er . . . that the one in love is always the last one to find out these things . . . 'cos I mean that if anyone had told me that I'd have got split between me and my wife I would never have believed 'em . . . could never have believed 'em . . . I still haven't found the real answer yet.

It is difficult to assess the influence which such unresolved issues may have upon second marriages, though clearly they often create lingering doubts for the individuals concerned. Certainly, problems occurring in remarriage might be confronted in the light of earlier experiences and where resolved unsatisfactorily may lead to further loss of confidence. On the whole, however, as we shall see below, the men and women in the sample tended to speak in terms of the positive benefits which might derive from an earlier unsuccessful marriage and 'learning by mistakes' was the maxim to which they most frequently resorted.

For most of the men and women there was a strong emphasis on the theme of divorce and remarriage as a private trouble. The passage from first marriage to demarriage to remarriage, whilst punctuated in some cases by numerous contacts with the public structures of the law and welfare agencies, was typically seen as a private trauma, something to be negotiated personally and to be come to terms with individually. Consequently, as our respondents told 'their' story, considerable attention and emphasis was placed on the retrospective nature of the account. This came out strongly when they were asked to contrast and compare first and second marriages, but was revealed more insidiously in the constant use of hindsight. 'Looking back on it now . . .' was the linguistic device most usually employed to achieve this. Through it they were able to engage in a continuing process of making sense of the past in terms of the present, whereby personal biographies were brought up to date and resolved into situations of stability and permanency.

Effects of marriage break-up

Careful scripting of accounts did not result in the editing out of painful and unpleasant experiences, however, and in common with Chester (1971) and Hart (1976) we found that divorce and separation had resulted in detrimental effects on both physical and emotional health. Over half of the divorced men and two-thirds of the women said that their health had suffered as a consequence of marital breakdown. For the men, the most frequently cited complaints were sleeping difficulties, weight loss and a tendency to consume more alcohol, along with nervous and emotional problems and difficulties with concentration. In Mr Moseley's case the symptoms seemed, in his view, to be linked to his continued uncertainty about his decision to separate from his wife.

> I lost . . . I don't know . . . about two stone . . . er . . . I couldn't sleep very well, uhm . . . I didn't really feel like eating at times . . . I don't know . . . somehow at the back of me mind, er . . . I knew it was for the best, you know, that it finished but er . . . why I just don't know . . .
> Q. Did you have any difficulties with your work, difficulties with concentration?
> Yes, I found it difficult to concentrate . . . er . . . I had a lot of headaches . . . obviously I got further behind with me paper work, so I had to bring it home . . . didn't always work.

In some cases, complaints of a more lasting nature were attributed to the marriage break-up. Mr Thompson still suffers from psoriasis:

> It started at the time that the marriage was . . . sort of . . . breaking up . . . at the beginning . . . that'd be, what . . . about 1969 . . . 1970 . . . and I'd just got a teeny-weeny little patch on me leg . . . I didn't know that I'd got it really . . . (   ) It wasn't until later, when it got worse . . . and the doctor looked at it . . . 'cos I'd got a bit on me scalp, and he said that he'd give me summat for it . . . so . . . he did, but it didn't work. I went to him

again with it recently 'cos it got worse and he said that a change of lifestyle, like remarriage, which is a big . . . a thing that you have to think about a lot, that sort of thing can make it get worse, and now it seems to be going away on its own . . . 'cos me worries are minimised . . . but I would put that down to the marriage thing . . . once you've got it, it's a difficult thing to get shut of.

Among the divorced women, problems with 'nerves' were the most common and were cited in over half the cases. In extreme form Mrs Chapman sums up the experiences not only of herself but of several other women in the study:

> . . . in fact I never came off nerve pills at all for about two year, I was constantly on different kinds from the doctor, y'know, and I got as . . . er, I was too frightened to go out to fetch 'em myself and I used to send t'eldest daughter up to t'doctor's, y'know, 'cos I were, er . . . what, scared of what may happen y'know, 'cos I got so that I was . . . getting I was just wandering across roads, y'know, anywhere . . . whether t'traffic were coming or not, 'cos me mind was er . . . what . . . constantly on . . . thinking about it all t'time, you know, trying to plan out what I were going to do and how it would turn out, whether I would get custody o' t'children and t'house or what, you know . . . I was trying to make me mind up, to push myself to go in for that divorce but then on t'other hand I didn't want to risk losing t'children and t'house because he'd kept telling me and telling me for years that if I ever did, I'd never get t'custody of t'children you see, you know, so, er . . . it were there like . . . at back o' me mind all the time.

Mrs Elliot, too, has had nervous problems, but like Mr Thompson and Mr Roberts is able to identify a number of other more lasting detrimental effects of her first marriage.

> . . . through all the beatings and that what he [first husband] gave me, I were at t'doctor's a lot, I had bad nerves and, er . . . t'doctor told me that what I'd gone through . . . it's as much I hadn't ended up in Middlewood [mental hospital] . . . and some of the illnesses what I've had now have all built up from that they say; they told Raymond [second husband] at t'hospital that they were all coming on through that what I've had . . . 'cos I've had peritonitis and all things like that, well it's all to do with nerves, well I've a nervous stomach and that, all things, you know, what . . . what I've had . . . are what I've had done to me, all built up.

It was apparent that the manner in which a first marriage had ended could have important consequences for subsequent physical and mental well-being. Chester (1971) suggests that for most divorced persons, personal miseries are greatest in the period before a couple actually separate and that the actual legal divorce is frequently experienced as both a welcome relief and the *culmination* of a period of recovery which has already been set in train by the separation itself. Our evidence shows, however, that the individual's perceptions of marriage break-up and the subjective meanings attached to it are closely intertwined with emotional, physical and health outcomes. For example, if we employ our earlier distinction between 'initiators' and 'recipients', it can be demonstrated that these different roles were linked to different consequences. In the case of the former, unpleasant and negative effects on health were usually experienced *prior* to separation, whereas for the latter, particularly those surprised by the sudden and unexpected departure of their spouse, the more problematic period came later. Thus for Mrs Thornleigh, an initiator, the first reaction to separation was one of undoubted relief:

> . . . it seemed as if . . . as though . . . everything had been lifted off my shoulders and I was glad that he'd finally gone . . . 'cos, you know, the last couple of years had been really traumatic . . . and, you know, healthwise, oh, I was at the doctor's and I was on . . . all sorts of silly tablets . . . even though, basically it was my fault, you know . . . but afterwards, after it was all over I felt a lot better.

For Mrs Hurst, however, who depicted herself in a passive role, the shock of her first husband's unfaithfulness and subsequent departure marked the beginning of a period of ill-health:

> . . . the doctor put me on tablets when my first marriage broke up . . . I was very nervous . . . and, you know, frightened of being in the house on me own at night . . . I were all right during the day, but when it got to night-time . . . you know, I used to think all . . . frightened of anybody breaking in and what would I do if anybody did break in, you know . . . and I tended to be awake most nights and er . . . I had an accident at home when I got me hand in the wringer and I had to go to hospital . . . and when I went to the hospital they said that I'd bottled me feelings up and it all come out after that wringer incident and I went hysterical and they thought that they'd have to keep me in, but luckily they managed to bring me round and they said that it was with me husband leaving me and the shock coming out afterwards.

In Mrs Hurst's case this complex set of difficulties compounded of shock, fear and loneliness lasted for over two years after her husband had left. When she went on to describe her unsuccessful *second* marriage, however, her reaction to the separation was quite different:

> . . . me second marriage was . . . him being cruel . . . you know . . . knocking me about and I just couldn't stand no more, you know, and er . . . Dr — said that if I didn't leave that I would be dead within six months (   ) . . .
> Q. How did you feel when you left him?
> I was more relieved, you know, to be away from him, you know, I didn't . . . I weren't upset or anything.

For others, however, the 'relief' of separation was short-lived and whilst some *initial* improvement in health took place this might be reversed when difficulties arose in the divorce procedure. Mrs Graham found that the initial relief of separation was 'marvellous' but then discovered that problems over access, maintenance and the sale of the marital home brought a return of her anorexia nervosa. Mrs Thornleigh, too, found that, despite the catharsis of separation, unresolved aspects of her marriage continued to plague her and have an adverse effect on her health:

> . . . when the divorce proceedings started there was a lot of hate and bitterness . . . and what we weren't going to do to one another was nobody's business (   ). It's not until your marriage certificate is taken off you and you get that paper saying that your marriage is dissolved, you know, that you realise that person is no longer a part of you and I think, no matter how well or bad a divorce goes . . . it's a traumatic experience.

Making a new life

For men and women alike this 'traumatic experience' produced a persistent emotional heritage which exerted an important influence upon subsequent relationships. For those who had not met new partners during first marriage these problems often bulked large in the early weeks and months after separation. Several men and women spoke of specific turning-points when they had confronted their situation head-on and self-consciously begun the process of making a new life for themselves. Mrs Fox:

> . . . it finally got to the stage where I had to shake myself . . . I weren't doing anything . . . and I were getting worse and worse and worse . . . and er . . . I had a good friend that used to come down and talk to me . . . she were the one that bothered . . . and, er . . . it really in a way shook me . . . and I thought . . . 'Well, it's

> about time that I started sorting me own life out now . . .' and, er . . . I did that . . .
> Q. You made a sort of conscious effort to do it?
> Er . . . yes . . . it were . . . a forced job that I had to do . . . I knew that I had to do it, you know, I mean . . . I were only twenty year old and, er . . . you could see the young lasses that I used to pal about with at one time . . . going out . . . and, er . . . I were stuck in t'house, and I thought, 'Well, that's it, I've got to *do* it, like it or not' and . . . it was hard, but . . . I did it . . . I finally pulled through.

Mr Bingham's attempt to 'get away and start a new life' took the form of a new job and a brief move to London. Mr Heathcote, on the other hand, stayed in Sheffield, but nevertheless found a new world opening up to him:

> I suddenly woke up one day and I thought to myself, 'Well, you're a bloody fool, you're only young' and then I met a girl, and another girl and then I met another and then for a period of about twelve months I went . . . I went riot, er . . . I had six girlfriends at a time, er . . . all of 'em wanted to jump into bed with me, which was incredible really when you think about it . . . er, unbelievable in fact . . . I was thirty-five, two kids, a dog . . . er . . . who wants me? I thought I was past it, over the hill . . . which, of course, is completely wrong.

To some extent the shape and form which this new life took was dependent upon the living arrangements of the invididual concerned. Nine of the thirty-one divorced women and eleven of the thirty-three divorced men returned to live with parents when their marriages ended. This had distinct advantages for custodian parents who were thus able to receive various types of help in looking after their children. Among the non-custodian and childless men and women there were further reports of sympathy and understanding on the part of parents, though some individuals recognised that their divorce was not really their parents' problem. Whilst for Mr Worthing the return to his mother and father's home after the break-up of his marriage seemed perfectly natural, Mrs Fox's parents were less sympathetic to her problem but nevertheless took her back:

> . . . I got to the stage where I went back to me mum and dad. They said I were wrong for leaving him and that I should go back to him, er . . . my father didn't agree with it, he's very, er . . . very old fashioned, we've never had any divorces or anything like that in our family, so I was wrong and my husband was right [but] I went back to them, well, I had nowhere to go . . . so, er

> . . . my mother and father said I could stay there as long as I wanted.

Mrs Turner, on the other hand, found her parents understanding, but recognised that she could not remain with them for long:

> Well initially, I went home to my parents and I think after having a home of your own, being a reasonably free agent, as you might say er . . . (   ) I decided that er . . . as well as I get on with my parents, I couldn't stay there permanently, so I'd got to make a decision to go somewhere . . . and I think I was only there about two months when a friend of mine, who I used to go to school with, contacted me and she said she'd got a cottage which she needed somebody to share the expenses with.

In a slightly different way, Mr Brown felt a certain responsibility towards his parents, whom he did not wish to burden with his problems; consequently, in the manner of many working-class young adults who are marrying for the *first* time, he found that meeting a new partner and going to live with her was an appropriate pretext by which he could regain his independence:

> I were made more than welcome at me mother's . . . open arms actually . . . but I felt a bit sorry for me parents . . . I know your parents bring you up and that, you know, but why should they have my troubles? You know what I mean? They've brought their family up and got them off their hands, they don't want another one on their hands, you know, so I were glad when I met Jean.

Those who went on living on their own or with their children after separation faced other difficulties. Whereas those who returned to parents appeared to suffer from a loss of personal autonomy and self-esteem, the women and men who lived independently were prone at times to loneliness and isolation. Both situations prompted the desire to form new relationships. The ambiguities of the state of demarriage seem, indeed, to have expedited and shaped this process so that it is possible to identify important differences between first and second courtship. As we have already seen in the case of the recipients, meeting new partners and developing new relationships was a difficult experience for some of the men and women we interviewed. One aspect of this which we have not so far considered stems from the fact that in all of the couples in the sample, one or other partner had custody of a child or children from a previous marriage. When second courtships were described to us, therefore, reference was frequently made to the part which children had played in the development of a relationship. Indeed, in many cases, courtship appeared to revolve around family life and, if it were to proceed, had necessarily to find a level within the established day-to-day routines of a pre-existing single-parent family. Several men and women had found that this created difficulties at some stage in their relationship, either initially, or in some cases later, when children appeared to intrude and make demands upon a couple's time and emotional resources. Second courtship therefore forms another important stage in the total process of family reconstitution and, indeed, has a significant influence upon the subsequent nature of stepfamily life.

For some men and women, meeting their partner's children for the first time was remembered as an uncomfortable and embarrassing experience, especially when it took place during the actual period of marriage break-up. Mr Bingham speaks of meeting his second wife's daughter:

> How can I put it? There were no hostility or owt like that . . . We met, we made friends, like, quite quickly really . . . it were a bit hard for me, I were . . . a bit embarrassed . . . she wasn't very talkative at first . . . well, you see, I were . . . dragged her away from a good home, er . . . her mother and I . . . and I were a bit embarrassed for her really, thought she might resent me.

For some couples, though, the embarrassment came later on, when their own relationship had developed further. Mrs Graham:

> I'd met him, obviously before he started to come back here and, er . . . for quite a while the children accepted this stranger because he only came perhaps once a week . . . and then towards the end of that year he was coming a lot more often. They could see that something was very much different . . . well, we had just fallen in love, we were older but we were behaving younger and we found this hard for the children to accept. You see you do all this before you have your children, you're sort of on cloud nine for two or three years and then when you have your children you sort of simmer down a bit . . . you don't always want to be kissing and cuddling and being in each other's arms . . . but, you see, we've done it the other way round and that was when a few complications started to develop.

Several other couples spoke of similar problems created by their children's recognition of their parents' sexuality. In the case of the Thompsons considerable ingenuity was necessary when it came to establishing sleeping arrangements during the early period of cohabitation. Mrs Thompson:

> Barry was sleeping in the back bedroom and Jeremy and I were sleeping in the little bedroom, which we were for quite a few

months because we thought it was . . . for Jeremy's sake . . . we didn't want to, er . . . we thought it would upset him, you know, because I mean there had been me and his dad and then for me to live with somebody else on the same basis, you know, you probably would just upset him. We thought that, if anything, it should develop more gradually than that . . . but, er . . . we had a chance of a double bed . . . well, what we did, when we moved him into the other bedroom, he was away at the week-end with his other grandparents and we did the room up, put his bed into it, got all his toys into it and, er . . . Barry painted some signs on the door, you know, 'Jeremy's Room' and did little funny signs all over it and things like this and then we set the teddy on the bed and wrote a little note out which said, 'welcome to your new bedroom', you know, and put it on the bed. And I think he was so pleased to see the teddy and all the trimmings and everything that I think he quite forgot that he was, sort of, he didn't feel pushed out so much.

For many of the men, a common reaction to the child or children of their new partner was a desire to offer help, guidance and encouragement. In so doing they quickly cast themselves in some sort of paternal role wherein they filled a gap created by the absence of a father or, in some cases, compensated for earlier paternal neglect. As we shall see in chapter 5, this was a frequent claim made by stepfathers in the sample, that they had imparted some interest, behavioural or personality trait to their stepchildren. For several men and also their wives, this process was felt to have begun in the earliest meetings, so that in retrospect it was possible to construct an account which emphasised the essential rightness and justification of the new relationship. For example, Mrs Browning describes the first encounters between her handicapped son, Martin, and Adrian, whom she subsequently remarried:

I think it was because Martin had never had anybody to play with him, his dad never played with him and when Adrian used to play football with him, you know, it were Martin that sat down and puffed first, 'cos he was that tired, 'cos he'd never had anybody to do that with him before (   ) Martin was still in napkins when I first met Adrian, er . . . he couldn't walk downstairs . . . he wasn't like a three-year-old . . . he's fetched him on in a lot of ways really . . .

Other women also illustrated this point by contrasting their new partner's behaviour towards their children with that of their former husband. Mrs Worthing:

Er . . . the first thing I noticed about him was his attitude to the

> children, he was so different . . . even though they weren't his there was something about him . . . he used to, er . . . play and talk to 'em, whereas my husband never had time, you know . . . he were so good with the kiddies and he used to have time to take 'em to the park . . . it were too much for my husband to take 'em to his mother's . . . the kiddies . . . but he [i.e. second husband] had a good relationship from the start with 'em and I liked that instantly.

Mr Hobson describes how his concern for her children motivated him to ask Pat to come to live with him:

> I went down . . . to their house . . . to visit. I went down there, saw what state she were in, you know, down there with the kids and that really got me, you know . . . so I said, 'What about leaving him, you know and coming . . . coming here,' which she did.

From these accounts it is possible to understand the central place which children might occupy in the courtships of the divorced and separated. In those cases where *both* partners had custody of children from a previous marriage the situation might be further compounded. For these couples, considerable emphasis was placed upon the worry and uncertainty surrounding the question of whether or not the children would get along well with one another. Mr Hurst's description puts it quite openly:

> I wanted to see how they'd get on . . . so I took them up there [i.e. to home of new partner] Saturday and Sunday, then the following week-end they came down here, er . . . she [i.e. second wife] wanted to see t'house, what I'd done to it, so, er . . . and I cooked for them the following week, you know, she cooked a meal up there, Saturday and Sunday, then I cooked down here, Saturday and Sunday and er . . . everybody got on very well, so, er . . . we knew then there weren't any problems.

Such a frank, experimental attitude seemed to characterise the courtship of several of the couples. Mrs Baker, for example, described how from the start 'the children were already mixing, we never did put them as a barrier between us.'

In fact, in a far more general sense, meeting a new partner after a divorce involved dismantling numerous other psychological and emotional barriers. A syndrome which we have chosen to describe as 'courtship as confessional' proved fairly typical among these second-time-arround relationships. Once again, the theme of learning by previous errors lies close below the surface and many of the men and women had obviously found second courtships to be of therapeutic value in so far as they provided an opportunity to discuss the past and construct some meaningful explanation of it. Some relationships had, accordingly, been marked by an open and frank intensity of personal testimony. Neither was this confined solely to the middle-class couples, in the manner of those narcissistic preoccupations so mordantly described by Lasch (1980). Instead, for middle and working class alike, courtship as confessional provided an important cementing of relationships within the process of family reconstitution. Several couples described how, even on a first meeting, they had talked about their respective marital experiences. Mr Graham:

> . . . we just got talking together, er . . . probably an hour, a couple of hours, talking together, er . . . she sort of told me, er . . . her side of the story about, you know, her breaking up and one thing and another.

This kind of openness frequently seemed to speed up the progression of the relationship; in common with the findings of Goode (1956) in his study of divorced women, we discovered that couples were prepared to act quite quickly in ways which demonstrated a commitment to one another. In some cases this was linked to the kinds of perceived changes in self which we have already discussed. Mrs Worthing:

> . . . we used to stop in and we used to talk a lot, you know . . . and talk about his marriage and mine . . . I suppose it progressed a lot faster . . . I were older and I looked at him . . . looked at people different from when I were younger.

The most obvious way in which this is demonstrated, however, is in the early onset of sexual activity. In Mr Stanley's case he had taken Valerie into his home, along with her illegitimate child, in order that she could work for him as a housekeeper and look after his children. Within a fortnight

> . . . I moved in with Valerie, probably sounds a bit quick . . . but when you're together day and night you get to know somebody a bit better than what you do just seeing them for a couple of hours at night time, you know, things happen . . . obviously it was just a physical attraction and your own needs – mine and hers – I suppose, came first, you know, sexual satisfaction . . . and then gradually as time went on it got deeper and deeper.

Sexual *problems* in first marriage might also be on the agenda for discussion and mutual disclosure. Mr Turner found that he could talk openly with his new partner:

> . . . we seemed to hit it off well, you know, we talked the problems through, we talked them out, which was a good thing . . . because she had problems as well . . . and that was the good thing, that we had been brought together and that we could talk them out, which was marvellous. Er . . . of course we've read books and sorted it all out which was . . . 'cos, you know, it's obvious that there must be a hell of a lot of problems for a hell of a lot of people by some of these books that have been printed.

Undoubtedly such exchanges had a cathartic effect for some of the couples and helped to create a platform upon which a new relationship could be built. Many men and women seemed to have found this a necessary prolegomena to any further developments. It is likely that this sort of openness is related to feelings of insecurity and doubt; having once 'failed' in a marriage it was as if some of our respondents felt that their own particular marital ghost must be repeatedly exorcised whenever they met a potential new partner. Mr Fox:

> . . . we got to know each other's little 'ins' and 'outs', different ways and different feelings and I got to know, well, her little lad, like, and I got to know all her life story . . . that makes a difference, knowing someone's life story.

Cohabitation

As new relationships developed, many of the couples began to think, often quite quickly, in terms of the possibility of living together. As we might expect, their decisions in this area were frequently informed, often in a highly self-conscious way, by the desire to avoid repeating the mistakes of the past. Over half of the divorced men and women described their initial thoughts on the subject of remarriage in strongly negative tones. Yet as we have begun to see already, a variety of public and private pressures combine to make the state of demarriage a structurally ambiguous one. Despite their self-imputed intentions, therefore, most of the men and women in our sample had found new partners within a short period of their marriage break-up. New partners did not necessarily mean remarriage, however, and many of the couples had weighed up the relative merits of cohabitation or life together in a *de facto* stepfamily. Some had taken the attitude of Mr Fox:

> I always said, if somebody turned round and said 'You'll be getting married again' – 'No chance!' I said, 'I'd live with somebody, but I don't think I'd get married again.'

Mrs Chapman held similar views after her first marriage ended:

> I said I would never get married again, in future I would either find somebody and settle down and live with them or I wouldn't bother with anybody at all . . . and I think I'd got that in me mind, so that when I did meet him [i.e. second husband] I was only going to live with him, so that I could be free if anything did crop up like me first marriage, we could just go and that would be the end of it, there'd be no divorce proceedings and all that bother.

Such calculated honesty frequently characterised the decision actually to begin living together. Once again we see how strongly pragmatic views overshadow more conventional and popular notions of romantic love. Relationships among the divorced tended to be described in ways which place great emphasis upon practical considerations and the constraints of a particular situation. Just as Mr Hurst had described the manner in which he carefully introduced his children to those of his wife, so too it is in rational and calculated tones that he outlines their decision to start living together as one family.

> . . . well, we were both on us own, er . . . well, you see, I were travelling up there three and four times a week to Foxhill, she didn't come down here, not unless I brought her down, because of travelling time and bus fares . . . we thought it were just a waste really to keep two houses on, you know, her having that up there and me down here, we were paying two rents, two lights, two gasses, you name it, we were paying it . . . so I said, well, you know, 'We could cut half of these expenses down . . . you give this maisonette up and come and live in t'house' that was what prompted it.

Though slightly more cautious, Mr Thompson arrived at a similar decision:

> . . . I kept my flat on for about four months after I moved in here, just in case it didn't work out, I'd still got a flat to go back to . . . then we decided it were stupid to pay two lots of rent and, er . . . so I really moved in here then.

For Mrs Vickers, however, who wanted to remarry rather than just live together, there were firm conditions attached to the arrangement, which clearly illustrate her desire to avoid the mistakes of the past. This is how she had described the domestic and financial arrangements of her new partnership to her parents.

> I says, 'It's going in our joint names and Alan agrees.' I said, 'If it doesn't work out, as long as I end up with a similar house with a

> no bigger mortgage than I'd got already,' I says, 'OK,' you know, that was one of the conditions that I made. And, er . . . that was it, I know it sounds awful, probably, having those conditions, but you know, if you'd had the sort of marriage that I'd had, this is one of the things that, you know, is sort of important to you . . .

Thirty-four of the couples lived together before they were married. Among them it is possible to identify a number of different attitudes and feelings concerning what we might call the theory and practice of cohabitation. For a few, living together was a necessary evil, occasioned by the need to wait for the opportunity to remarry formally. For the majority, however, remarriage was a less pressing issue; some preferred to live together, with, at first, no long-term plans, others looked upon the experience more consciously as a form of trial marriage. Several of these men and women reported a sense of stigma, manifested in the negative attitudes of family and friends towards their living arrangements, which undoubtedly influenced their eventual decision to remarry. Finally, a few lived together for extended periods, not wishing to remarry for more positive, ideological reasons, but were eventually coerced by external legal and economic pressures. The subjective meanings attached to the state of marriage by these cohabiting couples varied considerably, but each revealed a specific concern with the conscious reconstruction of family life in the light of a particular emotional and material heritage.

In general we found a fundamental allegiance to the norms of marriage in preference to cohabitation. This is an important key to understanding why the couples in our sample eventually chose to remarry formally, rather than live together. Continually we see them, often after only short periods of cohabitation and despite earlier resolutions, discussing the question of marriage. Their considerations were, of course, frequently precipitated by the disapproval and criticisms of other members of the family. If a couple were living together successfully it seemed only natural and right that they should secure public recognition of their relationship through the formal act of marriage. Quite apart from any feelings which might exist concerning the normal laxity of an adult couple living together without civil or religious sanction, many of our respondents reported pressures to remarry which were couched in terms of its desirability for the children concerned. These pressures, and the accounts which the men and women gave of them, embody the diverse, often fragmented and contradictory ideologies of family life which are current in our society. The decision to remarry therefore is at the heart of family reconstitution, since without remarriage the family life of the divorced does not attain full societal legitimacy. None the less, the subjective meaning and significance of remarriage did vary, from that of a *sine qua non* to a mere legal duty undertaken for purely pragmatic and instrumental motives.

One fear which some couples had was that in remarrying they might actually endanger their hitherto successful relationship. Mrs Bingham's comments illustrate this:

> We'd been very happy living together and I kept thinking, 'Will it change once we're married?' you know, because I'd heard so many people say that you're happier living together than you are married . . . you know, I thought, 'Will it change?' You know, I was afraid in case it . . . we wouldn't be as happy.

Even after eighteen months of living with Martin, Mrs Fox felt apprehensive about getting married to him:

> . . . we went down to the Registrar and we found out all about it . . . and I think we both were a bit dubious still, about, er . . . we were wanting to get married but not wanting to get married, you know, we were both a bit frightened of what would happen.

Whilst several of the men and women felt this way about remarriage, most of them in some way or other encountered pressures which made living together, with no prospect of matrimony, increasingly difficult. As Mrs Chapman put it:

> . . . if I'd have been left to me own I think I should have just carried on and carried on like I was . . . just not bothering . . . just living together . . . but it were me sisters at t'back of me to get married.

It was in fact pressures from other members of the family which were most likely to precipitate the decision to remarry between an otherwise unconcerned or procrastinating couple. Mr and Mrs Fox had discussed the possibility of marriage on several occasions, but had rejected it each time. Mrs Fox's father, however, persistently suggested that they should marry, particularly for the sake of her illegitimate child, Jonathan. Mrs Fox goes on:

> . . . and then one day I went down to Martin's [second husband] mother's and I was a bit down in t'dumps and she asked me what were the matter and I told her that me dad had been getting on at me for this reason and she said, 'Yes, me and Martin's dad have been talking about it and we wish you'd get married. . . .' Anyway I told Martin and he says, 'I don't know,' and we let it die for a couple of weeks and then we were talking one night and Martin says, 'Do you want to get married?' And I says, 'I don't

> know, I think so, I don't know.' 'Well,' he says, 'we've lived together for eighteen months, if we don't know each other now we never will.' I says, 'Well, it'd make us both happy.' He says, 'Aye, it'd make us parents happy as well.' I says, 'Aye and our Jonathan'll have a name of his own.' He says, 'Well, we'll get married . . .'.

Some couples found it possible to resist such pressures as long as outstanding and unresolved legal aspects of first marriage made remarriage difficult or inconvenient. In fact, this seems to have been one of the few benefits of a lengthy and protracted divorce, in so far as it pre-empted an expeditious and ill-considered second marriage. Nevertheless, several people admitted to feeling unwelcome attention because of their cohabitation and this appeared to be more difficult to deal with when a decision to marry had been taken but was being delayed for external reasons. Mrs Bingham, who had given little thought to remarriage at first, became increasingly embarrassed by the fact of her cohabitation as time went on. Typically, this might occur when coming into contact with some official bureaucratic agency or organisation.

> . . . I used to feel very embarrassed if it come out, you know, that we weren't married, you know, in the bank and things like that . . . you know, it used to come out that you weren't married, but you lived together . . . I used to hate that . . . it began to matter then, in that I wanted to be married.

Perhaps the most common problem, which we discuss in more detail in chapter 5, revolved around ambiguities concerning the surnames of children, which frequently cropped up in schools, dentists, doctor's surgeries and so forth. Difficulties of this type point to the existence of particular normative structures surrounding the family and indicate that in certain sub-cultural settings and among specific social class groupings, divorce, cohabitation and second marriage still induce adverse comment and stigmatising effects. Mr Brown, for example, was concerned about the negative consequences which his family circumstances might have on his career and stressed the advisability of remarriage.

> I've got a good name at my place of employment, well I don't want anybody saying, 'Oh, he's living over the brush with a woman.' I don't think you get any respect that way, you know what I mean, it's obvious . . . I shall get management and move up the ladder in time to come and, er . . . I just want to be accepted as a married man and that's it.

In other cases, feelings such as this were less prominent and living together was seen as a desirable alternative to remarriage. For some couples, therefore, the decision to get married for a second time was lodged in terms of practical expediency. In a society where the so-called private sphere is continually beleaguered by elements of a wider social structure in which marriage, rather than cohabitation, is the norm and which has a bureaucratic and administrative apparatus which makes the same assumption, then numerous practical disadvantages may stem from living in a *de facto*, rather than *de jure*, stepfamily. Accordingly, some couples who were otherwise committed to the idea of cohabitation without marriage, had decided to remarry, largely because of the relief from irritating ambiguities which would ensure. Mrs Thompson:

> We said we wouldn't get married anyway, we'd be all right as we were, just living together, because it didn't make any difference, but then, when it was almost time for my divorce to come through we decided, 'Well, it's best to get married, it'll save a lot of complications as far as form-filling and this, that and the other is concerned.'

Mrs Dunwell identifies a series of issues:

> I think I tried to kid myself on that I could live one of these lives like a lot of people do . . . they don't bother getting married the second time and still have children and everything and it doesn't affect them (   ) but we did want to live together, we wanted a commitment. I don't think it's *really* just for tax purposes that you have this . . . this legal bit of paper, you know, you'd lose out financially if you're not married, we were quite poor when we weren't married compared to what we are now . . . it's very complicated . . . if you're not married it makes it difficult, you know, people will come and call you one thing . . . and I got to the point at one stage where I didn't know how to answer the 'phone, you know, I'd say the number and they'd say, 'Is that Mrs Dunwell?' 'No.' They'd say, 'Oh well, must have got the wrong number.' . . . you know, that used to annoy me.
> Q. You thought that marriage would resolve that if nothing else, then?
> Oh yes . . . well it does, it definitely neatens the ends, you know, I mean, the amount of letters I've had to sit down and write to petty-fogging offices . . . you know, the post office and this office and that office, you have to write to, just to notify a change of name and marital status . . . it used to get me down a bit, all the different names and the different acts and people you have to explain to that you would rather not explain to . . . it definitely neatens off all the edges.

Mr and Mrs Pelham lived together for eight years before eventually marrying; both of them told how marriage had not seemed particularly important and how, in fact, they had been 'too busy to get it all arranged'. In perhaps the most overt expression of the pragmatic motive for remarriage, Mr Pelham explains the circumstances surrounding their eventual decision:

> Ann does a little bit of part-time work, but the firm who she does it for wanted a certificate from her for reduced liability national insurance stamp, I think it is . . . er . . . so she went down to social security to get this thing, this form or whatever it was and a woman there said, 'Ah, but you can't have it because you're not married.' So they got chatting and they got talking about what she was entitled to if anything happened to me . . . and it came out that she wouldn't get a widow's pension. So, purely for that reason, we decided to get married. Just at this time as well I'd taken out quite a hefty insurance, 'cos being self-employed I don't have a pension, I've got to make me own up, er . . . I'd just got all this organised and my solicitor said . . . 'From a will point of view your best bet is to get married and then make out a will, because if not, if you don't get married, even if you make out a will, your son might have some sort of a claim on your estate . . .' so we decided and that is the reason . . . that we went round to the Registrar Office and got married, it's as simple as that.

Remarriage

Family reconstitution, then, took place for a variety of motives and within a number of different settings. As we have seen, the reasons given for remarriage were diverse and various, yet in one important respect there was a uniformity to the accounts. All of the men and women in our study exhibited a conscious sense of 'world building', as Berger and Luckmann (1971) would describe it; they were actively engaged in the reconstruction of family life following the upheavals of divorce and bereavement. Within this common task they displayed a general tendency to make sense of the present in terms of the past. In this way they arrived at a subjective justification and legitimation of their family lives. In most cases this could be readily observed in the manner in which they were able to contrast favourably second with first marriages and in the ability to bestow a permanency upon the family and its routines within what was often quite a brief period of having come together. Accordingly, the warp and woof of stepfamily life was continually receiving attention, both in a practical sense and also most significantly on the level of attitudes, belief and legitimation.

In general it was those couples who had been ill at ease during cohabitation, or who had encountered structural problems of the kind described by Mrs Dunwell, who reported any significant change after their remarriage. For the majority the formality of the wedding had been a brief ritual interlude which had left the pattern of relationships substantially unchanged. As Mr Dyson put it, 'everything's gone on just the same'. Mrs Brown in fact felt it was less significant than she had imagined:

> Well, now it doesn't seem very important to me . . . it did before, but it doesn't seem important to me now.

Mrs Barratt, when asked if marriage had altered her relationship, used her reply to emphasise once again the practical realism which underlay the decision:

> I don't know really . . . we'd always . . . with being together it didn't make really make any difference to us, it were only a matter of us . . . in fact, it were only really because we wanted to put our name down for a pub and we had to be married, that we really got married . . . we were all right as we were before, it made no difference us being . . . it made no difference.

It is likely that this reluctance to acknowledge any change arises from a persistent scepticism about the permanency of marriage, deriving from an earlier experience of marital break-up. Thus whilst none of the couples rejected marriage *qua* institution, they fully recognised its fragility in individual relationships and were concerned to concentrate and work upon these, rather than to place any blind faith in an institutional arrangement of proven vulnerability.

One way in which this could be done was through direct comparisons between past and present relationships and family circumstances. Comparisons on a range of topics, including financial arrangements and domestic division of labour, were, in general, favourably disposed towards second marriage, as they were also when concerned with contrasting the personality types of different partners. Once again, the comments reveal a sensitivity towards problems encountered in first marriages and a desire to avoid repeating them, coupled with a greater degree of self-consciousness in examining the principles upon which the family, home and domestic economy are based. Mr and Mrs Baker exemplify this concern with 'learning by mistakes':

> . . . Harry and I are in a completely different situation than, er . . . me first husband and I (   ) . . . learning to give and take,

we've learned once, we've made the mistakes once, er . . . I'm not saying we'll not make 'em again, but at least once you've made the mistakes once, er . . . you've got a bigger chance of happiness really . . . understanding, because when I look back, I did make a lot of mistakes . . . there were times when I wouldn't give in . . . there were obviously times when he didn't give in either, but er . . . how can I put it, neither Harry nor I tend to stick to something that's unimportant and really it's the trivialities that we used to row about and now, if it's important enough to row, yes, we row, we have an argument, yes, and I probably lose me temper or he probably loses his temper but now, he comes round and so do I . . . whereas before, in us first marriage he probably would sulk for days, whereas now that's not important anymore. (Mrs Baker)

Mr Baker was aware of the pitfalls of slipping into the dull routine which he feels contributed to the break-up of his first marriage:

> You know, you can sit here and it's too much trouble to get ready to go out and now we don't . . . if we decide to go out, no matter how tired we feel, we get ready and we go out to where we said . . . 'cos it's surprising, you know, once you say, 'Oh I can't be bothered', it's falling into a rut again (   ) We don't want to get into that same rut as what we both got in from the first marriage . . . we've learned from us mistakes.

Mr Benson makes similar comments about his second wife:

> . . . she's quite . . . she's not an easy woman to live with, but it's worthwhile, you know, the pay-off is substantial, er . . . and she keeps me up to scratch and doesn't let me take her for granted.

In other cases the emphasis was upon the release from particular aspects of a former partner's behaviour, especially physical and mental torment. Mrs Roberts sums up the feelings of several divorced women in the sample:

> . . . only last week I'd not done something . . . only a small thing, I can't even remember what it was and I felt very guilty . . . I felt terrible and I thought, 'oh, he's going to go mad' . . . and he doesn't go mad and I was . . . for that moment I was expecting him to say, you know, be like what me first husband . . . and when I realised it was a really lovely feeling . . . and I said, 'Oh, I think I must have been brainwashed . . .' But I suppose when you've been married to anybody for . . . seventeen or eighteen years, you get conditioned and when you've got somebody who doesn't go mad and who just laughs and takes it in his stride, oh, it's nice . . . you've not got this churned-up feeling all the time.

In common with the accent upon particularistic explanations of marriage break-up, so too changes in family routines, domestic roles and financial arrangements were often attributed to the attitudes and personality of a new partner. Mr Thornleigh contrasts his two marriages:

> . . . there's just no comparison whatsoever, just no comparison, you know. When I look at it the first marriage was a complete shambles, you know, there was no co-operation, no co-ordination, nothing whatsoever, y'know, but in this house, y'know, everything just moves nice and smooth (   ) I've got more incentive. I've got a damn good woman for a start, y'know, er . . . she's more willing to put some work into the house, y'know, the social life is a lot better so therefore it falls back into the house, I'm more willing to do things and she is . . . so . . . if I say I'm going to do something, I'll do it.

The direction of change could, however, be in one of two ways. Some men and women, for instance, reported a move towards what Bott (1971) would refer to as a 'joint' conjugal role relationship, whereas for others the reverse was true, and second marriages were characterised by 'segregated' conjugal roles. Again, therefore, and contrary to our early expectations, there was no *general* pattern of movement towards second marriages in which heavy emphasis was placed upon sharing of household tasks and duties. The experience of marital break-up, as we noted earlier, tended to produce piece-meal rather than wholesale changes in attitude and expectations and was linked at a more general level to social class and sub-cultural patterns. Mrs Brown describes the attitude of her second husband towards domestic chores:

> . . . in me first marriage I did everything, but now . . . I mean . . . he helps me to wash up and if I wash the pots then he always dries them . . . and he helps me with the children and, er . . . helps me to do the bedrooms and makes the beds and things that need doing . . . whereas before I did everything myself.

Her husband attributes this sharing of the work-load to a conscious decision:

> . . . we both seem to muck in with the chores and that . . . we get jobs done together, you know, we go about them together, I should say, we help each other more than before, you know, in the previous marriage. But Jean and myself in this marriage, I mean, I feel that I want to be nearer to her actually.

In the case of some couples, however, the direction of change had been different for each partner. Mr Pelham felt that he had undergone a change in attitude in his second marriage:

> In me first marriage I did practically nothing and in this marriage I do more than I think I should, a lot more.
> Q. Why is that?
> It's just that the relationship has developed, you know, Ann doesn't stand for the things which me first wife . . . used to accept.
> Q. Is it just a case of that, or is it that you've changed your own views on that kind of thing as well?
> A combination of both I would think, I *have* changed, there's no doubt about it, I've changed a lot . . . I think for the better (   ).
> Q. What kinds of things do you get involved with in the home, that you didn't do in the past?
> Drying the pots, helping with meals, setting the table, Hoovering now and again, all things which if there's a job to be done and Ann hasn't got time to do it, then we'd muck in and sort it out between us.

His wife, however, was less convinced of the extent of his involvement and goes so far as to contrast it with that of her first husband.

> . . . if anything I would say Michael does less . . . he's less domesticated in that way than my first husband . . . and when he was there, he was more prepared to do anything, he wasn't such a chauvinist pig as Michael is (laughs) you know, in that Michael doesn't believe that it is his job to do things around the home.

By contrast, several men who felt that an unreasonable proportion of the domestic work-load had fallen upon them in their first marriages, were happier to report a more limited involvement the second time around. Once again it is possible to see how experiences in a former marriage may shape certain aspects of remarriage. Mr Smithson:

> Well, in the first marriage I used to do all the household tasks for a start . . . because she used to say, previous wife, that she just didn't like housework, and she didn't . . . I used to come home and start Hoovering up and everything, whereas now I'm married again and she does everything, you know what I mean? She's five kids and the house is always clean and tidy . . . everything's . . . I've just no complaints at all.

It should be noted that some of the men who were so clearly pleased with the fact that they had little to do around the house appeared also to have no concern with more liberal ideologies of role-sharing. Mr Parkes had taken little part in the domestic chores in either of his marriages and obviously thought his position enviable:

> Oh, I don't do nowt here . . . I don't do any work whatsoever . . . you know . . . if I wash the pots they put it on the calendar . . . You know, I don't do very much decorating, you know, I do all the painting . . . that's why it's so terrible (laughs) . . . and, er . . . it's very rare that I do anything regarding household chores. That's not being pig-headed or funny at all, this is perfectly true . . . it's just that . . . well, there's four girls at home . . . they all do chores . . . and the boys . . . they don't do many household chores . . . it's a woman's task and they do it.

Attitudes of this type were also borne out in some individuals' approach to family finances. Mr Gilmore:

> I handle the finances . . . whereas before I didn't. The previous wife used to do most of that, er . . . she saw to the majority of the things, the bills, etc., basically because that's the way she wanted it . . . she said she was a better manager than me – question mark – but, er . . . this time around, I handle the finance side . . . and that way I know exactly how we stand, how we're fixed and what to do about it, whereas before you . . . you had a very vague idea what was happening, you never really knew what bills had been paid, what hadn't eh . . . , so this time I've got the reins.

In general, however, it was in financial matters that changes between first and second marriages were most strongly emphasised. Several women who had in some cases undergone acute economic hardship in their first marriages were eager to emphasise the better circumstances which they now enjoyed. Again, this might simply mean a regular income or steady housekeeping allowance, rather than any more basic approach to money matters within the family. Mrs Worthing:

> I couldn't depend on me first husband, you know, you had to ask him if . . . if he'd put the mortgage away and things . . . and he said he had and he hadn't when you went to look. But with Ian, you know that he's done it . . . he's got a set wage like, and he puts everything away and I know how much money I can have and how much he has and I know that when a bill comes, there's money to pay it.

Several women described their good fortune at having found a second partner who was financially reliable and were able to use this dependability as another vindication of their decision to remarry.

Even so, as we shall see in the next chapter, family finance after remarriage is frequently subject to turbulence and disruption created by such additional complications as larger families, rehousing and maintenance payments. Once again some couples had been guided by earlier experience in facing the new difficulties created by stepfamily life. Mrs Moseley:

> . . . this time I was older, more mature, if you like . . . well I like to think that I am, the same with Graham and I don't think that he has any intentions of making the same mistakes as before . . . that he did . . . and I have . . . with money and things like that . . . I think that they do tend to be a constant irritant, especially in the younger years of marriage and . . . you know . . . I think that we've sort of got to grips with that . . . there comes a time in life when you've just got to get down to tackling the money problems and . . . er . . . I think . . . everyone goes through a very rocky stage with money in their marriages, they're very lucky if they don't . . . and . . . we've not let that happen this time . . . I mean, we pool everything, if there's anything that wants doing then we share it between us, which is something I've never had before . . . er . . . it's always been just left to me to tackle things the best way that I can.

Her husband, who took a less responsible and lower-paid job as a result of the emotional strain imposed by the break-up of his first marriage, admits that it has been a struggle:

> . . . we've had to watch ourselves . . . obviously . . . in fact it's took about two year really to get straight . . . and we're really on top now . . . living a great life at the moment . . . but at one stage we got to the stage where everything that was coming in was going out, er . . . we've had to wangle this and wangle that and take a loan out here and there, but we're all paid off now, so we're all right.

But whilst Mr and Mrs Moseley saw themselves as having reached a plateau of financial stability, in general, most of the couples' accounts were *less* conclusive. They revealed that in finance, as in the various emotional, psychological and interpersonal aspects of remarriage, the emphasis is upon a continuing process wherein family life is self-consciously stabilised and reconstituted. Mr Graham's remarks, in which he begins by answering a question on finance but goes on to talk in general terms about his experience of second marriage, illustrate this vividly:

> Q. Do you tend to organise your finances differently now to the way you did before?
> Yes, I do, er . . . although Jennifer sees mainly to the finances

> side, you know, the paying of bills and everything, but I mean, we always discuss, y'know, what's to be paid . . . uhm . . . I mean . . . she more or less . . . I go out to work and I bring the money home, sort of thing, and I turn the money over to her, but . . . er . . . it's not just as straightforward as that, I mean . . . it's not that I don't want anything to do with it or anything like that, but we find that it works easier and she knows roughly what the bills are and what's got to be paid and when it's got to be paid . . . but I mean, we still sit down and discuss . . . if bills are getting a bit too high, or . . . what we might have to reduce here, or what we could afford to pay for there . . . it's a bit of a struggle at times, I mean . . . you can imagine with family . . . it's not as though . . . we've . . . sort of, you know, sort of . . . started from just being young people, er . . . gradually coming to marriage and then had children . . . I mean, we've gone in right at the deep end this time, but I mean . . . we both knew what we were doing . . . I know I more or less went headlong into my first marriage, but this one were . . . I couldn't envisage me getting divorced again, once I'd got married to Jennifer, because, er . . . you can see ahead that bit more, uhm, you can sort of visualise, sort of thing, that . . . just which way things can turn, you know, by past experiences. You know, I mean, I can sort of see that . . . uhm . . . if something's up, if I've upset Jennifer, uhm . . . you know, it stands out a bit more now than it did . . . you know, I had no experience before . . . and that sort of keeps us on an even keel, you know, to a certain extent.

By now it will be apparent that the extent to which the couples in our study were able to keep their family lives 'on an even keel', as Mr Graham puts it, was heavily influenced by past events. In so far as aspects of first marriage were influential in shaping the individual's approach to remarriage and the attitudes, beliefs and routines contained within it, then it becomes impossible to make sense of stepfamily life without some knowledge of its antecedents. This is not merely appropriate at an investigative level, in terms of the piecing together of personal biographies, but is also sociologically necessary in so far as our respondents themselves were engaged in the process of making sense of the present in terms of the past. Family reconstitution should therefore not be construed merely as an abstraction or heuristic device, but represents practical and mental activity of a kind which is central to stepfamily life. Divorce and remarriage as a private trouble has been the theme of this chapter and throughout we have concentrated on the personal and often traumatic aspects of the individual experience. However hard our respondents may have tried to cast their accounts in a personal light, however, it is obviously necessary to explore the broader, structural constraints existing beyond the family, if the full implications of divorce and remarriage, for individual and society alike, are to be understood. We therefore turn in the next chapter to some of the legal, economic and material factors, which in standing on the peripheries of the private sphere, may also trespass into it.

Chapter 4

Stepfamilies in the public sphere

In the previous chapter we tried to demonstrate how the couples in the study attempted to make sense of the past and to recreate or reconstitute normal family life within the private sphere of their new partnerships. However, as we have already seen, it is rarely possible for the remarried to forget the past entirely or to make a completely fresh start. Both partners and children involved in a remarriage bring with them an emotional and material inheritance which can never be entirely ignored. Many of the most powerful reminders of this inheritance stem from their contacts with the public institutions which surround and shape family life: the courts and legal services; the Supplementary Benefits Commission and social service departments, employers, local housing and educational services. Thus the practical, material circumstances in which the remarried begin their new partnerships are frequently shaped directly by such public institutions. The process of divorce itself determines when they are legally free to marry once more, and the custody arrangements, family membership itself. In addition their place in the housing market, and their total income if it includes either supplementary benefit and/or maintenance may be a direct consequence of earlier marital experiences. Their individual and family identity and their perception of how well they coped as lone parents in the past is also greatly affected by relationships with social and welfare workers, doctors, solicitors and clergymen as well as their local community of neighbours and kin. As we suggested in chapter 1, the experience of divorce and remarriage brings many remarried couples and their children under much greater public scrutiny than their first married counterparts. Family arrangements which would normally be designated as private and, therefore, a matter of personal choice, are frequently shaped quite explicitly by legal and administrative policies and structures.

Although certain aspects of the apparently private domestic life of all families are to some extent structured by public institutions, it is apparent from a variety of evidence that some families experience a greater degree of public control than others. For example, a number of studies indicate that members of deviant family structures come under a much greater direct scrutiny by both experts, including sociologists, members of personal service occupations and, more generally, within their local communities. (Voysey, 1975; George and Wilding, 1972; Marsden, 1969). George and Wilding's study is particularly important in this respect. They argue that although experts, practitioners and the public alike tend to regard *all* one-parent families as deviant in some way, motherless families are expected to have more potential problems than fatherless families. Whilst it is widely expected that mothers left on their own with dependent children will be able to cope alone, albeit in reduced financial circumstances, George and Wilding's survey of community attitudes showed that there was much greater uncertainty about whether fathers could, or should be expected to manage on their own (George and Wilding, 1972). Many of the lone fathers in their study were aware of their deviant status, their isolation within the local community and the restrictions imposed by child care responsibilities upon their chances of meeting a new partner. However, even amongst this group sharing common disadvantages, some fathers came under much greater public scrutiny and control than others. Although all faced certain common problems, their consequences were not so severe for the fathers in their sample from social classes I and II. Not only did they enjoy better health, and a higher standard of living and were less likely to claim supplementary benefit, but they also turned to social workers for help less frequently because they generally had sufficient financial resources to pay for child care where they had no help from kin. Thus, in some important respects the middle-class fathers in their study enjoyed greater insulation and privacy from the public institutions which shape family life. Such evidence leads us to the tentative conclusion which will be tested in relation to our own data, that whilst family structures which deviate from the nuclear family norm will tend to experience closer public scrutiny and control, the greater the material and interpersonal resources of the family the more its members are able to insulate themselves from public intervention and dependence upon public institutions.

Fathers with custody of their children: a case study

As we explained in chapter 2, the intention and scope of our research and lack of knowledge about the total population of stepfamilies precluded the recruitment of a representative sample of remarried couples and there are certain differences between our study families and the remarried population as a whole. In particular, there are a larger than expected number of fathers in the study with custody of one or more of their children from their first marriage, including one, Dr Parker, who has custody of a stepchild of his first marriage. Fourteen of the thirty-three divorced men in the study had custody of some or all of their children; in five cases, custody of the children was split between father and mother (Brown; Dyson; Johnson; Stanley; Walker). Many of these men's earlier experiences as single parents mirrored those described by George and Wilding and it is evident that although remarriage has enabled them to share parental responsibilities with their new partners, for some at least, many of the consequences of deviant family status persist. We are, therefore, introducing the data presented in this chapter with a detailed consideration of the subgroup of families in which a custodian father brought some or all of the children of his first marriage into the new family. The experiences of this group illustrate most strikingly the continuing effects of the public sphere upon stepfamilies, especially in relation to custody, access, finance and contact with personal service professions.

Research on custody and access arrangements after divorce suggests that divorced fathers are given custody of their children in only a relatively small proportion of cases; indeed this state of affairs has stimulated the formation of at least two pressure groups campaigning for divorce reforms to protect the interests of fathers, *Families Need Fathers* and *Campaign for Justice in Divorce.* Eekelaar and Clive found that in England and Wales, only 10.3 per cent of the children of the divorce petitioners in their sample were living with their fathers at the time of petition and in only 3.7 per cent of cases were the children split between parents. As their research demonstrated that in the overwhelming majority of cases, whether contested or not, the court decision favoured a continuation of existing arrangements, it may be assumed that between 10 and 15 per cent of all divorced fathers have custody of children (Eekelaar and Clive, 1977).

Detailed consideration of the accounts of the fourteen custodian fathers in our sample helps us to understand more about the variety of circumstances in which the unusual arrangement of custody to father took place. In seven of the cases (Baker; Dyson; Hammond; Heathcote; Smithson; Stanley and Vickers) husbands were left with their children from the beginning of their separation, when, with or without warning, their wives left home. Mr Smithson's first wife had already left home for a short time. When she returned they began to look for a larger house together:

> We were buying [a house] in Hillsborough . . . we were laid in bed one weekend and she says to me, 'I don't think I'm going to like the house at Hillsborough. . . . I'll only finish up leaving you again.' I says, 'Who are you to tell me when you're going to leave me and when your're not going to leave me.' I says, 'Anyway if it's like that I'll give you a week to find somewhere. I think you ought to go.' She got a flat with some more girls at the Fiesta [nightclub] . . . I found out she was knocking about with this taxi driver. . . . When I found out about that I said we'd better call it a day and I went to live with me mother, took the kids and everything.

Mr Heathcote's first wife was also working at a nightclub at the time she left him. At the time he realised he had been working very hard, building up his own business and recognised that his wife's job 'had the sort of atmosphere, with people coming in and throwing money around'. She met another man and the day after she told her husband about him:

> . . . she rang him up and he fetched her. (sighs)
> Q. When was that?
> 3rd April 1975. I timed it badly actually, if I'd left it four more days, I could have claimed personal allowance for a married man for the whole of 75/76 and . . . but you don't think about things at the time, do you? (laughs)

He went on to describe the arrangements he made to look after the children:

> I was commuting, taking the children to school at nine o'clock or ten to nine then going to Woodseats having to get back home for quarter past three to pick the first one up from school and then back to school for the other one at half past three or waited for them both to come out together, our Raymond was a bit older, he walked home with some of his friends some times, er . . . and then it was arranging a baby-sitter.
> Q. How did things work our when you went to your mother's then?
> Well it was magic then 'cos mum was there, right, er . . . except that she worked and er . . . she left at half past seven in the morning and . . . to go to work well that was OK 'cos I'd usually see the kids off to school anyway, that didn't matter.

Mr Vickers's first wife left him with their two boys, the youngest eighteen months old, after her affair with their student lodger was discovered. She later said she wanted to return to try to 'make a go of it', and he agreed to this but she soon left again. When asked why the children had remained with him Mr Vickers explained:

> She made the excuse which most women I don't think would . . . that she couldn't afford to give them a proper home and everything else. She wanted me to move out of the house and leave her that. I nearly did but I was advised very strongly by the solicitor and I still thought she might well send for the children at a later date, but she never did.

When Mr Harper discovered that his first wife had been having an affair with a friend of his and wanted to go and live with him he told her that he would not let her keep their two children. She took them with her when she left a few days later, but he went and collected them immediately. Some three weeks later they met by arrangement she told him she thought he should have the children.

Two more fathers acquired their children a short time after separation (Hurst and Turner). When he discovered that his first wife had had a number of affairs, Mr Hurst left home and went to live with his parents for several months. He travelled back to his old neighbourhood to go to work and so, through friends and neighbours, was able to check up on his children:

> this friend of mine from up the road . . . he came down and said that, Martin, that's youngest, he's prone to having nightmares and . . . he were knocking him up at, I think it were either two or three o'clock in the morning, and er . . . he said he couldn't find his mam. . . . He [his friend] came down to try, you know, to get 'em up, and he couldn't get any reply, so he 'phoned Hackenthorpe police and they eventually came down and knocked 'em up. . . . She'd probably been drinking the night before and got in heavy sleep . . . she used to drink a hell of a lot. . . . Anyway they took a report on it and settle him back down, so the next morning I came and told them both they'd got to go and I took the kiddies with me back to me mother's because she wasn't looking after 'em properly.

Although his wife left their house to live with another man, 'a mate of his', the tenancy was still in her name and it took some time for him to have it transferred:

> I had to apply to Housing and inform them that we'd split up by which time I'd got me separation order through . . . and t'custody which made it easier for me to get this house so I had her name taken off the [rent] book altogether.

Mr Turner returned from work to find that his first wife and son,

Trevor, had disappeared. He eventually found her at her mother's in Manchester. He returned to live with his parents but visited Manchester regularly to see Trevor and, although he hoped for a reconciliation, it seemed increasingly unlikely. One Sunday he collected Trevor for a weekend visit:

> I went down on 16 April, it always sticks in me mind that day, it was a Sunday and, er, my wife wasn't in but her mother was . . . and she gave me a parcel of toys, so I thought anyway, one or two clothes for him to change into over the weekend . . . when I got . . . got to me mother's and took the things out of the bag, I noticed that the clothes had been recently washed and still damp . . . and I knew then . . . that was it, I was having him and he wasn't going back, not from my point of view, from their point of view as well, there was no doubt about it, so that was it.
> Q. What did you feel when you realised that?
> I felt pretty sick at the time actually, because I knew then again that things were . . . it was definitely finished, you know, I . . . I'd been rather optimistic I think against any hope really, of er . . . of reconciliation but . . . t . . . to find out that he's just, thrust, you know, that a child's just thrust there upon you (   ) but then again, I was pleased that we were able to . . . but me problem was now of course, how was I going to cope.

Mr Brown also returned to live with his parents after he discovered that his wife had been having an affair. After some months he met Jean, later to become his second wife. Soon after they had started living together:

> My wife rang me up at work and said that the boys were pining for me . . . she said 'They want their father'. . . . In her eyes . . . the girl's been the favourite. . . . And I said what did she mean and she said that both the boys wanted to come and live with you . . . and I says 'Of course they can, I'll come down and talk it over with you first' and I went down there and she'd got them packed . . . I said to Jean 'She's packing the lads off on me, what shall we do?' and she said, 'We'll have them, we'll have them both.' . . . So I took the boys back home and Paul fitted in great . . . 'cos all the lads were his age, and the other boy hadn't got a friend or anything . . . I could see he were missing his friends that he'd grown up with and I said to him, 'You want to go home, don't you?' and he said, 'Yes Dad, but can I still come . . .?' and you know . . . it were heartbreaking. And we asked Paul and . . . he said he wanted to stop with his Daddy because I'd been on nights regular and my wife had worked during the day, so actually I was

> his mother and father . . . I'd been in close contact with him all his life . . . and he really clung to me.

Mr Walker's wife walked out on him taking their children. When he visited them he was aware that his eldest daughter, Pamela, then aged thirteen, 'wanted to come home, to live with me anyway'. He went to court to get a variation in the custody order but,

> I didn't seem to have any chance at all, although the child wanted to come and live with me, they don't seem to like to split them up somehow, I don't know why.

He remarried in 1976 and soon after, Pamela did in fact come to live with them. Mr Walker himself is not sure exactly how it happened;

> I can't tell you the truth of it, I can tell you what Pamela told me and I don't think that's strictly true. She said she'd had an argument with her mother and her mother said she'd have to go . . . so I took the car over there, put all Pamela's stuff in and brought her back here. . . . Millie [his ex-wife] said she could come here and I brought her here and I think she's been happy ever since. I know which place she'd sooner be . . . but the reason for her coming here, I don't know whether it's correct, I have my doubts, on the threat of throwing her out.

Mr Johnson also acquired care and control of his eldest daughter when she was fourteen:

> She started to be a bit too much . . . a bit of a handful for my wife . . . she couldn't manage her . . . because she was starting to get a bit wild so I stepped in and brought her up here and that actually split the children up.

Mr Parker, who had acquired a stepdaughter through his first marriage, became a 'week-end father' to his daughter and step-daughter when this marriage ended. Because of his first wife's failing mental health, he was aware of the possibility of future crises and changes:

> When I became resigned to the fact that the marriage was over, I recognised a . . . sort of realism on my part, and a commitment to carry on forging a worthwhile life for myself . . . I mean occasionally things happen . . . like at one point I thought I was going to have to take the girls . . . I thought there was going to be a crisis and I thought my former wife was going to offload them to institutions. And at that point, I contemplated . . . marrying a girlfriend I had at that time, although I didn't love her and didn't really want to marry her . . . to provide a home for the girls, luckily it never came to that.

The crisis came later, after he had remarried. His ex-wife's health had obviously deteriorated and on a weekend visit:

> We questioned the girls like we'd never questioned them before . . . we thought that it was unseemly I suppose, but I found out things that . . . you know, made it really out of the question for us to take them back.

Thus, the custodian fathers we studied acquired their children immediately or very shortly after their marriage ended when they were either left with their children, 'given' them by their wives or in Mr Hurst's case took them away because his wife had not been looking after them. Within a relatively short time these children were apparently settled with their father, often with a grandmother doing much of the routine child care. A second group of custodian fathers re-assumed responsibility for one or more of the children of their first marriage at a later stage after they had remarried, usually because there were difficulties within the children's own home. However, it is often hard to tell from the available accounts the extent to which such moves were initiated by either mothers or children. These two groups of custodian fathers faced distinctive but different problems which were likely to affect their life in a new family. The first had faced, although mostly for only a short time, a period as single fathers subject to their particular problems and conflicts, and as a result may have had exaggerated expectations of the way in which remarriage might alleviate their difficulties. Indeed, as we have seen, Mr Vickers made what he later designated as a 'disastrous' rapid and short-lived second marriage for this reason, whilst Mr Smithson lived for a short time with another woman before he finally remarried. The second group of fathers, therefore, found themselves having to absorb, sometimes at very short notice, a new and relatively unknown child into their newly formed family. It is not surprising, then, that some of the common potential conflicts of stepfamilies as they are shaped and managed in the public sphere are most clearly illustrated with reference to these fathers.

Even where the parent without custody is unhappy about the arrangements which have been made, there appear to be powerful pressures deterring him or her from resorting to a contest over custody. The fact that most children remain with their mother after divorce, that this is felt to be the most natural arrangement, is likely to deter many fathers from even contemplating applying for custody. On the other hand, women who, for whatever reason, leave their home and children may feel themselves, and be regarded as, unworthy of responsibility for their children. Although, the principle of no-fault divorce has operated since the implementation of the Divorce Reform Act, 1969, behaviour may still be taken into account in dealing with access, maintenance and so on. In addition there is considerable evidence, as we saw in chapter 3, that those who have experienced marriage breakdown and divorce continue to apply notions of guilt, innocence and moral worth in their own explanations and accounts of the decisions that were made either informally or in court. Thus a number of custodian fathers whose wives could be designated in some way as 'guilty' women, because they had left home, or had been unfaithful, made it plain to their wives that they wanted, and had a prior right to their children. In some cases, the threat of unwelcome courtroom revelations strengthened their argument. Mr Baker's informal arrangements with his wife broke down. He went to court to obtain separation, custody and maintenance orders knowing that his wife's father:

> . . . always said that, if ever it came to a court case, he'd always . . . back me against her.

Similarly Mr Heathcote made use of a private detective to obtain the necessary evidence to petition on the grounds of adultery. Before the divorce went through they discussed custody of the children:

> I told her she couldn't have 'em and er . . . that I'd fight her through every court in the land if she tried for 'em, but I would have done, no matter what it cost (a) because she wasn't in at night when they were in bed (b) because the fella she'd gone off with had got a criminal record, he'd been down the line for burglary and theft, er . . . and his police record which I was given a copy of showed that he was a man who moved around a bit.

Mr Heathcote's account also illustrates how fathers petitioning for custody, even if it is not contested, may be advised to bargain or compromise to ensure that the court upholds their wishes:

> I did ask me solicitor before we came to the divorce hearing about er . . . asking for maintenance, er . . . in my mind she was earning a very good income, she still is er . . . and then as far as I was concerned, if . . . if she'd taken the children, I'd have had to have paid maintenance, why shouldn't she and there had been two or three cases through the courts where the mother's had in fact had to pay maintenance and I thought it was only fair, in this particular case, since she . . . was the guilty party if you like, as far as the law is concerned anyway, er . . . that she should in fact contribute towards the upkeep and education and what have you of the children, and my solicitor said if you go for her on that,

> she'll just . . . counter it by . . . asking for the custody of the kids, and what do you want? I said I want custody of the kids, he says . . . forget the maintenance.

The formal award of custody

Although accounts of contested custody or access disputes are often featured prominently in newspapers, the great majority of divorcing parents make their own arrangements for the care of their children. Custody or access were disputed in only 10 per cent of cases in Eekelaar and Clive's sample. However, it is necessary for some parents to have their decisions and arrangements to be formally ratified through the courts when, for example, the custodian parent wishes to take over the tenancy of the matrimonial home or to claim a variety of benefits. Formal award of custody is also seen by some as a kind of insurance for the custodian parent in the event of any future dispute. For example, although Mr Smithson was uncertain of the formal procedures involved and felt frustrated by his solicitor's apparent lack of action, he knew that his former wife had put 'no access required' on her divorce papers. He believed she had done this because she wanted proceedings to go through quickly so that she could remarry. Some time later:

> . . . she moved up from London . . . and she must have thought, 'Well I'm not far away, I'll go and 'phone him up and I'll have the kids for a weekend,' I said, 'Oh, no chance, she's not starting that, she doesn't want them so she can get married and everything.'

In his confusion, he had completed his own forms differently, allowing her reasonable access, so she took the dispute to a solicitor but eventually gave up all attempts to see them after her eldest daughter told her on the telephone that they did not want to see her.

In our own group of custodian fathers, custody of children was only effectively contested in two cases (Brown and Walker). Although Mr Turner's first wife formally contested his custody of Trevor, she did not turn up in court so that, as Mr Turner described it:

> . . . the court was cleared and my solicitor put my case and . . . within a matter of minutes I'd got custody of him, there was no problem . . . [it] absolutely amazed me.

Similarly, Mr Brown's custody problems, which continued throughout the period of the study, necessitated making a compromise:

I could have got all three kids because, er . . . she'd tried to take her own life twice with an overdose and I think . . . with her going out and leaving them I'd got witnesses saying that she'd been leaving 'em for six hours every Friday night, so I think she'd got everything against her, you know . . . if . . . if I'd have plugged for them kids, I'd probably get them, you know, but I says, no, I says I'll just have Paul.

Because it is so unusual for custody to be given to fathers they often come under much greater scrutiny during the custody hearing. Mr Heathcote gave the judge a characteristically detailed description of his domestic arrangements:

The judge wanted to know who took the children to school, so I says, I do, who sees to the children when they come home from school, so I says I do, er . . . and then . . . then . . . my solicitor then butted in and said, 'Is it true you are an Insurance Broker?' 'Yes,' I said, 'but I'm self-employed, I can take off whatever time I like to look after the children, . . . no argument,' . . . I said, 'in the evening, . . . we are with me mother, and me mother is there, I says if I have to go out on business they're not . . . I see that they're not left on their own, . . . they never have been, they never will be.' (   ) He then said, 'Well what happens during the summer holidays?' I said, 'Well . . . during the summer holiday that's just gone . . . I took the children away for a fortnight's holiday er . . . I came back it was bank holiday and so me partner told me to have the rest of the week off so effectively I was away for three weeks er . . . me mother took them away for a fortnight to the caravan at Cleethorpes, the other week me sister came over and er . . . me wife also had them for a couple of days so between them they were well looked after.'

Mr Baker's custody was not contested but he had to appear in judge's chambers after his divorce hearing:

I went into private chambers at twelve o'clock and the judge were . . . more or less misinformed then, because he thought that I was applying for custody, he didn't realise that I had already got custody, until about half-way through the interview, and that is when it dawned . . . so he starts asking about this house, you know, how many lived here and how many rooms and that, and I explained all that bedroom situation and he seemed quite satisfied with that . . . then he said were they ever left on their own, so I explained that Janice [his second wife] works Wednesday, Thursday and Friday and we have to leave at 7.30, so more or less for three quarters of an hour, they're on their own, Wednesday, Thursday and Friday morning, so he just says, well how old are they, so I told him Alan was twelve, so he says he's quite old enough to look after himself and the others, and that was that.

There were three cases where custody was contested; although Mr Walker's attempt to gain custody of his daughter Pamela was unsuccessful, with her mother's agreement she later came to live with him after he remarried. Mr Harper's wife contested custody at the time of their separation. His case was apparently strengthened because by this time he had met his future second wife and would thus be able to demonstrate to the court the 'normality' of his domestic arrangements:

Just by chance I mentioned to the solicitor that I would be applying for a divorce, because I might want to get married again and he said, 'Well that's great because it helps the case,' so Mary went with me to court and I got custody.

Mr Brown's successful attempt to obtain custody of his youngest son has been a continued source of conflict between him and his ex-wife. When he was first interviewed in May 1978 he felt that although his wife had 'fought for Paul all the time' he felt that now that he had legal custody of him that the issue was settled, even though he was aware that:

. . . she still tries to get at me through the children, you know.

By the time the Browns were visited for their second interview in September, relationships with his ex-wife had deteriorated. There were difficulties about access arrangements:

She'd have Paul every other Saturday . . . and we'd say 'Bring him back at half past five' and she'd be two hours late with him and . . . she used to really muck us about, and I said to her, 'If you can't bring him home on time, then don't bother having him because it was stated that you should bring him back within a certain time, you know . . . and I used to go down for Douglas and Mary . . . and she'd go out . . . she wouldn't be in . . . when it was my turn she wouldn't let me have them . . . she'd just go out . . . so I haven't been to see them for ages.

He also described an incident which had taken place outside Paul's school the week before the interview:

Last week we had a terrible experience with the ex-wife coming up to the school and she assaulted Jean . . . terrible, outside school.
Q. And what happened there?
Oh she tried to drag Paul off Jean and everything and er, she hit Jean . . . she's about five foot nine and she's very tall, you know

> . . . and Jean's very small and . . . she didn't expect any trouble at all, I think . . . and it was a surprise more than anything, and she was heartbroken. It took us ages to get over it, you know.

They had also been told by Paul that when he had once visited his mother she had made him say into a tape recorder that he did not like living with his mother and father.

Although Mr Hurst was given custody of his four children when he divorced in 1977, a year later two of the girls had returned to live with their mother. Mr Hurst's description of his ex-wife's wanting contacts with the children demonstrates his bitterness and declared intention of trying to keep them apart:

> At the time of the divorce, she was, er allowed access by arrangement with me and she used to come down and see them on Sunday afternoon . . . then it got to a stage where she used to arrange to see them and I used to bring them up and she didn't turn up. Well she did that about two weeks running . . . then she'd come up a week and then miss a week . . . two weeks, so it finished up that I wrote her a letter, and said that if she wanted to see them she must do so by appointment.

Sally, his second daughter, renewed her contact with her mother when she found herself in the same class as the daughter of her mother's boyfriend. She visited her father every weekend and told Sally about her mother's new home, so as Mr Hurst explained:

> She knew that [her mother] had got a new house which she'd rigged out with new carpets, new three-piece suite, colour television and so she decided on a weekend visit and she said that she wanted to go for this weekend, so I let her go . . . that it would probably pacify her, that she'd probably stay the weekend and forget about it.

Sally then decided that she would like to live there permanently. Understandably Mr Hurst found it hard to recognise that there might be any reason beyond the improved standard of living motivating her, although he was clearly worried about the effect her decision might have on the other children and hence the stability of his new family life:

> Everything there was new, you know . . . and I think she'd been promised a bike and a holiday with the school and this, that and the other . . . but I didn't stand in her way. And at the same time I asked the other three if they wanted to go and nobody did, so I left it at that.

He told his ex-wife that:

> . . . if Sally went there to live that there'd be an arrangement whereby that she wouldn't pester to have the others over there as well, you know . . . to upset the family life that I've got here. Obviously I don't want this side upsetting and I don't go upsetting their life and I don't want her going and doing it here . . . it's as simple as that, and that's why I'd rather them not see her and let them forget her altogether.

After Sally had moved her younger sister Lesley went missing one weekend. Eventually they found out that she had gone to her mother's. Mr Hurst felt she had gone 'to see Sally, it wasn't to see her mother' but some months later she moved there permanently.

These accounts demonstrate how non-custodial parents' continued contact with their children, including the payment of maintenance, can provide an obvious arena within which unresolved conflicts, particularly about custody, are acted out. In most respects the problems of access experienced by custodian fathers are no different from those of the divorced mothers in our study and will, therefore be discussed later in this chapter. However, the feelings expressed by some of the custodian fathers about their ex-wives' failure to make use of agreed access illustrate very sharply and vividly the sense of ambivalence experienced by many custodian parents about their children's continued contact with their other parent. These feelings of ambivalence are heightened when the more usual pattern of custody with mother as full-time parent is reversed.

As we have already shown, it is still relatively unusual for divorced fathers to have custody of their children and the custodian fathers in our study only did so when their ex-wives had failed as mothers in some respect. As Voysey has suggested, public moralities of parenthood require parents, particularly mothers, always to put children first. The belief that a 'good' or a 'natural' mother will want to be with her children all the time makes it difficult for many people to understand the feelings of women who run away and leave their children, who publicly do not wish to have custody of them, or who do not visit very regularly. The fathers themselves often have very contradictory feelings. On the one hand they may be very critical of their wives, perceiving them as unnatural and lacking in ordinary love and care for their children, but on the other as we have seen from Mr Hurst, they feel threatened by their ex-wife's continued involvement with the children; at a symbolic level at least, the paramountcy of a mother's investments in parenthood persist despite formal legal arrangements. Mr Smithson, for example, seemed affronted that his wife should write 'no access required' on her divorce papers in order to accelerate the progress of her divorce, but had also taken considerable pains to deter her from visiting his children. As we have already seen, Mr Hurst found that renewed contact between his children and their mother led to a change in custody for two of them, disturbing the precarious unity of his newly created family.

Fathers may also be critical of their ex-wives' 'selfishness' in relation to their own perceptions of their children's needs. Arrangements for Mr Heathcote's ex-wife to visit the children appeared to work satisfactorily, but he commented:

> The one thing I don't understand . . . and I don't think I'll ever understand is that apart from [arranged visits] she never contacts the children. She never rings up to see . . . if they're all right . . . say if it was Raymond's birthday today, she might [ring up] either this morning before he's gone to school or, say this evening to say 'Many Happy Returns', all right but she wouldn't come up to see him, to give him his present . . . he'd have to wait 'til the next time she was seeing him before he got his presies . . . which the children feel, I'm sure they do.

Similarly, Mr Baker described his wife's visits:

> She'd have them for an evening and . . . you know, she never really wanted 'em for a long time and this used to burn me up, you know, I think she could have done more to . . . have them a bit more, . . . they couldn't understand why she didn't bother with 'em so much. . . . she won't have a permanent arrangement to see them, she just likes to ring up . . . you know, when it suits her . . .
>
> For five months we hadn't heard from her, we didn't know why . . . well I say I didn't know why . . . she's been saving up for a new car and television . . . it happened last year . . . she didn't see them for three months and when she turned up she'd got a new car . . . this year it's been five months.

Mr Baker was particularly angry that at the custody hearing his ex-wife had lied to the judge both about the frequency of her visits to the children and the maintenance she paid:

> He went on to access and maintenance, so she says er . . . 'I see the boys at least once a week' well this were a lie in itself, as I say, she'd seen 'em about three times in two months, up to this divorce case, and since the divorce case, she's only seen 'em once.
> Q. Did you say anything at that point?
> No, I just wanted the divorce to go through, you know. But the . . . she said er . . . she sees 'em at least once a week, er . . . that she paid the £4 which she does, and she said every so often she

> buys them clothing when she can, well this in itself again was a lie but, as I say, I let that pass.

However, after she resumed visiting, he admitted:

> . . . personally I'd like it that she never saw them again, you know, 'cos as I say, the house runs smoothly.

If, as we have suggested, idealised typifications of parental roles cause custodian parents to judge their ex-wives harshly, they also make them sensitive to their own performance as parents. They may feel particularly vulnerable to public criticism or judgments of the way they are looking after their children. Contact with social workers was particularly significant in this respect. Where custody was disputed they were aware that they were 'on trial' as parents, peculiarly accountable to visiting social workers for their performance of the constituent activities of parenthood. In their uncertainty about their performance as lone parents, some fathers placed enormous reliance on the comments, compliments or 'good reports' they had received from social workers, sometimes repeating an account of the same incident or conversation in all three interviews many months apart. If they were vague about the exact title or function of the social workers who visited them, they were very much aware of how a social worker's approval strengthened their case in a legal dispute. Mr Hurst described how the probation officer:

> . . . had them all in one by one and asked them, and they all said that they wanted to stay with me . . . so er . . . I got a glowing report.

When he was given custody of his children, they were put on a supervision order and he recognised the social worker's very infrequent visits as continuing approval of how the children are being looked after:

> Q. Did you have any dealings with social workers at all?
> Yes . . . that Mrs C. . . . probation worker . . . she was . . . she still is my social worker, but er . . . she never calls on me or anything, she knew that I were doing me job OK (   ). . . .
> She visited me twice I think in what . . . four . . . five months, she knew that they were getting looked after OK so she said there were no need for her to visit so much, the only provision that she made was that if I had any trouble to contact her . . . and that was the working relationship that we had.

Mr Brown, aware of the social worker's duty to be impartial, found sufficient reassurance from his social worker's comments to continue to press for custody of his son, Paul:

> She got Legal Aid, obviously you know, and then er . . . she tried to cause a hell of a lot of trouble with Paul, you know, by dragging Paul back you know, so I went to a child welfare officer, Mr G. and he says, 'Look, I can't "side" with anyone,' he says, 'I've got to take her side as well as my side and the child's,' he says, 'I'm not thinking about you two at all,' he says, 'I'm thinking about that child's interests.' Well he came to see Paul and er . . . he says, Obviously I can tell how Paul's acting, you know,' he says, 'he's happy here,' he says, 'I'm not going to put . . .' he says, 'Why should I disturb him from here, if he wants to be here he can stay and live with his father, you know.'

He gave a more detailed account of this incident in the second interview:

> When she realised that Paul . . . did want to stay with me . . . she tried a helluva lot to get him back . . . I went to see . . . went through the proper channels . . . because she obviously wasn't thinking of him . . . just herself and to hurt me. But I'd put his life and future before anything so . . . I went to see a probation officer . . . great chap . . . and . . . I had a good hard long chat with him, and asked him how I went about it . . . dragging him through court or anything like that . . . I didn't want to go through a solicitor . . . you know . . . a child doesn't want to have to go through experiences like that.
>
> So, I went to see this probation officer and had a heart-to-heart with him, and after I explained it . . . he came over to see us at Eckington, and he said, 'Look, I'll tell you if Paul's going to stay with you, I can see for myself you know.' And he spoke to Paul and had a look round the house . . . and then he said, 'Look, I can see that the child's happy', and he said, 'That's all I want to know' . . . and went to the school and everything . . . obviously Paul was happy so . . . and he said then, 'Well that's that, I'm satisfied.'

It is perhaps significant that none of the custodian fathers or indeed any of the men in the study made adverse comments about their contacts with social workers. However, many of the women we talked to were extremely critical of their treatment by social workers.

Generally, we may conclude from our consideration of the custodian fathers in the study that the legacy of particular problems faced by single fathers indirectly continues to affect their domestic life after remarriage. Where there had been conflict over custody it persisted in access arrangements and, on occasion, in financial matters. The ambiguities and complications of post-divorce relationships with a child's non-custodial parent tended to be exacerbated in such cases because of such beliefs, fathers believed that their ex-partners 'ought' to be more involved with their children and continued to worry whether their children might be 'better off' if, because of changed circumstances, they returned to their mother. Fathers were more likely to have retained or gained custody of only some of their children, so bringing in train the further complications of split custody. In a number of ways the accounts of the custodian fathers communicate a sense of vulnerability whose origins lie in their experiences as single fathers. Taking part in this study may have provided them with an opportunity to discuss continuing difficulties and to seek further confirmation of their good standing as parents.

Custodian mothers and fathers without custody

Thirty-two of the women in our study had been divorced and only one, Mrs Turner, had had no children. All but two of these women had custody of all of their children. Mrs Elliot's two eldest illegitimate children now live with their father in London and John, the son of her first marriage, lives with his father. Mrs Pelham still found it very difficult to talk about the circumstances which led to her son, Mark, staying with his father:

> I have a guilt complex about it definitely and especially about . . . my little boy . . . er, you know, I think that's the worst thing, that's the worst decision I ever made . . . It was a choice between Michael and my son basically . . . it's very difficult to sit and tell you how things happened day by day or week by week.

When they decided to split up it was agreed that she would keep the children. Her first husband went to stay with parents and because she was living in poor accommodation and having difficulty in finding a child minder it was suggested that Mark should go and stay with them temporarily. She began to realise that Michael, her new partner, 'didn't particularly want him' as he had 'lost his own son' of a very similar age. She was undecided about what she should do and on one occasion went to try to collect Mark from her husband and his new partner's home:

> I remember once going where they were living to get Mark and that . . . I had a terrible do with this woman . . . which ended up in Mark screaming and me coming away crying.

Because of strongly held ideologies and stereotypes of appropriate male and female parental roles, responsibilities and investments, the experiences of such non-custodial mothers provide a complementary, mirror image account to those of the custodian fathers discussed above. When Mrs Elliott and Mrs Pelham described their feelings and experiences of being the kind of 'defective' or 'unnatural' mothers who gave up their children they translate into personal human terms some of the negative images of their ex-wives conveyed by the custodian fathers in the study. However, in this section we focus on the more typical patterns of relationship between custodian mother and non-custodial fathers from two complementary perspectives, as the experiences of the thirty-one custodian mothers are compared with that of the eleven non-custodial fathers in the study.

Custody and access

When parents split up most children stay with their mothers. Because this is what happens most frequently and is widely felt to be the normal or natural course of events, many separating couples do not even consciously consider or discuss the alternatives and, as we have already seen in the first section of this chapter, patterns of custody which deviate from this norm may bring special problems. Very few of the divorced women in our study reported any conflict, or even discussion with their ex-partners about custody of their children although many of them, in common with other single mothers, faced severe accommodation, financial and also health problems during the early months of their separations (see also Hart, 1976; Chester, 1971; Marsden, 1969). The divorced women in our study who had suffered physical violence in earlier marriages were among those who experienced the greatest difficulties. Although we asked no direct questions about 'battering', the accounts of thirteen of the thirty-two divorced women in our study include reference to occasions when they had been physically assaulted by their ex-husbands. Whilst some, including Mrs Fox, Mrs Chapman and Mrs Browning, gave their husbands' behaviour as a direct reason for their separation, others included descriptions of severe assaults as if they were an incidental, perhaps inevitable, part of married life. After particularly violent incidents, or as in Mrs Hurst's case when her second husband's violence involved injury to her children, such women left home with little or no preparation, returning to their parents, or other relatives. Thirteen of the divorced mothers in the study lived with relatives, most frequently parents, for a time after their first marriage ended. Until Mrs Chapman regained her house following a court injunction she and her children were split up amongst accommodating relatives:

> Q. So you went to your sister's did you?
> Well me, me eldest daughter and t'youngest little girl, we went to me eldest sister's and me other two children went to stop with me other sister 'cos there weren't room for us all in one house, you know er . . . so we were split (   ). T'court eventually did turn t'house over to me and . . . they made an injunction out against him that he couldn't go nowhere near t'house, while I was living in it. So we went back home, you know, and started us life more or less as . . . up once more, me and t'children.

Mrs Hammond also found it very difficult to find accommodation after she left her husband and, as a result, she left two of her children with him, whilst the other two were fostered by her sister.

For the divorced women formal legal disputes with their ex-partners over custody were very rare. Mrs Hobson was the only woman who had to fight for custody of a child through the courts. Soon after she left her first husband he came and took Stephen away. When she went to fetch him from school she found her in-laws waiting in the school yard. When this attempt failed:

> We had to go to court to get him back. And me own husband said that he wanted him putting in a home and I stood up in court, I said, 'Over my dead body' and my solicitor made me sit down.

If established generalised norms about parental role obligations help determine which parent in ordinary circumstances should look after and have custody of children when a marriage ends, they do not seem to provide a comparable solution to the problems of role ambiguity faced by non-custodial fathers. There is little agreement amongst experts, practitioners and most significantly non-custodial fathers themselves about how they should continue to relate to their children generally and about more specific matters such as access visits, birthdays and so on. Expert rhetoric stressing the paramountcy of the child's interests in determining subsequent patterns of relationships (Goldstein, Freud and Solnit, 1973) is matched by the obvious concern felt by non-custodial fathers in the study to do what was best for their children. However, there is generally less clarity about how to determine and serve the best interests of children so that in Britain today, as in other industrialised societies with high divorce rates, there is a variety of possible responses to the problems and contradictions of being a non-custodial parent. Such variations may be understood in terms of the interaction of two important factors; the continuing level of conflict between the separated parents and their active commitment to a continuing parental role. A number of therapists and commentators have suggested that disputes over children prove a continuing arena for the discharge of unresolved conflict between the separated or divorced parents (Weiss, 1975; Epstein, 1975). The resolution of such conflict depends in part upon the partners' own emotional resources and personalities but is also greatly affected by the manner of their marriage breakdown and separation. In chapter 4 we distinguished between the 'initiators' and 'recipients' of marriage breakdown, modifying a distinction first made by Hart (Hart, 1976). Many of those who cast themselves as 'recipients' appear to have had little time to prepare for what happened and, if their separation occurred very abruptly, they had few opportunities to discuss either its cause or its consequences with their departing partners. By contrast those who described their decision to separate as a joint one, or when it followed a temporary separation imposed by one partner working away, or when couples went on living together for some time after the final decision had been made, they inevitably discussed, and argued about, what had happened to them as well as being able to make plans for the future. In addition when a deserting partner returned for a short time to 'try again', even if their attempt was unsuccessful, their experiences were more akin to those who separated by mutual consent. They had many more opportunities to make sense of the past by expressing their anger and conflicts during this period and the day they actually stopped living together was more of a planned event. As a result they were less likely to use disputes over children as an arena for continued conflict and had already begun to rehearse their roles as separated parents during this intermediate period.

Although we hold a number of generalised expectations in our own society about the 'good' parent, which in this century have been much influenced by experts of various kinds (Rapoport, Rapoport and Strelitz, 1977, chapter 2), there is evidence from the Newsons' work that class and community differences abound. In traditional working-class communities, despite some changes (Klein 1965), fathers remain less closely involved in the everyday care of their children than some of their middle-class counterparts, whilst the Pahls' study of the family life of senior managers portrays fathers who frequently had little day-to-day contact with their children, seeing their role primarily as one of economic provider (Pahl and Pahl, 1971). Thus, fathers who have had relatively little direct involvement with their children before their separation will find it more difficult to sustain a continuing relationship with their children afterwards. Personal guilt may also play a part in this, so that those most aware of their past family failures, including 'deviant' non-custodial mothers, will find it easier to withdraw completely. The interaction of these two variables, continued level of conflict between ex-partners and the degree of involvement of the non-custodial parent, may be viewed diagramatically (Figure 4.1).

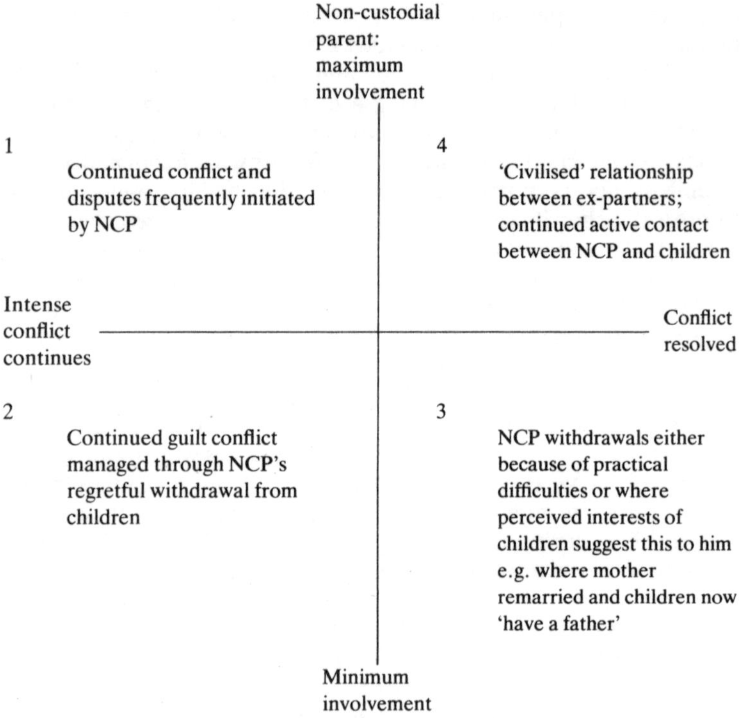

NCP = Non-custodial parent

Figure 4.1

1 Continued conflict over custody and access

As we have already seen, the most bitter conflicts over custody itself were experienced by a number of the custodian fathers in our study. Where mothers had custody continued conflict between ex-partners was expressed through disputes over access which persisted and, not surprisingly, were often exacerbated by the mother's new partnership. Many of the custodian fathers had also experienced lengthy disputes about access arrangements. From the father's point of view, where the marriage was finally ended because his wife had had an affair his regret and jealousy were sometimes rekindled by the knowledge that she and their children had settled down in a new household with 'the other man'. Even after divorce old wounds are re-opened when an ex-spouse forms a new partnership. She is finally 'no longer available'; she may now be living in better circumstances than the father himself, if he has not remarried, and his children have acquired a new father. From the mother's point of view her ex-husband's rights to, and exercise of, access act as a continuing reminder of the past at a time when she is intent on building family life anew. It is significant that many of the complaints voiced about access by couples in our study focused on the way in which both the actor, the non-custodial parent, and the activity – visits, meetings and so on – intrude upon the everyday web of family life in a way which frequently symbolises, for them at least, their differentness from unbroken families. The more this is resented, the more likely they are to find fault with details of the non-custodial parent's arrangements and behaviour, so that the focus of conflicts, on occasion sufficiently entrenched to be brought to court, is often some apparently trivial detail of the time or duration of an access visit. Although Mrs Moseley's ex-husband was granted reasonable access at any time, he had got into the habit of seeing his children on Saturdays. When the Moseley's bought a caravan on the Lincolnshire coast, they started going away at the weekends:

> Of course he got a bit uptight 'That's not fair weekends is my days . . .' I've tried to tell him that there's no reason why he shouldn't see them at night . . . I mean . . . they could come here and drop their school things and be in town for half past four, they could go to the pictures, the parks, museums, anything . . .
> Q. You're not happy with the present arrangements really?
> Well if we want to go away, he said he was going to cause us trouble about us going away at weekends, which I think is unfair to the kids. . . . he said he didn't see them for long enough. Now half past four to nine o'clock is longer than ten o'clock to half past two by anyone's watch isn't? [It is in fact the same].

It was frequently the second partners, the stepparents of the children involved, who seemed most resentful of the non-custodial parent's intrusion into their family life. When he first got to know his wife, Mr Farmer felt that her husband took liberties with the children but felt reluctant to become involved until their relationship was more settled, perhaps because of his lack of previous experience as a parent:

> He used to just come to the house, her house . . . pop in now and then . . . now and again when it suited him . . . he pulled up in t'lorry and talked to t'kids . . . So I thought, 'When you get, you know, living with this lass like, we can manage without him, it's best if he has no contact at all.'

After they were married, he told the children's father not to come to the house again, clearly resenting the continuing influence he had upon the children and, indirectly, upon all of their lives. Similarly, Mrs Vickers complained that her stepchildren were often unsettled after visiting their mother:

> I suppose that I resent her interference . . . I think it would have been far better if she had left them alone and she saw very little of them. . . . Over the last three years she's sort of put pressure on . . . she has them nearly every holiday and I find it unsettles Colin . . . it's very difficult when he comes back. . . . She's the only thing that I regret about the whole thing, that she is *there* you know.
> Q. You'd prefer to see her fade into the background would you?
> Yes, mmm . . . even in spite of the fact that it gives us an opportunity to go away on our own . . . I'd be quite willing to give that up if she'd sort of have no contact with them whatsoever.

2 Conflict: the non-custodial parent withdraws

The resolution of the kinds of conflicts outlined in the previous section poses special difficulties. Where a marriage has ended acrimoniously but without the opportunity for both partners to express their feelings to each other and to make some shared sense of what has happened to them they are increasingly unlikely to be able to resolve their difficulties and to learn to co-operate with one another in the best interests of their children. In many communities, their own inner feelings of guilt and hostility are confirmed by public expectations and stereotypes of appropriate post-divorce relationships and behaviour. In a localised close-knit social network of kin, neighbours and workmates, despite an official morality of 'irretrievable breakdown', blame and guilt are assigned to individuals through gossip and 'sides' may be taken in a way which would make it difficult for either party to be seen to be modifying their original views or to sustain amicable relationships with their ex-partners. In such circumstances, the withdrawal or exclusion of the non-custodial parent appears as an increasingly attractive solution to their problems. As we shall show in chapter 5, the custodial parent's remarriage is seen by some as providing children with the second parent they needed, thus increasing the non-custodial parent's marginality. Informal attempts may be made to persuade the non-custodial parent to stop seeing his children or an application may be made for a variation in access arrangements on the grounds that continued contact is not in the child's interests. Mrs Graham described a recent episode when one of her daughters seemed so upset after a visit to her father that they took her to their family doctor:

> [He] said, 'She just wants to think that she's never got to . . . *got* to see him again.' You see the very fact is that he *can* see them again, at the moment, he doesn't see them, but the fact that he can, seems to worry them all.

She concluded:

> We're still having trouble with my former husband, you know, we've got to get it that he doesn't have any access to the children you know.

Although action through the courts remains as a last resort, parents and stepparents may discourage contact in more subtle ways. Describing with relief, almost with pleasure, the gradual elimination of contact with a non-custodial parent, Mrs Farmer speaks of the pattern of contact between her children and their father:

> Two of them have seen him a couple of times because they get on his bus, you know, he works on the buses, but otherwise they've never seen him . . . you know he got reasonable access to them, but he's never taken the kids . . .
> Q. So how do you feel about that?
> Well, now I'm married again I think I'm glad that . . . it is . . . like that because I think . . . the kids get a more stable home life if they've got a stepfather . . . and [if] they're going to see their own father as well . . . for access then . . . I would imagine that it's very hard for them to accept their stepfather whereas our kids were . . . just cut off from him, you know, and they've accepted my second husband . . . you know . . . look on him as father.

The issue was generally discussed in terms of the children's needs and preferences and a number of mothers suggested that for a variety of reasons, their children did not want further contact. Mrs Elliott was asked:

> Now that you have got married again does Jean ever see her father?
> No.
> Q. Can you remember the last time they saw each other?
> He's never seen her, not to talk to, whether he's seen her on a a bus or . . . seen her on t'street I don't know.
> Q. How do you feel about that, would you prefer them to see each other?
> No. She always says that's her dad, this husband I've got now . . . she says that's her daddy see . . . and we've told her that he's adopted her and we've shown her her birth certificate and she cut it up, she says, 'I don't want that,' she says, 'he's my dad.'

The non-custodial fathers in the study painted their own picture of the difficulties surrounding part-time parenthood and many felt the inevitability of a gradual loss of contact with the children. Although Mr Thornleigh was separated from his ex-wife in 1973 the conflict between them continues and is focused on disputes about access and maintenance:

> Q. How much maintenance were you paying?
> Er, th . . . about er . . . a . . . at the time I think about £2.50 a week, you know, per child . . . and er . . . on . . . on the wages, you know, I was . . . I am getting then, that was a lot to me . . . you see, what with being in lodgings as well and paying maintenance out . . . I haven't seen me children now for about er . . . three year.
> Q. You've not seen them at all in that time?
> No. They have been up here . . . but Andrew seemed to resent it, you know, it'll be mainly because of what she's . . . put into him, you see, but er . . . Jane . . . I know for a fact that she's been trying to find me. When I once saw her, and she told me . . . that she made her own way round here, she knew the street, you know, she'd walk up and down and look for the house, but she didn't know which house it was.
> Q. So you just bumped into the children once or twice and nothing more than that?
> Well, it was planned with Jane because er . . . er . . . call it a little bit under-handed if you want . . . I was once at me mother's and she knew that Jane came on a certain day . . . you know, so I planned it, that I'd be there when Jane came, you know, that's when she told me.
> Q. Did Jane continue to visit your mother then?
> Yes, and then eventually . . . my ex-wife has since stopped the children going to see her now.

3 The non-custodial parent withdraws in his own or the children's interests

In a number of cases the non-custodial parents described how they had lost or were losing contact with their children either because of practical difficulties, for instance where the children had moved to another part of the country, or where the perceived interests of the children suggested this.

Since Mr Roberts's ex-wife moved south he has found it much more difficult to visit his children regularly:

> I see them approximately once every three weeks, so I don't think that I see them enough, um . . . I would say that it used to be once

> a week . . . now it's once every three weeks, with the odd week thrown in when they're on some sort of holiday.

He has found it diffiult to define his role as a non-custodial father and expects their move to the south to make this worse:

> I can't see any aim . . . in being involved with me children . . . or what, any aim on their life. For years now, really these are just going to be blank years for me 'cos I've got no contact with what they are doing at school at all . . . the out-of-school activities . . . I'm like an outcast from all that, even though I see them and speak to them and I write to them . . . I still seem to be an outcast, because they've gone so far away.

Mr Roberts could, however see some benefits for his own marriage in what had happened:

> Although it hasn't done me a favour, it's done our marriage a favour, by them going down there.

Mary (his second wife):

> . . . tended to think we were seeing a bit too much of them and they weren't being allowed to settle into a pattern . . . ( ). There was conflict caused by them coming regular . . . and since they've been gone, it seems to have . . . this household seems to have tempered down a bit.

Mr Graham was also aware of how his contact with his children affected his second wife:

> Jennifer's a bit apprehensive about it, which is understandable . . . because she always gets the feeling that when I go over there I come into contact with my former wife and that obviously upsets her ( ) . . . She's always got this bit of a fear that at the back of her mind, you know, she doesn't like me talking to my former wife at all.

Mr Graham had found his first visits to his sons after their separation very awkward and embarrassing:

> It wasn't at all easy just to go and knock on the door and say 'Can I see my son?' ( ) . . . But I just used to try and call down sometimes during the day if I knew they were . . . sort of . . . going to be at home, just to see him.

As his sons are growing up they appear to him to be growing away from him:

> I've found out that David doesn't seem to be too interested. I mean . . . he's sort of getting to the age when he's wanting to be

> out with his friends . . . I don't think he's forgotten me but . . . the fact that I left him . . .

His ex-wife had also made difficulties about her children meeting his new partner and although Mr Graham spoke optimistically of making more regular arrangements in the future, it is difficult to envisage any real change.

Mr Fox now has almost no contact with his daughter:

> Since I've known my second wife . . . I've known her, what three years now and, er, I think I've seen me daughter twice 'cos me and the first wife made arrangements a long time ago, that I wouldn't see her 'cos she used to live on the other side of Sheffield, before she came to flit up here. Last time I saw her, well, it were me nephew's party . . . and me daughter were there like, and she remembered me and kept on saying 'That's me dad, that's me dad' and then I think we saw her . . . about a week after that and I haven't seen her since.

When they first separated, his visits were fairly regular but he found them very disturbing:

> I were upset sometimes like because I could go up there and she didn't want to bother with me, didn't want anything to do with me . . . (   ) then I'd go up another time and she were round me all the time and I were upset both times . . . I used to talk to myself and say 'Well you can't blame her in a way 'cos she only sees you once every week' and after so long I tried not to let it upset me.

When they moved to another part of Sheffield:

> I had to catch two buses, and it took a couple of hours to get there. When I got there she played with me like and I took her for a walk, I enjoyed it but I never saw her again in quite a few years.

Later his ex-wife remarried and she suggested that if he did not go and see his daughter there would be no need for him to pay maintenance:

> I thought about it and said 'Well, she's my daughter, I want to see her' and then I thought 'If I keep on seeing her it might upset the applecart 'cos me wife's got married again' . . . I thought about and studied the situation like and I says 'Right, she's got her life to lead and I don't want to keep upsetting her, so fair enough' and so I just discontinued sending up the money.

4 Non-custodial parents remaining in active contact with their children through flexible access arrangements

Mrs Baker, Mrs Dunwell, Mrs Hutchinson and Mrs Thornleigh are all examples of parents for whom conflict with their ex-partner is a thing of the past and who, though aware of potential problems, described a variety of patterns of contact with their ex-partners which encourage fathers to maintain relationships with their children. Their attitudes towards their ex-husbands range from Mrs Thornleigh's very positive:

> We have a fantastic relationship now . . . it's unbelievable, you know, we can talk like best friends can talk . . .

to Mrs Hutchinson's clear distinction between her feelings about him as ex-husband, so that she did not wish to know where he lives, and the recognition that:

> . . . he is father to me children, I'll give him that, but that's about the only nice thing I can say about him.

Mrs Hutchinson had made use of the courts to formalise contacts in a way which now works very well:

> Well, in the first place there wasn't an order made and he could see them when he wanted, obviously 'cos we lived in the same house and then when, he moved out he came up every day and then he got to be a real nuisance and started knocking me about again, so I went back to court and I had a custody order made out for him to be able to see them on Sunday afternoons . . . well I don't stick to that 'cos he doesn't live in the district any more.

This more informal arrangement sometimes interfered with their own plans on Sundays:

> . . . 'cos it's really the only day that we've got all together . . . me Roger and the kids . . . we look forward to that and he knows that . . . and he's getting a lot more thoughtful now.

She was surprised to find that her second husband was jealous and didn't like her ex-husband visiting the house. Having recognised the potential conflict, she took steps to resolve it:

> Well, he doesn't come to the house, 'cos the kids they play out a lot and if he wants to see them usually he only has to walk to the top of the road and they'll see him . . . he doesn't come to the door any more . . . I can't understand why Roger is jealous. But I went along with it 'cos I know what jealousy can do and I've watched what it can do to other people.

She is also aware of the difficulties her children might be having in continuing to relate to their father. She described how Nicholas questioned her about her own contacts with his father:

> . . . he came to me and said, 'Er . . . you don't see me Dad any more do you Mummy?' . . . and I said, 'No, not very often, I see him now and again and . . .' . . . I mean . . . I always speak and say 'Hallo' and perhaps he'll ask me if the kids are all right and I'll stand there . . . a lot of people think that's funny 'n all, but they can go and . . . tickle . . . 'cos I talk to who I like you know . . . and he says, 'I'm glad that we don't live with me Dad any more 'cos I didn't like that when he used to hit you,' and I said, 'You don't remember that,' and er . . . he said, 'I do and I once come downstairs when he were hitting you and your mouth were bleeding and I'll never forget Mum,' and I said, 'Oh don't talk about things like that, it's in the past,' so . . . he obviously remembers . . . now . . . whether . . . Robert genuinely remembers or Nicholas told him what he remembers . . . but the kids are both . . . pretty quiet towards him. . . . No, the eldest of me two daughters always did love her Dad . . . and he made a lot of her, you know . . . when she were little . . . really made a fuss of her . . . and I think that she's just beginning to realise that . . . now . . . she sees that we didn't just break up just to be awkward, and upset her. . . . But I never have explained to her why we've broken up. . . .

Mrs Thornleigh's 'fantastic' relationship with her ex-husband developed out of a period of great bitterness and upheaval, both before and after they finally separated:

> There was a lot of bitterness, the first few months, you know, whilst the divorce was pending and everything . . . he was going to take me to the cleaners and this, that and the other and he wanted this, that and the other and the, you know, one day I said to him, 'Look, you know, you're being a bit silly, you're going to end up with nothing,' I said, 'You be fair . . . the only people you're spiting' – he wasn't going to pay the maintenance and he wasn't going to do this and he wasn't going to do that – 'is yourself and the kids . . . I can support myself . . . you know it's only yourself you're spiting' and we had a really good talk and from that day onwards, we get on fine now. We get on like a house on fire.

Mrs Dunwell's decision to leave her first husband evolved from her recognition of her dissatisfaction with their marriage. As we have seen, in a characteristically businesslike way, he made arrangements to buy her a small terraced house:

> In his mind to purchase another house would be eminently sensible . . . the mortgage was quite small, but eventually, if I wanted to sell, I would have capital there for me.

Although he gradually seemed to accept their impending separation and dealt with the financial aspects of it very efficiently, he was deeply distressed by the news that Geoff, subsequently her second husband, was to move in with her shortly afterwards. A day or so after Geoff had moved in with her, her ex-husband came to see her:

> . . . he was very, very upset, more than at any time that we'd discussed splitting up and the actual leaving . . . I said 'You must have expected that eventually I would make a new life for myself' . . . 'Yes,' he said, 'it's a bit like a person dying you know, if you know they're dying, it doesn't help when they actually do die . . .' that was the nearest I've seen him myself you know, he'd never sort of presented . . . the emotions behind it before as he did then.

However, by the time they got round to filing divorce petitions they felt able to do so without the help of solicitors because,

> [We] . . . agreed what was to be done about the children. We had an evening where I went over to his house and sorted out exactly . . . what we decided was good for the children.

Generally, she feels their separation:

> Wasn't as dramatic as it could have been 'cos it was carefully planned, both by me and my husband 'cos I told him a long time before. And the housing was carefully arranged because of the kids and the money that he'd give me.

Mrs Dunwell's account of her former husband's contact and relationships with their children, including a foster child, Lesley, demonstrates her concern, which she admits is sometimes tinged by guilt, for his needs and feelings as a father as well as those of the children. The pattern of their contact has altered with changes in his life:

> He used to have them . . . he was at university then, he used to have them on Wednesday afternoons as well . . . in the afternoons, which used to be helpful and the kids enjoyed that.

Now,

> It's alternate Saturdays and Sundays because he gets his shopping done once a fortnight, so that we arrange for them to have an alternate Saturday . . . that also means that it's flexible . . . If he rings and says he can't have them on a Saturday and would I mind, it nearly always works out that it's convenient so we can swap that and change as needs be.

Such sharing includes Christmas:

> . . . he had them Christmas Day last year and they stayed overnight and then came back for Boxing Day morning. Um . . . that's the first Christmas Day that I've not had them, which was a bit . . . I didn't enjoy that at all but I apparently had them the last two Christmas Days before that, and they didn't go until about eleven, so I got them opening their presents and everything which was . . . fairly normal.

Although these arrangements work well, she is also aware of actual and potential sources of difficulty. In some respects their attitudes and methods of discipline differ:

> The . . . two girls . . . went through a phase when they were very rude . . . I don't think it was particularly aimed at Michael; but they were just going through that stage at school . . . they let loose on him and he couldn't cope with that. Because I suppose when you only see them one day, you expect them to be *nice* but of course, that day's no different to them, so they're not.

In the future things may change:

> I envisage difficulties later on when they'll be wanting to go with their friends, you know . . . one of them goes to dancing on a Saturday so she's there for two hours of the day, and once or twice another . . . has said she'd like to do something that her friends are doing . . . it's going to pose somewhat of a problem later on.

Although Mrs Baker had been hurt and shocked when she discovered that her first husband had been unfaithful, they talked a good deal before they eventually decided to separate:

> If I'd have, if we'd have stayed together it would have gone from bad to worse because it was already implanted in me mind and people had already started talking and that was the end of the marriage. I still thought a hell of a lot of him, he did me, he moved me in here, he gave me nearly all the money from the house, sold the contents from the house, he made a good allowance for the children, we don't argue about them . . . it just broke up.

Although he now lives some distance away her ex-husband still sees their children regularly, but his relationship with his children is now more distant than that described by Mrs Dunwell. Initially, Mrs Baker had expected his contact with them would diminish:

> I said I hoped that when he got promotion he would move a bit further away than he was . . . and he was a bit cross about that . . . and so I said, 'Look I think that children need to be able to be in a permanent position with one set of rules' and he agrees.

In return Mrs Baker tries to fit in with his arrangements whenever she can:

> Q. So when do the children see their father then?
> Well, they're seeing him this weekend actually . . . er . . . they saw him at . . . they didn't see him at Easter . . . he came and took them out for a couple of hours about a month ago . . . just after we were married, about a month ago . . . And he saw them at Christmas . . . had them for a few days at Christmas and he's seeing them for three days this weekend, before he goes on holiday . . . and he's arranged to take them for a week's holiday in the summer holidays. . . . But . . . before he arranges anything with me he always asks me if I've arranged anything, and what dates have I arranged, and I . . . tell him, and he asks me if it's all right if he takes them on holiday in such-and-such a week, and what can you do when anybody's co-operative like that? There's nothing that you can . . . You say, grand, the kids'll love it.

Thus, in this case, the potential for conflict has been resolved as the divorced couple have gradually negotiated a new web and balance of relationships in which the children's family base is their mother and stepfather and their non-custodial father has come to play the role of benevolent uncle. His decreasing involvement with the children of his first marriage is compensated by his new commitments as a stepfather in his second marriage.

Mr Thompson's 'civilised' divorce followed a similar pattern and his account of his relationship with the daughter of his first marriage illustrates how this emotional withdrawal feels from the non-custodial parent's point of view. He sees Tracy regularly, but:

> my wife has remarried and there's a nice tight little family group, and to be quite frank you know . . . I think that . . . I should leave them alone . . . and be more of an uncle to her than her dad, because the other fella's got to bring her up and, er, he's not a bad bloke you know . . . I like the fella himself, he's a pretty reasonable bloke, so I think she'll be all right. I mean he won't bring her up like I would, she'll be more sedate and I think she'll probably be more posh . . . I think she'll probably end up being a bit superior . . . He's a doctor or something or other . . .
>
> . . . I think I should stay away, otherwise t'kid 'll get confused, you see, all through her life she's not seen a lot of me, so I'm a backwards and forwards person to her, so I just keep it that way.

The accounts and observations we have presented illustrate the variety and diversity of access arrangements experienced by the divorced parents and their children in our study. We have tried to develop a typology of access patterns and relationships which takes into account both the personal and structural factors affecting post-divorce relationships. The level of conflict which persists between ex-partners after separation, as well as the degree of involvement of the non-custodial parent are to some extent both matters of personal history and preference. However, it is important to remind ourselves that such decisions and responses are also greatly affected by the prevailing social attitudes, beliefs and norms structuring post-divorce relationships. Margaret Mead has pointed to the contradiction between the official morality of lifelong monogamy and recent increases in divorce which has meant that few alternative moralities have emerged to help structure the post-divorce relationships of parents and children. She observes that in the United States prevailing social norms tend to encourage patterns of avoidance between ex-partners:

> Among the older generation, there is some feeling that any contact between divorced people somehow smacks of incest; once divorced, they have been declared by law to be sexually inaccessible to each other, and the aura of past sexual relationships incriminating. (Mead, 1970, p. 121)

The couples in our own study came from a variety of backgrounds and different local and occupational communities. For a few, so-called 'civilised' relaxed post-divorce relationships were a reality, although others showed their awareness of such a pattern as an apparently unobtainable ideal. Many others had little or no contact with their ex-partners whilst a few were still locked in formalised conflicts over custody, access and financial matters. Our discussion of the relationship between the personal and the public sphere, in chapter 6, will include consideration of the ways in which official, community and class moralities underpin personal decisions, strategies and responses in this area. However, as a final point, it is important to note the extent to which the difficulties of some of the couples in the study, notably the Thornleighs and the Bakers, were compounded when one partner had managed to resolve the conflicts with an ex-partner, whilst the other had not. Where an 'ideal' of amicable resolutions exists, then the partner still in conflict, usually the man, who is challenging the norms of uninvolved fatherhood through his refusal to give up custody or curtail access, compares himself unfavourably with his more successful, 'mature' partner. As a result our argument that the new domestic and family unit created by remarriage can only be understood in terms of the emotional and material inheritance brought to it by *both* partners requires some elaboration. Consideration must be given to the differing experiences and attitudes of the two partners and to the effects they may have on each other. Where their experiences are similar their shared beliefs and responses will be confirmed and strengthened; where they differ, their beliefs and practices are more likely to be challenged and undermined and to be set against some external 'expert' opinion or public morality about such matters.

Financial matters

Since the time of our study many of the financial aspects of divorce and remarriage have been widely discussed in government and legal circles. In retrospect, perhaps, we did not pay sufficient attention to such matters at the planning stage of our own investigation. However, although we did not ask detailed exhaustive questions about sources of income, domestic budgets and expenditure, it became increasingly evident that for many couples the complicated and uncertain structure of their family budget and their own housing situation acted as a constant reminder of their past marriages. Thus, the data presented in this section will illustrate and extend our earlier arguments, that the material inheritance of the past, which continues to shape the everyday domestic life and potential conflicts of remarried couples, is itself structured by the policy and practices of public law and welfare institutions.

Most of the couples we studied formed new partnerships within a relatively short time of leaving their first partner. As a result some partners inherited, literally in a sense, debts and financial complications from their partner's ex-spouse:

> When my husband left, the week after he left I got two bills . . . I always thought we should have had some money for these bills. We hadn't got a penny and I tried the social security and they said they'd stop it out of the money I was already receiving and I was only receiving about £9.00 I think, it weren't very much. It were just pointless, so Ian helped me to pay. (Mrs Worthing)

Her husband had had no children in his first marriage and his wife had worked, so that his attitudes to money and patterns of expenditure were altered very drastically when they started living together:

> I've got a lot more money (now) but I've got a lot more to do with it.
> Q. Are you finding it a struggle financially?
> I wouldn't call it a struggle, but er . . . there's absolutely *no* chance, none whatsoever of saving.

He described giving his wife £100 a month for housekeeping while,

> . . . the mortage and the insurance and the rates comes to another £100 so that's £200 written off . . . before we start. Then another £30 put away for the electric, and gas and telephone, £30 a month usually covers that . . . that just leaves about another £20/£25 a month for meself.

His wife receives £10-a-week maintenance and also child benefit:

> She doesn't say her money is for the children. When they're stocked up with clothes and things, then she'll probably go out and buy me a shirt or herself some shoes with it. If I'm a bit short I might say 'Can I have this week's £10 for taxing the car?'

The Hursts' family budget is also tight so that they depend a good deal on the regular arrival of maintenance and child benefit. Mr Hurst is aware that he is now making a much greater emotional and economic investment in his home life:

> Now, you know, finances, if they are available . . . I'm starting to spend it in the home.

He had recently taken on an additional part-time job as a salesman, 'which keeps me busy on a Wednesday and Friday night and Sat'day morning'. Mrs Hurst was on her own with her children for some time before they met and is well used to financial stringency. Although at the time they were interviewed they were very short of money because their child benefit book had been temporarily withdrawn some weeks earlier, she spoke with gratitude of the way she was able to share her problems with her husband:

> If I worry [about money] then I tell him and he tries, we try to work it out between us, it's not all one-sided you know . . . we share us money; if he's got it then I can have it and if I've got a bit then I help him with it.

Normally, she would use her child benefit 'to buy food and that in the week'. Mr Hurst gets his earnings from his part-time job monthly 'so we have to wait while the end of the month'. Her ex-husband had recently begun to pay regular maintenance:

> I wrote him a letter and said that it were no good to me at the end of the month, and that I wanted it at the beginning of the month.

She has recently begun proceedings, for which she had paid a legal aid fee of £15, to get her maintenance increased from £10 a week. In their interviews, both Mr and Mrs Hurst referred several times to the problems created by the loss of their child benefit book, withdrawn to be altered after Mr Hurst's daughter went to live with her mother, and their need, as a result, to borrow money to make ends meet. Their experience illustrates very clearly the uncertainties felt by those whose sources of income include maintenance or welfare benefits, which are often unreliable and seem very much out of their control. Mrs Hobson is also unable to rely on the arrival of her maintenance payments:

> I should receive £11.50 but he's got in that much arrears . . . I were lucky last week, I got £25 and I'm still keeping me fingers crossed 'cos he still owes me some more.

When it fails to arrive she has to rely on her child benefit, paid out on Tuesday, until her husband is paid on Thursday, when she meets him from work to do the shopping. She also has a close relationship with a neighbour:

> If I can't manage in t'week, she'll lend me something y'know and if she can't manage I lend her something.

Whilst she was still on her own Mrs Farmer had been reliant on supplementary benefit:

> I used to receive a Giro cheque every week and this was payable on a Saturday and I found week after week I wasn't getting my Giro on the weekend I wasn't getting any money and I found that really difficult. . . . I would have to go down to the social security and tell them on the Monday, that me cheque hadn't arrived and then usually they said that they'd put it in the post so I'd get it the day after which was fairly useless because I'd had to borrow all weekend. In fact some weekends, there wasn't anyone to borrow off.

For the Hursts the temporary loss of their child benefit had been sufficient of a disaster for them to consult a social worker, who had promised to help out but had not been able to produce results. They had even contemplated asking their MP to get their child benefit book back but they knew, as with Mrs Hurst's current maintenance application, that there was little to do but await the outcome of the mysterious bureaucratic procedures which they felt powerless to influence.

Another important aspect of the material inheritance of the remarried is their position in the housing market when they begin to live together. Eekelaar concludes that where a mother has custody of children 'an examination of the way the English courts have approached this problem shows that the home is seen as a potential benefit for a spouse exercising the children's function' (Eekelaar, 1978, p. 179). A recent study of the views and practices of divorce court registrars showed that most registrars would try to retain a home for the children wherever possible (Baker *et al.*, 1977).

Although local authority council tenancies are not covered by the Rent Acts and therefore exempt from the provisions of the Matrimonial Homes Act 1967, Section 7 which gave the courts power to transfer a tenancy from one partner to another at the time of divorce, in many instances local authority tenancies are transferred to the mother of dependent children. In general, therefore, divorced mothers are more likely to stay in the matrimonial home, whilst their ex-partners find new accommodation. Thus, when a mother in possession of the matrimonial home finds a new partner they will usually start living together in her old home, even if they move subsequently. Although this may provide the children involved with some continuity, so that they avoid changes of school and the loss of friends, it has disadvantages for the new partners, who must start a new relationship in a domestic setting which has strong associations for one partner and reminds the other of the one whom he has replaced. However, it is often made very difficult for them to move, and although over half of the couples in our study (22) were now living in homes new to both of them, others had very little choice. In this respect the Grahams seem particularly vulnerable and much of their second interviews were taken up with the way in which their everyday lives were constrained by financial problems, which arose from her retention of the matrimonial home.

Some eight years after her first husband left home, Mrs Graham is still involved in complicated legal battles with him, which she sees as a continuation of the conflict which had eventually destroyed her love for him:

> He's killed every ounce of everything I had for him, and believe you me there was an awful lot. . . . Now he's doing such awful things, through solicitors . . . now he's messing us about with the house, he's still getting at me and the children . . . in a different way now.

After lengthy battles her solicitor succeeded in keeping the house for her, although she has to buy her ex-partner out:

> We pay him an amount per month until we've paid off what he's settled with us at . . . it's all been drawn up on agreement with solicitors . . . it'll take about six years to pay him.

In effect, this now means that the Grahams have no alternative but to stay there:

> . . . it's just a pity that um . . . [pause] . . . um . . . this house needs so much doing to it, to keep it in . . . in good order. I mean . . . we couldn't *possibly* get another house for this price . . . you see, we took this over at £6,400. Well, my solicitor told me last

> week um . . . um . . . he showed me a Henry Spencer um . . . house and it was a semi-detached in Ecclesall, no garage, no central heating and it had gone for sixteen thousand. He said this is . . . 'We're sitting on a . . . a goldmine really' and he really did *fight* to keep this house for us . . . but . . . I . . . I also feel that even if we were to sell this house and perhaps make that much profit . . . pay my husband off what he wants . . . we still couldn't afford a house, because I mean . . . we wouldn't get . . . get anything under about twelve or thirteen thousand. And then you'd . . . probably get the same problems, that would probably want something doing to the kitchen or the garden'll need doing so . . . we're probably better sitting tight and trying to cope.

One of their main problems with the house is that there are 'too many memories':

> We're in the same house, none of the wallpaper or anything's [changed] we're just trying to start now but I mean we've no money to start with . . . I mean we've lived with this wallpaper for six years and you know you can't, um, live with memories for six years. We sort of want to get a different image, to see if we can blot out the past.

Their financial problems have been compounded by Mrs Graham's ex-husband's failure to pay maintenance regularly:

> I think he paid six months out of last year and the year before about five months. But . . . I mean . . . they can't seem to do anything about this . . . but now, as I say, he's made up this last three months. So whereas my solicitor had said 'Well, look, he's not paying you, the agreement is that if a fortnight elapses, you don't pay him' . . . we've not paid him but now he's paid us his three months, we've go to find three months' money [laughs]. And we've not put it by in any way because we've had other difficulties cropping up between which we've used the money for.

Their budget is further stretched by Mr Graham's maintenance payments to his ex-wife and two sons:

> I've just been to court about the maintenance . . . to try to get a variation but they turned it down . . . but I can't afford to pay it so I'm er, I'm sort of paying what I can you know . . . because it's a struggle at the moment.
> Q. You tried to get it reduced from £15 did you?
> Yes, but the magistrates felt that, well, they couldn't see any reason why it should be reduced. They just weighed up all the incomings and all the outgoings and one thing and another and they said I could afford to pay it.

> Q. How much do you, in fact, tend to pay?
> Well, about £7, about half. That's not paid every week . . . the priority to the two boys but I wouldn't mind if it were just for the two boys, but it's for the former wife as well, and that I just don't agree with . . . she's managing to get out and I don't think she is as hard up as what she probably makes out to be.

Thus, whilst their continuing financial reminders of the past centre on their house, for others, including the Thornleighs, maintenance payments, and their relationship to access, are the primary focus of dispute. As we have already seen, Mrs Thornleigh has managed to build a manageable relationship with her ex-husband; she receives regular monthly maintenance payments, 'forty-three pound on the fifteenth of each month'. However, Mr Thornleigh's ex-wife has taken him to court twice to secure increases in her payments. Although he is just able to pay it,

> . . . there isn't much left to . . . have a wage packet worth . . . y'know when all me outgoings are taken out, not much at all. I've no savings at all, I can't afford to save.

As his wife explains, this affects their relationship:

> I would say I'm more financially better off than what Keith is . . . I earn more than what he earns, but he knows that if he wants anything and it's there, he knows that I will give it him. . . . We're going through a very sticky patch at the moment. His salary isn't very high and he's got maintenance to pay . . . and it rather demoralises him to know that he has got to ask me. . . . If he is pretty broke and I'll say 'Come on, I'll take you for a meal' . . . then he'll turn round and say 'Well why should it be you?' and I just kind of say 'Well, one of these days it'll be you again' . . . it really upsets him.

His feelings of resentment are compounded by his ex-wife's denial of access:

> I'm maintaining the children, but I'm not allowed to see them, I mean it's all wrong . . . she'll take the money but she won't let me see them which to me is all wrong.

The connection between payment of maintenance and rights to access was considered by a number of the divorced people in the study. In some respects maintenance is perceived as the non-custodial parent's investment in his children, an investment on which he has a right to expect a return. Mrs Chapman and Mrs Vickers described how being paid maintenance directly by an ex-partner could 'buy' the right to see their children when the money was collected or delivered:

> He used to come down and pay the maintenance money which he should have paid through court, you know, for the youngest one and, er, he did see her then. (Mrs Vickers)

Attempts to obtain a variation in a maintenance order were also interpreted in this light, so that Mrs Snow's ex-husband began to demand access again after she had pressed for an increase, whilst Mrs Smithson refused an increase because she did not want her ex-husband to start seeing the children again:

> When I started asking for more maintenance, he decided he was going to come and fetch her . . . the last time was two years ago and it was mostly that 'if I'm going to pay maintenance, I'm taking Susan' and she had a tantrum . . . and I shut the door on him . . . . . . so I went to the doctor's and got a medical certificate to say that . . . it was detrimental to Susan's health to see him and he's never been since. Besides, I stopped claiming maintenance, I thought it it's going to make . . . all this upset, I'd rather not bother claiming the money. (Mrs Snow)

> I went before the courts . . . and he just asked me questions and then he said that there were no access and he asked me if I wanted some money . . . and you know . . . I said, 'No I don't want it.' (Mrs Smithson)

For many of the men and women, the potential financial problems and conflicts with their ex-partners have been resolved because, over a period of time, they have entirely lost contact with their former spouses, whilst a minority have developed patterns of contact and communication as divorced parents which ease their continuing economic relationship. However, it is evident from the significant minority whose problems persist that maintenance arrangements, because of their links with custody and access, provide powerful reminders of the past and, on occasion, a ready arena for continuing conflict between divorced parents.

Chapter 5

Parents, stepparents and children

Introduction

Concern for children as 'Society's most valuable resource, people's most precious "possessions" ' is, as the Rapoports point out, an important element of contemporary ideologies of family life. (Rapoport, Rapoport and Strelitz, 1977, p. 35). The legal principle of the paramountcy of the child's interests, employed as a criterion for the resolution of individual disputes over custody or access, also has a more general social significance. Consequently in their review of research and popular writing on parenting and child development, these writers are able to point to a number of widely held 'conceptions' of parenthood which are, in differing ways, part of both expert and lay public moralities of parent-child relationships. The effects of parental conflict, separation and remarriage have become, in C. Wright Mills's terms, public issues, because they are seen to affect children and because of the conception that society as a whole is in some way accountable for 'its children' as a national resource and responsibility. It is not surprising, therefore, that most research on stepfamilies has been concerned with either the problems faced by stepchildren or has involved comparison of children from step and other families in terms of school performance, social adjustment and so on.

As we explained in chapter 2, we were anxious to avoid placing too great an emphasis on the problems of stepfamilies, especially in the way in which we presented the project to those who took part. From informal comments and discussions, however, it soon became apparent that few people believe that sociologists could possibly be interested in the circumstances and rituals of ordinary family life, so that throughout the study we have tried to avoid asking leading questions about the problems of remarriage and being a stepparent.

DC's contact with the couples and the structure and content of the interviews were intended to encourage remarried parents to designate and discuss the questions which they *themselves* saw as important. The design of the third interview was not finalised until DC had had the opportunity of a number of informal discussions with the study couples. There was, of course, a considerable overlap between 'expert' and our remarried parents' own preoccupations. It is clear from our data that many of the particular problems raised by experts, for example issues of naming and the stepparents' right to discipline, are an important part of the daily domestic decisions and routines of the couples to whom we spoke for the purposes of our study.

Because our investigation was primarily concerned with what remarried parents said about having children in their new family, it must be realised that the data about children presented in this chapter derives from *parents'* own views, opinions and observations. Although DC met many of the children involved, they were not questioned or observed directly; rather we were interested in how their parents and stepparents 'saw' their children and how they viewed their development. More importantly, we were interested in the criteria they used to discuss and evaluate their children's experience of the new family created by their remarriage.

Much of the American clinical and survey data on stepchildren assumes that the development of a child whose parents are separated as a result of either death or divorce and who subsequently acquires a stepparent suffers vis-à-vis his or her counterpart from an 'unbroken' or 'intact' home. The economic, domestic and emotional consequences of parental divorce are documented by social scientists, and have become an important part of widely held folk beliefs about the effects of childhood experiences on subsequent development and adult personality. Bad behaviour or poor progress in school, adolescent delinquency, difficulties in making and keeping friends of the opposite sex, as well as a variety of adult eccentricities are all frequently explained as the result of a 'broken home'. Such beliefs are legitimated in a variety of academic research and literature and in the occupational ideologies of many personal service workers such as teachers and social workers, as well as in popular fiction, TV drama and so on. Thus, as Goode's (1956) study of divorced women showed, the decision to divorce is seen in a much more serious and important light if children are involved.

There is considerable evidence that for many of the divorced parents in our own study feelings of guilt and uncertainty about the consequences for their children of their decision persisted for a very long time. There is much less expert evidence, however, about the effects of parents' remarriage than there is on divorce, so that the content of professional opinion and folk wisdom remains much less clear. While divorced parents tend to justify their decision on the grounds that their children would suffer more from the continuing conflicts of an unhappy marriage, remarried parents emphasise the way in which their new partnership has restored some of the benefits of normal family life, especially daily contact with a second parent. It follows, therefore, that the more closely moral justifications for remarriage are based on the restoration of 'ordinary' family life, the greater the sense of dissonance which results when the material and emotional inheritances of the past inhibit the conscious creation of a normal family life based on an ideal of the unbroken nuclear family.

As Busfield and Paddon's (1977) work demonstrates, children in our society are seen as an indispensable part of family life. Accordingly, we speak of couples 'having a family' in a way which implies that those without children are not worthy of consideration as a 'family' at all. Thus, when couples with one or both sets of children set up house together they may be preoccupied with the early stages of their new partnership, but they are also an instant family group which involves a variety of new relationships and liaisons.

The more strongly parents feel that their children's past has been shadowed by the conflict, change and instability of marriage breakdown, so clearly at odds with idealised notions of a stable, placid and uneventful childhood, the more they will tend to invest in the immediate re-creation of a normal and happy family life with their children. In trying to make sense of their earlier family history and of how it may have affected their children, the parents in our study often made reference to both the potentially damaging consequences of their divorce and the benefits which they believed would follow from the restoration of 'ordinary' family life.

We asked parents a number of questions both direct and indirect about the effects of the past on their children, including:

> Thinking about children in general, not just your own, how well equipped would you say they are to deal with situations like divorce and remarriage? (Interview 2)

> Parents often wonder what kinds of attitudes their children are going to have to subjects like family life, love, marriage and sex and so on when they grow older, do you think they will be very much influenced by the fact that you were [both] married before? (Interview 3)

If concern with the damaging effects of divorce and belief in the wholesome consequences of ordinary family life are posed at either end of a continuum (Figure 5.1), the parents' answers give some idea of the range and diversity of their feelings, not only about the continued effects of the past, but also about the strength and success of their commitment to rebuilding an identity as an 'ordinary' family.

Separation, divorce and remarriage are, from the child's point of view, at variance with beliefs about good child care which stress the importance of continuity and stability.	Remarriage brings a measure of normality to the child, recreating the financial, domestic and emotional circumstances of an 'ordinary' family.

Figure 5.1

When we consider what parents said about their children, the extent to which they had succeeded in recreating an ordinary family life for them was critical in categorising feelings and experiences on a whole range of child-care issues. There are, of course, a number of factors, both structural and emotional, which affect the degree to which 'normal family life' is either a possible, or desired aspect of identity for the study couples. It is however important to stress the degree to which remarried parents shared in the experiences and common problems of having children with their once-married counterparts.

Although we were unable to compare our material with a specific 'control' group of unbroken families, our parents' responses to issues raised in the third interview, in particular the children's physical, educational and emotional progress, matters of discipline, pocket money and friendship, demonstrate clearly how similar their experiences were to those of first-married parents such as the families in the Newsons' studies. As a consequence, we believe that our data not only sheds light on the particular values and concerns of remarried parents and their partners, but also adds to our understanding, as sociologists of the family, of the preoccupations and public moralities of parents generally.

Previous family experiences and family structure

The extent to which a newly cohabiting or remarried couple can offer the children in their new household an 'ordinary' family life and upbringing, which does not differ in any significant respect from that of their counterparts from unbroken marriages, is dependent on a number of interrelated factors. The most critical is obviously the structure, social composition and earlier family experiences of the members of the new household. So strong is public imagery of the ordinary family as transmitted in advertising and so on, what Leach (1967) has called the 'cornflakes packet norm', that it is common for individuals whose family relationships and arrangements differ from this desired norm to experience some embarrassment on public occasions when they appear as a family group or in circumstances when their family role is the defining element in their identity. This applies not only to stepparents but also to many other family groupings and relationships which deviate from commonly accepted norms. Thus childless couples frequently complain that they are expected to be trying to start a family and are pitied for their failure to do so; children from one-parent families sometimes experience stigma at school (Ferri, 1976) and many parents with handicapped children find the public scrutiny of strangers and acquaintances trying (Voysey, 1975). The consequences of this failure to conform to the norms surrounding patterns of marriage and family-building are not simply a matter of public embarrassment but also affect the everyday routines of child care and family life itself. Amongst the significant variables for stepfamilies are the relative ages of the new partners in relation both to each other and their children and stepchildren, and any children of the *new* marriage.

Only ten of the men and five of the women who took part in the study had not had children when they entered their present partnership. Of this group, three of the men and five of the women had not been married before (Messrs Elliott, Farmer and Deam, and Mrs Heathcote, Kennedy, Parker and Prior). As a result they differ in two important respects from those who were already parents. First, they could not call upon any experience of parenthood, of what children are like and what is involved in bringing up children, when they became stepparents themselves. Second, they attached different meanings and significance to the decision to have a child in their new marriage. There are, of course, significant differences between men and women in this respect. In general, as the Newsons point out, what constitutes being a good mother, as opposed to being a good father, is much more clearly and closely defined. A mother's role obligations in our society are held to be at once both more specific and more encompassing than those of a father. Despite some recent concern with fathers' role in child care, such expectations promote a domestic division of labour in which mothers not only bear responsibility for everyday care, but also for how children behave or 'turn out' generally.

Becoming a stepmother

As a result women with little previous experience of children who become stepmothers face a much harder task than stepfathers. For whilst stepfathers' role obligations in relation to social expectations of fatherhood seem much more diffuse, stepmothers, by contrast, will usually be expected to take on the many domestic duties involved in daily child care and will also be immediately accountable in public as principal custodians of their newly acquired children. Thus in the case of formerly motherless families, the arrival of a second wife and mother is a crucial step in family reconstitution. The pursuit of an 'ordinary family life', as defined by prevalent social norms and public moralities, is much more difficult for a motherless than a fatherless family. Whilst the custodian father is relieved of either unnaturally 'feminine' responsibilities, or reliance on other female relatives, his children find reassurance in belonging to a family group which conforms more closely to those of most of their peers. Although many parents and stepparents in our study referred to a period of difficulty when settling down together, in the parents' eyes at least, most children readily accepted the arrival of their new stepmother. The realisation that the family's reconstitution was inevitably incomplete, that in significant respects stepfamilies could not fully conform to the norm of the unbroken nuclear family, affected adults, especially stepmothers, more than children. The accounts of previously childless stepmothers tended to stress their own earlier experiences of children. Before her marriage, Mrs Kennedy had looked after her future stepchildren as a nanny, which she felt reflected her interest in children:

> I've always sort of been interested in children . . . you know when you're a little girl you like babies and you play with toddlers and look after them, and I'd always babysat, not only for money but I'd got to know the children and looked after them . . . I was brought up to think of family life, so I suppose, yes, I always intended or wanted to have children.

Mrs Turner had been married before and saw herself as a potential mother because she assumed, as most women do, that she would eventually have children:

> When you're young you think that you'll get married and you'll have children, but it is a thing that I've always wanted, it was just a case of settling down and getting comfortable more or less, before we did.

These women also use their subsequent experiences of having children of their own to confirm their authenticity as mothers and to make sense of encounters and difficulties with their stepchildren in a way which suggests that it may be particularly important for previously unmarried stepmothers to have children of their own in their new marriages. Mrs Heathcote was the only one who, at the time of the study, had not yet done so. She described how her stepdaughter, Sally, has sometimes,

> . . . hinted that she thinks it would be nice to have a brother or sister . . .
> Q. What are your feelings on that subject?
> Um. . . . If it happens, it happens. . . . If it doesn't, it doesn't. . . . If it happens it'll be super, but if it doesn't, you know we've already got two.
> Q. Are you trying to start a family?
> Not *trying* no, but then again not trying *not* to . . . [laughs] a bit complicated.
> Q. Would it make a lot of difference to you, do you think, having a child of your own?
> Mmm, it'd be super, it'd be great.

Mr Heathcote's comments demonstrate more clearly how much they would like a child of their own:

> We've tried for bloody ages . . . right . . . beginning to give up . . . don't get me wrong, I don't mean give up in that way [laughs], you see Jane's got to the age now where it's possible that she might not have any kids. . . . Some couples can go through life and never have any kids and yet the bloke next door . . . they're having kids you know . . . every other day, . . . I don't know. . . . But I think if we were to have another child, it would cement the relationship, between the two children and Jane *more* than anything else . . . will you come back in two years' time when I've been trying a bit harder? [laughs].

Where possible stepmothers were also at pains to stress how young the children were when they first looked after them:

> Well I did know Emily from when she was three and I don't think I missed out particularly from not knowing her before then, because I think at three the child's personality is pretty obvious and before that I think . . . judging by Ben [her own child] anyway they are all pretty much babies you know, they do predictable baby things and so on. . . . (Mrs Parker)

Mrs Kennedy was asked whether she felt she had missed out through not knowing her stepchildren when they were small:

> Oh yes, in fact I always say I'm very jealous of Kirsty . . . that she

> bore my children, you know [laughs], OK I've had one but it's not the same, but I've got a perceptive sort of imagination . . . and I can . . . many times if an incident was talked about by Barry when they were children, and it crops up a few years later, I'm *there* knowing it all and if they ask me and Barry's not around, I'm able to talk about it quite happily . . . I mean I had Katherine when she was, what, only eighteen months old and I had Victor when he was about six, I know those two then, and had them also to look at to imagine what the older ones were like, when they were little.

Mrs Turner was very clear about what she felt she had missed by not being with her stepson from his early years:

> I've sort of come in at this . . . as he is now he's nearly ten, so the baby years and actually getting to know him through the years . . . they've all been missed. I mean he's quite old for his age, quite intelligent and I suppose it's like getting to know another person, he's not a child that you can . . . how can I put it . . . he's not a young child that you can gradually get to know as they develop, he already has, and I think in that respect it's harder . . . you know, he's got ideas, set ideas and things like that and it's a case of both of us really adjusting to each other, I think.

She was aware that she had already had considerable influence on him in the time that they had been living together as a family:

> I think Paul [her husband] would admit he was spoilt, absolutely . . . it was a case of 'can I have?' and it was given no matter what. Also I think he's lost an awful lot of weight that he had got worrying him; he used to be very upset 'cos people called him 'Tubby' but he was allowed continually to eat and eat and never stopped . . . and he's cut down now to just meals and perhaps a bar of chocolate at night, and he's a lot happier for it.

Becoming a stepfather

The stepfathers in our study may be divided into four groups: the unmarried; those previously married but with no children; non-custodial fathers; custodian fathers. Mr Deam, Mr Farmer and Mr Elliott were bachelors who became stepfathers as a result of their first partnership; in addition seven other married men had no previous experience of fatherhood. Mr Farmer and Mr Elliott present contrasting pictures of their experiences as newly married stepfathers. Mr Farmer, like the stepmothers described above, was aware that his eldest two stepchildren were 'nearly grown up':

> The two eldest ones are teenagers, put it that way, so they've more or less made their own way, haven't they, so there's not a lot of impression I can make on them.

In particular, unlike their younger siblings, they had been more influenced by their father:

> The eldest two, they can remember their Dad and that.
> Q. Whereas the youngest ones don't?
> No they're not . . . he hasn't had much bearing on them, we can try and shape them, but we can't the other two.

Mrs Farmer had already been sterilised before they met and as a result he is a frustrated 'natural' father who is able to describe his own ideal family very vividly:

> I'd like me own, naturally . . . if we'd, say four little toddlers say at two-year intervals, two . . . four . . . six . . . and eight, . . . something like that, . . .
>
> I like to see little 'uns 'cos they're not that old you can't get 'owt across to them . . . they tend to pick things up from you, you know they take your point of view and if you say they should do this and they shouldn't do that, and if you're quiet they're quiet and if you're adamant they're adamant, you know what I mean . . . and they sort of take the point of view of you as their natural father.

By contrast, Mr Elliott, with three children of his own, as well as his stepdaughter, Jean, is able to see himself as father to all four, anxious to give them what they want and to spend as much time with them as possible. Jean, his stepchild, was only three when he first knew her and he feels this has helped them to feel they are an ordinary family:

> Q. I know that you're taking part in this study and answering questions about being a stepfamily and so on, but do you ever consciously think of yourselves as one?
> No I don't.
> Q. So It's not something that you really think of very much?
> No I mean at work one or two of them might say 'Oh, he's got married to a woman who's got a kiddie' so I say, 'So what, I have, what's difference?'
> No I don't conceal it from anybody, because Jean accepted me . . .

The experiences of the men who had no children in their first marriage were very similar. Only Mr Moseley still has no children of his own, something which he still regrets. He had wanted children in his first marriage but his wife became 'too career-minded'; Mrs Moseley had been sterilised before they met, but she was aware that he would have liked children of his own:

> I know that he would have liked a family of his own definitely, but he's not bothered now 'cos he's . . . he says that he thinks it's a bit late in life to start thinking about a family at our age anyway.

In general the remaining men, who became fathers for the first time in their second marriage, felt, like the stepmothers, that the younger the stepchildren were at the time they met, the easier it had been to build a relationship with them. Mr Dunwell felt closest to his youngest stepdaughter:

> Q. Would you say there was much difference in the relationship that you have with each of the children?
> There is, yes, I think it's mainly due to the fact that I've been with some of them for a greater proportion of their lives . . . I'm closest, definitely closest, to the youngest girl. . . . It tails off, definitely does tail off towards the eldest.

Mr Worthing's awareness of the difference between knowing his youngest daughter since she was fifteen months old, as compared with Sarah who was three when they first met, has been sharpened by having a child of his own:

> Q. Do you ever feel that you've missed out from not knowing them when they were very small?
> Yes, more so since I've seen David growing up, but I knew Susan from thirteen or fourteen months . . . , still to all intents and purposes a baby, but I did miss them being as small as what he is.

Stepparents who had acquired their stepchildren at this early stage saw themselves as being more fortunate than those in 'typical' stepfamilies, whose problems and differences from ordinary families were all too visible:

> I think you get a lot of people in my position who've started to be a stepfather to somebody . . . a mother wouldn't bother 'cos it would be just an ordinary child 'cos they're all her children, but somebody like me who takes her over . . . I just regard her . . . like I've done with the baby . . . like me own . . . but a lot of people tend to spoil them when they're the stepfathers 'cos they try and impress them, but they're both treated exactly the same as far as I am concerned. (Mr Snow)

Mr Worthing distinguished his own family from

> . . . the kind of relationships that you either read about or see on

> television, they always seem very strange and strained and one thing and another, and generally speaking that's because everything changes when the kids were ten and eleven and older and that's when you know, there's obviously a gap between that child and the new father and that child and the other children.

In a number of different ways parents' comments and answers to our questions about their family life with their children illustrated how the age of children at the time of a remarriage affects the process of family reconstitution. Even where the family had not been together long at the time of the study, if their children were young they tended to talk more confidently and expansively about the everyday family routines and rituals they had established together. Neither stepparents nor their stepchildren were as likely to question the legitimacy of their parental authority and they also had fewer and less persistent anxieties about the long-term effects of their divorce and remarriage on their children. In general they spoke naturally and unselfconsciously as parents, whilst the remarried parents of older children tended to think more carefully about the everyday conduct and decisions involving the children, pursuing a course of what we have called 'conscious parenthood' which contrasts markedly with the spontaneity the Newsons define as a key characteristic of normal parenthood (Newson and Newson, 1976).

This may be illustrated by considering the issues relating to the expression of physical affection and attitudes towards nakedness within the intimacy of the family group, as well as to discipline generally. Our decision to ask questions about such matters was prompted by the frequency with which they were mentioned by the stepparents whom Maddox interviewed. In general our parents' answers differed more because of individual and sub-cultural attitudes to physical contact and norms about nakedness than because of the existence of steprelationships *per se*. Nevertheless, many discussions of how particular family norms emerged demonstrate that where children were young, say under five, when they began to live together, it was easier to establish patterns of physical familiarity dependent more upon parents' own views and experiences than on any constraints imposed by the steprelationship itself. In this respect there are no significant differences between those marriages involving partners who were already parents, whether custodian or not, and those who had had no children when they married their present partners. It was, however, very common for habits and attitudes towards undressing and nakedness to be modified and renegotiated within the new partnership as part of the construction of shared life-worlds. Many parents described how they had brought into their new family life old, familiar habits of their previous partnerships. In addition they were often aware of how their own attitudes and behaviour had been affected by their new partner's rather different views. Mr Smithson realised that his own views stemmed from his childhood:

> Well, they don't see us undressed, not totally naked . . . I've always had a thing about that ever since . . . probably 'cos when I was small I never used to see me Dad or anything, and I don't like them to see me like that.

Mrs Fox's habit of bathing with her son Jonathan started when he was a baby and now fits into their domestic routine:

> I usually bath him Sunday nights . . . and we have a babysitter and then me and Martin go out, and Jonathan's always been in the bathroom with me since he was, like, old enough to sit up on his own and I've never stopped him . . . [he] plays with his toys in t'sink and then gets in and washes himself . . . I think he'd be about six months old when he first came in with me.

He does not bath with his stepfather, but Mrs Fox thought this is because 'when Martin gets in the bath it's straight in and straight out'.

Mrs Baker was very conscious of how her second husband's more open attitude towards sex and nakedness had affected the whole family:

> Harry's very relaxed about sex. I think it's always been swept under the carpet a little bit where I come from, even from my last husband. . . . There was a proper place and time to talk about sex . . . but he doesn't go flashing himself in front of Patricia, he makes sure he's discreet in front of the boys, we don't go round naked in front of them . . . I think in general it's a pretty easy atmosphere and Harry's a big knocker watcher and Patricia watches her Dad looking and turns round and says 'I saw you' [laughs] it's easy . . .

Mrs Kennedy realised that her husband's first wife, Kirsty, had been much less open than herself and made a conscious effort to alter the children's attitudes:

> Oh we're very open about it, in fact, it's very funny because Kirsty wasn't, but I've always thought, 'Well, damn it all, they're my family and my children and though they haven't come out of my stomach they may as well learn what the human body is about'.

The wide variety of attitudes and routines described by the

couples in the study illustrate both the diversity and range of individual choice which it is widely believed families may enjoy within the private sphere of their own home and family circle, but if stepchildren remain in contact with their non-custodian parent such private matters become more public as some stepparents feel accountable to the 'other' parent. Whilst it is generally believed that neighbours or close kin have no right to know about, or pass judgment on, their attitudes and routines, it is, after all, 'none of their business', non-custodian parents may be felt to have a continuing interest and involvement with their children, which makes such matters more public. Children who stay with their non-custodian parents in fact experience two private spheres or domains whose values and habits in relation to physical contact, nakedness and so on may differ markedly. Dr Johnson described the differences between her own children and those of her husband's first marriage who visit regularly. Although her son is now growing older, she described how he had,

> . . . recently, asked me to turn round when I happened to be there and he was putting his pyjamas on. He doesn't take any notice of us prancing about in the nude and Jessica. . . . But the other three . . . and Derek's wife . . . it never occurred to us . . . but her three are very prudish, and she actually wrote and said, 'Peter was very embarrassed on his visit this weekend because he saw you without your clothes on in the bathroom' and I thought 'Oh dear, another hang-up' and it hadn't registered with us at all.

Mr Hutchinson's attitudes towards being naked with his stepchildren were affected by his daughter who,

> . . . came up and told me, and this is what stuck in my mind, she said she'd been in t'bath, and Derek, that's her stepfather had come in t'bathroom and she said that she wouldn't have minded if it had been me . . . 'cos we all used to bath together and I know it hurt her a lot wi' Derek going in. . . . If my daughter hadn't have said that I probably wouldn't be so wary, so it was summat that had never entered my head, but it had entered hers and I could see how it had affected her.

The unusualness of their children's circumstances and experiences also affected parents in more general ways, forcing them to consider and discuss matters which might otherwise be avoided and ignored. We asked them whether they thought their children's attitudes to subjects like sex, love and marriage might be influenced by their parents' divorce and remarriage and many mothers, particularly, suggested that their circumstances had not only forced them to talk to their children about sex and so on, but had also made it possible for their children to consider such matters in a much more direct way.

In general, then, we would wish to suggest that the age of their children at the time when new partners set up home together is a very significant factor in determining the extent to which families may either wish, or succeed, in establishing patterns of ordinary family life which approximate closely to those of unbroken nuclear families. A second, significant factor is the number and relative ages of the children in the new stepfamily unit.

In our discussion of the demographic characteristics of the study families we noted that they were larger than average. There were three main reasons: a number of parents already had more than three children in their first marriage; some couples had additional children in their new marriages; some family groups included the custodial children of both parents, i.e. stepsibling families. Of the fifteen families who had four or more children:

> In four cases the custodial parent had already had four or more children in their first marriage.
> In five cases family size was increased because of the one or more babies of the new marriage.
> Six were stepsibling families.

The earlier marital histories of Mrs Hutchinson, Mrs Moseley and Mrs Parkes show some of the common features associated with high fertility. All three came from working-class homes and married young; Mrs Parkes was one of sixteen children; Mrs Hutchinson and Mrs Moseley have additional children not currently living with them. The domestic and social environment of all of these women both in their families of origin and of marriage had been in some measure affected by poverty. As Askham has pointed out, the mechanisms by which economic deprivation is related to high fertility are extremely complex (Askham, 1975). However a number of studies indicate that,

> For both the non-manual and manual groups . . . economic aspects of life were significantly related to the number of children women had. Those who had experienced husband's unemployment, job insecurity, or inadequate income had more children than those who had never experienced these difficulties.

Dunnell concludes, therefore, that:

> These findings tend to support the idea that economic insecurity and poverty may have some causal link with high fertility. (Dunnell, 1979, p. 26)

Thus for some of the couples in our study the children of their new marriage should be seen as part of a more general pattern of high fertility. However the decision to have further children after remarriage made by other couples was important because of the light it shed on their beliefs about having children and sharing parenthood together.

Remarriage and the decision to have additional children

In their recent book on the factors which have influenced family size in post-war Britain, Busfield and Paddon stress the importance of examining the meanings attached to 'having children' as well as the number and spacing of children. They argue that it is, 'how individuals perceive and assess their present and future circumstances as well as the importance that they attach to them when making decisions about family size and spacing that counts' (Busfield and Paddon, 1977, p. 252).

From their data they suggest 'children are considered essential to married life' (ibid., p. 134) and that a married couple is not really a family without children:

> When asked about having children most people draw upon a set of ideas that links getting married, having children and having a family to one another, making all seem mutually interdependent. Underlying this set of ideas is the belief that a married couple with children constitute a natural, normal and complete family. Without children a married couple are not a proper family. (Ibid., pp. 135–6)

By definition all the couples in our study were already 'a family' as one or both partners had brought children from their first marriage into their new partnership, so that their reasons for having a further child or children together must draw on other sets of ideas related to their beliefs about the nature of parenthood itself and their own earlier experiences of different types of parental involvement. For such parents, if they are still young enough and able to have children, the important issues are, whether? when? and how many?

As we have suggested elsewhere, second courtships include sexual contact at an early stage (Burgoyne and Clark, 1980). For those who are still able to have children, the mutual discussion and sharing of past biographies might include considerable reference to the experience of wanting, having and bringing up children. Consequently when, as a couple, they began to construct a new joint prospective biography (Berger, 1963, pp. 68f) whether to have a child or children together was frequently discussed from the start. It should be emphasised that both partners bring to such discussions and decisions very different past experiences, if, for example, one is already a parent and the other is not or if one partner is now a non-custodial parent. In addition they are both coming to terms with changes in their parental role which inevitably follow from their new partnership; for example single parents are able to relinquish sole responsibility for their offspring; non-custodial parents acquire 'new' children and non-parents have their first taste of parental responsibility. In addition, as the Rapoports indicate, the nature of parental involvement changes as the children themselves mature and develop (Rapoport, Rapoport and Strelitz, 1977). Thus partners may have already been blood and/or social parents, or, alternatively, never have been parents at all. If their new partner already has custodial children they become full-time social parents or if he or she has non-custodial children with whom they have active contact, they become part-time social parents. Perhaps this can be put more simply in a diagram (Figure 5.2). If we also distinguish between 'blood' and 'social' parenthood in terms of the way in which parenthood is felt to fulfil certain needs, it is possible to isolate the circumstances in which it might be most important to have a 'child of one's own' or '*our* own child'.

A *Needs arising from beliefs about the significance of blood ties*

1 It is important to reproduce something of oneself to go on in the future.
2 To mingle one's own genetic inheritance with that of a loved partner is to create the unique product of a particular relationship.
3 To give birth to, or less strongly, to father a baby offers biological/psychological fulfilment.

B *Needs arising from beliefs about parenthood as a pleasurable, socially desirable role and activity*

1 Confirmation of adult status.
2 Setting seal on a specific partnership (cf. A2)
3 Being a parent within a 'normal' family is regarded as a significant and valued aspect of social identity;
   - the daily activities of family life with children are regarded as intrinsically satisfying;
   - children are a source of fulfilment and future investment for their parents;
   - children give a sense of continuity and investment in the future.

Clearly, being either a stepparent, foster parent or even an adoptive parent cannot satisfy those needs derived from beliefs about the importance of blood ties. However, some understanding

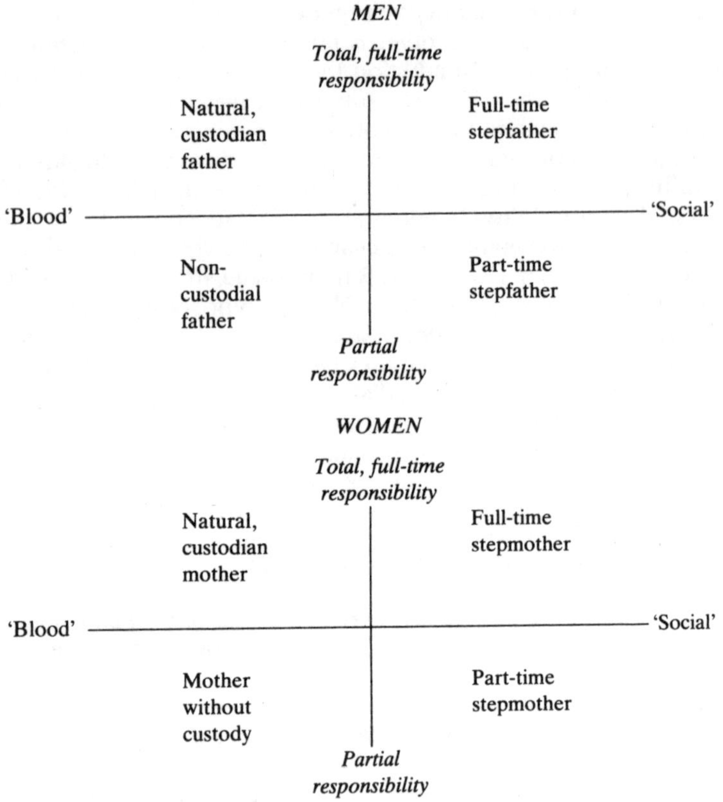

Figure 5.2

of stepparents' beliefs about the perceived limitations of social parenting may be derived from examination of how important having either a 'child of one's own' is for stepparents or 'having a child together' is for the remarried couple. Amongst the study families generally a slightly larger proportion of the middle-class couples had a child within their new marriage than the working-or intermediate-class couples and this was also true of the 'large' families with four or more children isolated above. It would, however, be unwise to draw any firm general conclusions about the effects of economic and class factors on the decision to have additional children from such a small-scale study. There were, in addition, other differences between families with a baby of the new marriage and those without (Table 5.1). Not unexpectedly almost all the families in which custodian fathers married childless women had already had babies in their new marriages (Table 5.2)

Table 5.1

	Average age of wives at time of study	Average family size at time of study
Child(ren) of new marriage	31.7 years	3.2 children
No child of new marriage	34.4 years	3.3 children

From our earlier discussion of those who had not had children at the time when they became stepparents, it is evident that it is particularly important for them to have a child of their own, and unlike stepparents who are also non-custodial parents, they do not have to support children from a previous marriage. Thus, in so far as economic circumstances determine the remarried couple's decisions about further children, stepfathers may be able to consider additional children more easily than non-custodial fathers. Recently a number of pressure groups have drawn attention to the plight of the second wives of divorced men who have to pay maintenance for both their children and their ex-wives and, thus, cannot afford to have children in their second marriage. In addition, the second wife's earnings may be taken into account when assessing maintenance. In their policy statement the Campaign for Justice in Divorce argue:

> Under no circumstances should a second wife's efforts to support and enrich her marriage be diverted, directly or indirectly, to the benefit of a former wife. . . .
>
> A second wife's right to have children of her own should not be denied by limiting her husband's ability to support her. (Campaign for Justice in Divorce, 1979, p. 10)

Although the Campaign for Justice in Divorce is a pressure group defending one particular set of interests, and their policy statement raises a number of complex issues, it does draw attention to the large number of second marriages which must inevitably seem defective or second-best to the partners because they cannot allow

Table 5.2

	Custodian fathers	Custodian mothers	Stepsibling families
Child(ren) of new marriage	4	11	3
No child of new marriage	1	11	10
	5	22	13

'having children' to follow 'getting married' as it does in the ordinary course of events.

Having babies in a new marriage may also be largely determined in other ways by one or both partners' experiences of parenthood. Individuals may try to 'replace' children they have lost contact with. For example, as Mrs Elliott's children from her first marriage had been taken into care, her present husband believed that, 'She'd had her children taken off her some years ago in her first marriage and she wanted to defy t'authorities, so she had another two.' Mrs Elliott has now been sterilised but she felt she 'would have had another baby if I could, but I couldn't . . . but I would like to.' Only three of the non-custodial fathers, Mr Gilmour, Mr Graham and Mr Pelham had had children in their remarriage at the time of the study, so that there is less evidence that non-custodial fathers who have lost contact with the children of their first marriage try to replace them through having more children in a remarriage. It seems that in most cases such stepfathers are able to derive sufficient fulfilment from the social aspects of parenting presented by their acquisition of stepchildren. For example, although the Gilmours were expecting a baby at the time of their third interview, Mr Gilmour felt that it had been his wife's decision, although she described it as a joint one. Mr Gilmour was asked,

> Q. What about more children?
> There's one on the way [laughs].
> Q. Oh, I didn't realise that. Congratulations.
> Yes, June next year and . . . I hasten to add, it was planned, discussed and decided upon . . . I lost [laughs].

Mrs Gilmour commented: 'at first we thought we weren't going to have any but now . . . we both changed our minds and it's what we both wanted.' However, having accepted the forthcoming baby, Mr Gilmour was able to articulate ideas about the benefit she might bring:

> I think it will bind us together quite a lot . . . I think in a way they cement a marriage . . . providing that you've got a foundation to cement together in the first place, yes, I think they're a good thing . . . and I enjoy kids anyway.

In other respects the decision to have a child is also affected by the partners', particularly the mothers', experiences of being a parent in their previous marriages. Thus, if they know that they like having babies and perceive themselves to be good mothers, they may welcome the opportunity to have more if their present financial circumstances permit. Other women felt more ambivalent about having further children, especially if they believed that having or bringing up children had in some way precipitated the breakup of their first marriage. Thus when Mrs Thompson was asked about having more children, she admitted,

> I'd like some more, actually, I mean Barry knows I'd like another one but I think it would be too disruptive . . . you know I'm sort of frightened that the same sort of thing might happen again, and we're sort of starting from scratch . . . like this house . . . we haven't got much furniture . . . all that much to be practical . . . I really need to go on working.

However, her need to work is not simply because of financial problems:

> I'd love to have another baby, but the thing is it makes you so much more dependent on your husband, doesn't it? And, much as I'm sure that Barry would support me I still want to keep my bit of independence, more now than I ever did when I was younger.

She explained this in relation to her first marriage:

> You know, I see that it just got worse when I left work and had Jeremy . . . when I'd left work and when I was cooped up at home all day and I just don't want . . . really don't want the same thing to happen, I mean not that Barry's anything like me first husband but I just think sometimes it's inevitable that it happens.

In this section we have considered the most salient features of remarried family structures affecting parents' and stepparents' images of their own family life. We have suggested that previous experiences of parenthood, including *not* being a parent, affect the degree to which the remarried pair want and are able to perceive themselves and their children as like an 'ordinary' family. Thus, the more closely the family group itself approximates to public images of the 'normal' family, the more easily they are able to present themselves publicly as just an 'ordinary family'. Similarly, the younger the children are when parents divorce and remarry, the easier it is for their new family group to rebuild an ordinary, unremarkable domestic life together. These parents and stepparents believed, and gave evidence to the fact, that very young children were able to accept change more readily and retained few memories of earlier events, so that within a very short time, for their children at least, their new life together had become natural and permanent. Consequently these remarried parents were more confident than those with older children. Their confidence and identity as an 'ordinary family' were also unlikely to be undermined by any continued contact with the children's non-custodial parent. Some of the study couples had been together for several years by the time they were interviewed and their accounts of their life together and evaluation of the children's development frequently demonstrated that, like Mr Elliott quoted earlier, they did not really think of themselves as a stepfamily.

In addition, the decision to have further children of the new marriage is also associated with the couples' desire to conform to the norms of ordinary family life; formerly childless stepparents, particularly stepmothers, enhance their legitimacy as parents through having a child of their own whilst many couples described these additional children of the new marriage as bringing the various members of the family group together into a 'proper family'.

Parents' evaluation of their present circumstances and the quality of family life

Typically we hold parents accountable for the nature and quality of the family life experienced under their roof because it is they who have taken the decisions involved in marrying, finding a home, having children and so on. In our own society most individuals perceive family roles and projects as central elements of their personal life, individuality and identity. Thus for most people, their own evaluation of the constituent elements and activities of their family life becomes a critical factor, contributing to their sense of self-esteem. Consequently, in the case of the remarried, the extent to which they themselves, as well as their partners, children and significant others evaluate their family life positively will affect their views and opinions on many aspects of their life as a family with children a great deal. In their answers many of our informants referred to aspects of their partner's and their children's evaluation of their life together as well as to others whose opinion counted: kin, friends and, on occasion, teachers, social workers and others.

We have considered some of the special features of setting up home for the remarried in earlier chapters, but their experiences and evaluation of daily domestic routines are significant in this chapter in so far as they make a significant contribution to parents' perceptions of the quality of their family life. In the second interview we asked men and women to compare their present and earlier partnerships in terms of how household and financial responsibilities were shared. It was clear that couples were anxious to show that they found their present partnerships more satisfactory. Whilst some women praised their second husbands for being more domesticated and taking greater responsibility in the home, others were delighted by husbands who did not interfere. What was common in their accounts was their desire to demonstrate their contentedness with their present arrangements. In particular, as we saw in chapter 3, parents mentioned their new partners' involvement with the upbringing of their children, stressing either the advantages of being able to share their responsibilities after a period as a lone parent, or comparing their new partners' greater interest and involvement with that of their previous partner. Conversely where either one or both partners mentioned the problems and difficulties related to family life with their children, such difficulties frequently appeared to undermine their sense of identity as an 'ordinary' family. When questions were asked about the details of everyday domestic life, nearly everyone who took part in the study described their lives together in vivid and enthusiastic detail, confirming their positive commitment to building a family life together. Some, like the Bakers, used their past experiences of each being single parents to develop new patterns of responsibility, others returned, thankfully, to a more traditional division of labour. Mrs Baker described her second husband:

> Harry has . . . he's tried to be a mother and a father to his two, you know if a button wants sewing on, he can sew a button on, or will iron a shirt, in the same way I can put a plug on or dig the garden, and we are both equally balanced in those things, and the children find us equally capable of sorting out any problems they've got.

Mr Shannon described his decision to remarry after the death of his first wife in rather different terms:

> I tended to regard married life as the norm and that therefore . . . I thought it might be more damaging to the children, not to have someone that they could regard as a mother, than to be on their own. There were difficulties in having housekeepers and my looking after the children and clearly they were losing out on home cooking and this kind of thing . . . and the benefits that come from having someone in the house that can look after you and do your mending and prepare your food and all this kind of thing and this is . . . artificial if it's done by a housekeeper.

Many of those who had formerly been single parents described their relief at being able to share some of the pressures and problems of parenthood. Mrs Smithson felt that in her first marriage, she always had to,

> Stick up for the kids . . . 'cos me husband was always on to them, you know, so I stuck up for them and they *knew* and they used to play me up then and I didn't . . . we used to be falling out.

She especially appreciates being able to share her children's future with her second husband:

> And he'll talk to you, you know . . . say Alice . . . she's growing up and he thinks she should have . . . a few more privileges than the other four now, you know what I mean, that she should have an extra hour, something like that . . . 'cos she's thirteen next, so you can't treat her like the rest of them . . . and so we've been talking about this . . . she's wanting, er . . . to go out to youth clubs and that and he's more scared about it than what I am, you know . . . I said to him, 'Well, let her go . . .' 'cos he'll laugh about it and say, you know when they're about sixteen and there's a boyfriend coming to the door, and she'll be saying, 'Well I can go if me Dad can come' [laughs] he's er . . . he thinks about it a lot more than I do, you know.

Mr Smithson is also aware of being able to help her with her children:

> It makes me feel a bit better that she's asking me to deal with them, you know what I mean, she's not like . . . wanting to deal with them herself . . . she'd rather . . . you know, which pleases me. I like it like that. (   )
>
> Linda'll sometimes come and sit with me, you know, she tends to hang round me a lot. But apparently, Mary was telling me that when she lived with her husband she were the odd one out, she never got any . . . what's you call it . . . he never showed her any emotional, you know . . . as though he wanted her or anything like that and she was definitely the odd one out, and of course when she came here, I took to her a right lot, you know what I mean, she really enjoyed it.

Mrs Hutchinson's description of her husband's involvement with her children concludes with the comment,

> I think really they're benefitting more than I am from this marriage [laughs] if you know what I mean, there are more of them for Roger's love to be shared out between, but they all seem to be flowering.

She has noticed a change in one son:

> I've noticed a big change in him since we've been married, because before that he was . . . a demon . . . and I couldn't do very much with him at all. If I wanted him to behave I'd just got to keep him in where I could see him which wasn't very fair, but if I let him out he got up to all sorts of mischief and now he doesn't.

Her descriptions illustrate how she has been able to share some of the pressures endemic in bringing up four children in a way which meets her own standards.

> Q. Is there much difference in the relationship that the children have with you and your husband; do they come to you for different types of things, would you say?
> More often than not, they'll go to him first and if he can't help them then he'll send them to me, if they want to go out anywhere they don't ask me they ask him (   ) and usually I'm busy so that it's obvious that they'll go to him to ask a question first because I'm . . . they've got a lot more thoughtful like that . . . if I'm doing something they don't come pestering me like they used to.

Mrs Moseley also values the support with the children her second husband has given her, using visits to school as an example:

> Q. Do you find that you and your husband talk very much about family matters, particularly the children and their upbringing?
> Oh yes, that's something . . . that I never had before, you see, with me ex-husband 'cos he used to say 'Oh well, it's up to you that' you know . . . and that was that. But I mean Graham, will go down to the school with me on open days and things like that, which my ex-husband didn't do, I always ended up going on me own. So I think really that they've got a better . . . more stable background now, you know, than they've ever had.

New partners were also felt to have brought new leisure interests into the family. Mr Hutchinson proudly described how his own interests have,

> . . . rub[bed] off on t'lads . . . different things . . . they'll start getting a screwdriver . . . and I've no need to ask them if I want anything done in t'garden and they *want* to do t'garden on their own.

One of Mr Thornleigh's stepsons, Nicholas, had taken up cycling:

> I used to race, so we hit if off there together and he's always coming to me with broken spokes and such like and I'm putting it right for him . . . straightening the gears up, you know. And Neil's interested in music and I love music so we hit it off there together.

Many of these comments on leisure interests and activities illustrate fairly traditional views about gender differences. Mrs Gilmour sometimes found her son's interests hard to follow:

> Well . . . he's all cars at the moment, a bit beyond me you know

> [laughs] but we play together . . . I used to go and play football with him and everything like that. (   )
> Q. Do you think that since you got married again your present husband has passed on a lot of his interests to Derek?
> Oh! Definitely, yes.
> Q. What sort of things?
> Model aeroplanes . . . and racing cars, of course. I didn't know anything about them . . . anything mechanical . . . they're both interested in that sort of thing . . . anything on wheels, you know.

For this reason Mr Graham seemed rather sorry that both his stepchildren are girls:

> Q. Would you say that you'd passed on any of your own interests to the girls?
> Interests? Not really . . . it's difficult to pass interests on to girls, isn't it? It's not like boys, you know . . . you get playing football or things like that, there's no interests that I could pass on to them.

However, Mrs Baker's involvement with a brass band resulted in her stepsons taking up the trumpet:

> That's a hobby that they've got off me. Alan's in the band now and Ian will eventually go down when he's good enough to.

Mrs Shannon also felt that her stepsons were,

> interested in what I do . . . in my hobbies and interests that I have outside the home and things I'm enthusiastic about . . . I like anything to do with the literary world and I think that perhaps that has encouraged them to explore that world, which they may not have done perhaps otherwise.

In their comments on their partners' involvement in bringing up stepchildren, many parents stressed the way this enriched the partnership itself and spoke appreciatively of being able to discuss family matters with their new partners.

Mrs Worthing described how she talked to her husband while he did some decorating:

> . . . he's been doing a lot in the house lately. I go up and sit on t'bed and talk, and always . . . at night, if he's been on afternoons, I always wait for him to come in and we have a talk then, er, when he comes home at night we usually wait while the kiddies go to bed you know, 'cos I like it when it's sort of, a step forward, like Susan . . . all of a sudden today this morning I've noticed she knows a colour; she used to be terrible, everything were green, and this morning she said 'Your trousers are blue'

> . . . and I thought that were great (   ) and I couldn't wait to tell Ian.

Similarly, Mrs Hobson found they often talked when they went to bed at night:

> If we're sat up in bed . . . and we were talking about Stephen the other night, you know and he's progressed a lot since he's been to that school.

Mrs Dunwell appreciated the quality rather than the quantity of her conversation with her present husband:

> I won't say I talk more because Geoff's quite taciturn and I don't see a lot of him, with him working so long, so I don't talk more to him, I talk more *in depth* to him, you know. In the first marriage we tended not to speak about anything that was important, there'd be a lot of talk because he was there a lot of the time, but it wouldn't be . . . you know . . . deep, anything that really worried me, I probably wouldn't think about . . . discussing it with him.

One of the consequences of couples talking about their family life in this way is that they make each other aware of how they are appreciated. Mr Hobson described getting on very well with his stepchildren:

> Q. Was this kind of affection something they hadn't had from their own father?
> . . . As I say, the impression I got from Patricia [his wife] is that he wanted them in bed when he got home (   ) he never even spoke to the children, no kissing or caressing, anything like that . . . never saw him speak to them.

The material we have presented so far illustrates how parenting and childcare were used as means of family reconstitution but for some of the study couples difficulties and conflicts over children were sufficiently serious to give rise to feelings of uncertainty about their partnership and the family life they had created.

The most significant area of difficulty and uncertainty for the couples in our study related to the management of children. There is little comparable information about the experiences and conflicts of parents in unbroken families so that it is difficult to assess the extent to which the problems outlined and discussed below are a direct consequence of remarriage itself. It seems probable, for example, that the results of parents' holding rather different views about bringing up children, illustrated in our discussion of the Foxes and the Grahams below, might be very similar in unbroken families.

Many of the couples felt that they differed from one another in terms of how strict they were in matters of discipline. In most cases their evaluation of who was the stricter parent was congruent, which suggests, as we have shown above, that these parents may have talked a good deal together about the way they dealt with their children. For example, Mrs Brown described how their children,

> go to their Dad 'cos they know he's soft and he will nearly always say yes (   ) when they think that I'm going to say that they can't do something.

Mr Brown readily acknowledged that he was generally less strict with both his own son Paul and his stepson Timothy:

> Timothy can be a little . . . Dennis the Menace, you know, but I've seen Jean chastise him and really tan him hard on his backside, and I've felt it for him, you know what I mean, and I've thought, 'Oh crikey' as if he were my own (   ) you know I've thought, 'Oh Jean, don't hit him' you know . . . because I don't hit him.

Similarly the Hutchinsons hold different views about using physical punishment and both Mrs Shannon and Mrs Thompson felt that they tended to resort to smacking children because they lacked the traditional authority which enabled their husbands to control by words alone. Mrs Shannon could not recall her husband using physical punishment as,

> I think he could quell them with a word, if they needed quelling.

Mrs Thompson commented that,

> in families in general, that it's the mother who does the telling off all through the day or all the time that they're with the children and then father comes along and he only has to say one word and . . . quiver and quake . . . you know, and Barry only has to say something and Jeremy looks at him in amazement and he thinks 'Barry's told me off' and he instantly stops what he is doing.

When such differences were recognised couples were often able to resolve conflicts by agreeing to back each other up. Mrs Dunwell described their approach to disciplining the children:

> We abide by each others' decisions . . . don't always agree with them . . . but you abide by them in front of the children. We don't often disagree, just one or two . . . particularly with Rachel, I think . . . I'm saying that you mustn't be so heavy-handed, not in front of her . . . and he's saying, 'But she deserves it' and I say, 'Yes but you can't see . . . you just can't quite see what's going on in that kid's mind.'

The Heathcotes were also aware that they were still working out how to share their responsibilities. Mrs Heathcote was asked:

> Q. Who normally deals with them, when they do something they shouldn't or get into trouble or anything like that?
> If I'm there I do, and sometimes if I think perhaps we ought to discuss it and then I (   ) I'll perhaps tell them off and say to them that I'm not leaving it there and that I'm going to have a word with their father about this, you know . . . and then we'll discuss and both talk to them.

Her husband appreciated her involvement with his children:

> My first wife used to expect me to go home and reprimand them, three or four hours later, and you can't do that, you've got to do it there and then. (   )
>
> My children know how far they can push me and when I've had enough, that's it and they back down. With Jane . . . it's early days yet I suppose, although they've known her, what, for two years, and of course . . . she must feel (   ) a bit insecure . . . not knowing how far she can push the kids, and they probably feel exactly the same with her. But of course, they're learning.

His awareness that the early stages of the new relationship between stepparents and their children can cause problems is echoed by many of the other couples who had been together much longer than the Heathcotes and who referred to early difficulties which had now been overcome. In particular, stepparents felt that they lacked legitimacy as figures of authority because they were not 'real' fathers or mothers and, on occasion, were reminded of this fact by others.

Mrs Thornleigh describes how her husband has said to her,

> 'If I were their father, I would do more', I mean, if they were younger then I think he could discipline them, probably smack them, but I think that's one thing he won't do. (   )
> Q. Is that something you talk about very much?
> Not so much now, we did at one bit, but you know . . . they don't seem to be difficult . . . half as difficult to keep under control as they were.

Throughout his third interview, Mr Thornleigh showed how aware he was that he was not 'their Dad' but he felt that his problems were now safely in the past. In contrast to his continuing problems in gaining access to his own non-custodial children, he insisted that,

> here, everything's absolutely perfect, no troubles at all, we all get on smashing you know . . . they call me Keith, and I wouldn't

> expect them to call me Dad 'cos I'm not their Dad . . . and you know it's all first name terms . . . smashing.

Mrs Hobson described in glowing terms her husband's immediate assumption of parental responsibility for her children only to find that he was reminded by a probation officer enforcing a supervision order connected with custody that he was not 'really' the children's father:

> I leave [disciplining the children] to him you know . . . since after we were married he's always corrected them, you know . . . well he . . . they take more notice of him than they do of me, they seem to be playing me up more.

Mr Hobson described how,

> The probation officer once asked me what I would do when he grew older and if I asked him to do something and he turned round and said, 'You aren't my Dad' you know, this kind of thing, but we'll cross these bridges when we come to them.

For a small number of couples, notably the Foxes and the Grahams, such problems seem to have potentially serious consequences. In each case *both* partners referred to conflict. In their interviews they described their disagreements in some detail and for both couples such conflicts appeared to threaten their belief in the permanency of their relationship.

In the main part of his third interview Mr Fox mentioned fairly casually that his wife thought his methods of discipline 'rather old-fashioned' and he described himself as taking responsibility for discipline:

> Q. Who normally deals with him when he has done something that he shouldn't do?
> Me mostly . . . [laughs] and then I get into trouble for doing it . . . and it seems funny but he can make it up with me . . . I can shout at him and hit him [and] he'll come back to me, but if Ann does, he won't have 'owt to do with her for a long time.

When he tells his stepson to go to bed he does, but,

> When Ann's in it's a different kettle of fish altogether . . . she tells him to go to bed . . . and it's 'oh no' and he starts playing her up, so I have to sometimes turn round and say, 'Come on, bed.'

Mrs Fox complained of her husband's lack of understanding in his dealings with Jonathan but also felt guilty about contradicting her husband in front of the child,

> When our Jonathan's poorly . . . he's mardy, *very* mardy . . .

This last fortnight . . . he goes off food altogether when he's poorly, he'll drink a tap dry . . . but he plays wi' his food then and Martin gets rather angry wi' him . . . like at t'dinner table t'other day, I forget what it were we had to eat . . . but instead of telling his Dad that he didn't want it, he were moaning so . . . Martin shouted at him and the tears come and then I said, 'Well you shouldn't have done that, he's not very well and you know he's poorly' and . . . when I thought about it after . . . I should have held me tongue and waited while our Jonathan had gone out and then told him.

It was not obvious until later in their interviews, when they were asked about having further children, just how seriously both Mr and Mrs Fox viewed these problems. Mrs Fox tried to imagine how having further children might affect them all:

If we had another one, a boy *or* a girl, and Jonathan'd be eight and be starting Juniors then . . . he'd get his nose pushed out . . . but I don't think that would bother him, especially if it were a little boy 'cos many a time he's said, 'I want a baby brother to play with.' (   ) And if I had another one, I'd have to run about after our Jonathan, anyway with whatever he wanted, and then there'd be Martin and there'd be . . . so he'd have to cry 'cos I can't be in two places at t'same time doing t'same thing and . . . in a way I think discipline'd just be t'same in t'end (   ) . . . I might protect him a bit . . . motherly instinct you know . . . but I don't think I would protect him you know if he or her were Martin's, I think I'd say, 'It's your son as well as mine, if you think he's doing wrong, tell him.'

When asked about having children of his own Mr Fox replied:

We've thought about it, yes, I mean . . . I keep saying that I'll be a grandad like, before I'm a father, but it all depends on Ann really, if she wants to have them, then she'll have them, and if she dunnt want them, then she won't have them. We've talked about it but . . . in the last six months we've been having a bit of an upset so it's been put off for a bit longer . . . she's right like, she says that she's not having any kids and bringing them into the world wi' the attitude that we've got at the moment like and I know she's right.
Q. What is the problem then, in that respect?
Just . . . a few arguments . . . one or two things have just cropped up that we've had us arguments about, one or two good arguments, shouting and bawling at each other and everything . . . and sometimes we shout, well argue, in front of him and that's upset him a bit.

Mrs Fox was also worried about the effects their arguments might have on Jonathan. She was asked whether her son had any particular problems or worries:

> Well me and Martin's had quite a few rows, well not rows but disagreements lately, you know . . . with telling him one thing and me looking daggers and he listens to us and he knows what we're saying ( ) and me sister says, 'You never know, he might have heard summat he dunnt like and he's thought about it, and worried about it.'

Mr Graham described their problems very clearly, laying much of the blame on himself:

> Well actually, I'm fairly stern meself and I know I am . . . I've a tendency to fly off the handle if they've done anything really . . . well, if I feel that they've done anything really wrong, I fly off the handle and then I probably find that it's not as bad as what it seemt to be. I'm not normally a violent person or anything like that, you know . . . well, I would say I'm fairly placid you know . . . but sometimes they . . . you know, if I've had a hard day or something like that and I sit down and watch television and they start making a bit of a row, then probably I'll start playing hell. ( )
>
> It's probably *me* really, if the truth were known, it's probably me that's not used to them, I mean they've been together all four on them like, with their mother and then I sort of come on the scene and I've got to get it together with them like.
>
> Q. Have you found that being their stepfather has created special discipline problems for you?
>
> No, not really, the only thing that does sometimes cause problems is the fact that if I do correct them I'm probably a bit sterner . . . than what I should be, then Jennifer'll jump down on me and she'll say I wouldn't correct me own like that, you see, and this is the only problem I've found being a stepfather.

His wife described a recent incident where she felt he had been too strict with one of the girls, but her main concern was the way that they tended to argue in front of the children, because,

> There's very little time now we're on our own ( ) we usually try not to [argue] in fact Martin's the one who, when we first met said, 'I don't like arguing in front of the children' and if anything, he's the one that's done it most *in front* of the children, in fact he doesn't seem able to control himself now, if he's got something to say he says it, because very often I say to him, 'Look they're only in there, shut the door and come in here and say what you want to

say' and it's me that's gone the other way now, I try to get it so the children don't hear all the time because it must be very upsetting for them.

At various points in their interviews they both referred to their conflicts over the children. Mrs Graham described her husband's feelings and the conflicts they created in her:

> I think he could do without the girls altogether. He's accepted them because they were a part of *me* , but really I think Martin's all for me, he wants my time all the time . . . you know, he wants me all the time and he can't understand why I can't give one hundred per cent of my time . . . I've got to sew a button on, or I must do this Guide uniform, there's always something. I wish I could give him one hundred per cent of my time you know . . . I wish that . . . if I could have my time again . . . I wish that I could have two or three years just enjoying meself with him.

It is evident even from these edited extracts that the problems described by the Foxes and Grahams are complex in both origins and resolution. It is particularly difficult to estimate the extent to which they are a direct consequence of remarriage as such, although the couples' previous history and family identity provide them with a ready explanation which makes use of such categories. It is also clear that whilst many of the remarried parents we studied found few differences when they compared their problems with those of unbroken families, for others the legacy of the past persisted and continued to affect their experiences and evaluation of their daily domestic life together.

The enjoyment of privacy as a family: continued public control and 'passing' as an ordinary family.

As we suggested in chapter 1, privacy and autonomy are held to be valued aspects of family life in contemporary industrial societies. There are, however, fundamental differences in the degree of privacy enjoyed by family groups in different social strata or sub-cultures. On a number of occasions, notably in chapter 4, we have commented on the ways in which some family groups which deviate from the norm of the unbroken nuclear family may experience greater public scrutiny, both formally and informally.

Single parents, for example, often depend on informal help and support from close kin, especially their own parents or neighbours, and as a result, all those elements of their family life outlined in previous sections may be open to greater informal scrutiny by those who give help. There are, of course, considerable variations in patterns of neighbouring, degree of intimacy with kin and so on within our society generally. These affect normal and deviant family groups alike, so that such scrutiny cannot be regarded as a distinguishing feature of stepfamilies alone. The experience of being under such surveillance was, however, described by many of the couples in a way which suggested that it undermined their efforts to become an ordinary family. Such couples also described making conscious and deliberate efforts to 'pass' as an unbroken family in order to avoid such scrutiny.

In the second interview we asked whether any of their relatives, neighbours or friends were themselves divorced or remarried. Despite general protestations that they knew little of their neighbours' 'private' lives, all the people we talked to knew divorced and remarried couples themselves even if they were the first in their own family to divorce; several of these described themselves as the 'black sheep of the family'. Many people mentioned the number of children in their children's school who came from broken homes or referred to public discussions of high divorce rates in the media. In the same way that the divorced and remarried in their neighbourhood were visible to them, they were aware of being labelled themselves. Mrs Smithson described being asked questions about their family relationships which she clearly felt would not be asked of a first married couple:

> a lot of people say, 'How do you get on with them?' you know . . . 'Do you like them as much as your own . . . do you love them as much as your own?' (   ) a lot of people ask us . . . in other words what they are saying is, do you tend to stick up more for yours than for his.

Mrs Graham also commented.

> . . . people can be very cruel, you know . . . without knowing it, and it gets very involved when you start giving one name and then another name and you've got to say, 'Well, I was married before' and you know . . . you go into the long rigmarole . . . it's terrible.

Mrs Graham's concern about their public appearances as a family is demonstrated by her pride in her daughters' behaviour with strangers:

> . . . I'm proud of them when I'm out, because they give people the impression that we've always been as we are . . . they always call themselves Graham, the eldest does officially, she's called at school, but the other two are called Gowers, but if we're ever out, they seem to *know* themselves that we don't want

embarrassment, so if anyone asks them their names, they just say that it's Graham and Michelle does, and . . . I think they know that people ask questions if they say the other, and they've had this once or twice and they didn't like it.

Other parents also described their children's accommodation to the complexities involved in the use of either surnames or particular family names. Mr Heathcote was happy that his children still called their stepmother 'Jane' but described how,

. . . in front of their friends they call her Mum, right. And on one occasion they forgot and called her 'Jane' and their friends looked at them gone out . . . calling their mother Jane. And it would *appear* that on the surface . . . they put a front up, you know . . . they are Raymond and Sally . . . this is their home, and this is their Mum and Dad . . . and the fact that Jane is not their real Mum is none of anyone's business.

Mrs Moseley's children differ in what they call their stepfather:

Leslie's always called him Dad . . . that's the youngest, and Tina and Karen and William have always called him Graham, but . . . the funny thing is if they buy a birthday card or anything like that . . . it's always 'Dad' that's on it, like, er, anniversary cards 'to Mum and Dad', you know.

Names also pose formal problems in the public sphere, notably at school, but also wherever relationships have to be described, as Mr Farmer explained:

The word I don't like is stepfather . . . I think it's a terrible word that . . . even if you have to cover up . . . you don't *have* to, but I think it's better to, you know, like at work and things like that . . . 'cos you know, it's all these forms when you have to fill them in like tax and that . . . you know . . . you put . . . 'father, yes' and then they send it back and say 'are you guardian or stepparent?', that you're not their real father . . . you know what I mean . . . all this . . . it's like explaining to everybody all the time, like when you are in a queue at the back and everybody's listening in . . . you get that feeling . . . I hate that word so . . . I just make out yes . . . that to all intents and purposes . . . act to all t'neighbours and that . . . there's no comeback see . . . they think that I am their father, and I wouldn't like anyone to know, not that I've anything to hide . . . but I don't know . . . like if you say to people, 'Well, I've married somebody else wi' four kids' they give you a funny look, like.

A number of parents had problems about what their children

were called at school. Mr Moseley, amongst others, found it difficult to get the school to write to his wife using her new married name:

> . . . all right the kids' surname is different to ours at the moment, and we've rung up school and told the teachers but they still keep sending letters to Mrs Savage.
> Q. You found this annoying did you?
> I don't mind for the first once or twice, but particularly after you've phoned and told them and we filled forms in for them all, Karen as well when she was at school, at least twice in a year, so far as I'm concerned there's no excuse.

Mr Hobson was somewhat baffled by the school's policy dealing with his stepchildren's name:

> Well, such as the teachers at school, they let them write Hobson on their lessons and things like this, and I went up to school, to her headmistress about Paula . . . and while I was there I mentioned this and [she] said she wasn't allowed to put them on the register, but as far as the school was concerned they are called Hobson in their lessons but as far as the register is concerned they still have to be called by their father's name.

It is partly to avoid this sort of confusion that Mr Hobson would like to adopt his stepchildren. He had already talked to a solicitor, who had told him,

> . . . it would be very difficult . . . I don't know why . . . I think they're not keen on adoption nowadays.

Under the provisions of the Children Act 1975, stepparents are to be offered the opportunity of joint custody with their partners rather than adoption itself, a fine distinction clearly not understood by Mr Hobson or, for that matter, many others:

> . . . even if we can't get them under adoption . . . see if we can get legal custody of them . . . for meself.

Mr Hobson also wanted to adopt his stepchildren to give him, and them, greater certainty about the future:

> I think it would give me and the children a bit more security, you know . . . well, perhaps I'd like to feel more secure, put it that way. No, I've come to love them so much, I wouldn't like to see them . . . see anything happen to them, I mean you know . . . there's always a chance if anything happened to Patricia . . . I'm not expecting that their own father wants to take them back, but there's a possibility he'd take them away from me, into a home or

something like this is this is . . . something . . . I would really hate.

Mr Elliott is the only stepfather in our study who actually adopted a stepchild. Mrs Elliott explained why he decided to do so:

> Because when we went to the doctor's or in a public place you know they'd say 'Hello Mrs Elliott . . . hello Jean . . . this is Jean P., Mrs Elliott's daughter', you know and it sounded horrible and I were embarrassed really and I thought, 'Oh, people will think I weren't married when I had her but I was . . . it was my previous marriage,' so I told Raymond and so he said, 'Right that's that, we'll have that stopped,' and he went to see . . . how you've got to go about it . . . and he went to the births and registry office and they sent him down to court to get this paper (   ) and, oh, sent a social worker . . . a lady came to look round the house and get Raymond's details . . . where he worked and everything . . . see if he was a suitable father for her . . . and it were passed in court and there were no . . . the judge said that he thought that she'd got a . . . good Daddy to take over, which she has.

A stepfather's adoption of his stepchildren is one of the clearest and certainly the most formal and legally binding method whereby remarried parents can 'make' their family group into an ordinary family. Parental rights and duties are formally transferred to the stepparent, the children's names are changed and they receive a new birth certificate. Such adoptions are, thus, a legal means of obliterating the past and consciously building anew so that the new family group appears, in terms of names, and functions, in terms of parental rights and duties, like an unbroken family. The Houghton Committee questioned the wisdom of the increasingly widespread practice of stepparent adoption because it led to: 'the legal extinguishment . . . of a legitimate child's links with one half of his own family.' This was 'inappropriate and could be damaging' (Houghton Report, Cmnd 5107, 1972, para 105).

Although very few of the remarried parents we spoke to talked about adoption specifically, in the use of surnames at least, most were anxious to avoid drawing attention to the way they differed from ordinary families. This issue of names offers one specific illustration of how some couples wished, and encouraged their children, to 'pass' as members of an unbroken family. It is significant that whilst all such families might do this to some degree, simply to transcend potential complications in transitory social contracts, for others names had a much deeper significance.

Mrs Graham's comments, quoted above (see pp. 174–5) illustrate the extent to which rebuilding a new family life in which the past would be forgotten and undetectable had become a major goal in her life. Attitudes towards names are, therefore, frequently indicative of much broader sets of ideas and values. At one end of the spectrum there are those, like, for example, Mrs Dyson and Mrs Fox, who are already anxious about the unwelcome disclosures about the past which must be made *within* the family circle, whilst at the other the Dunwells happily retain three surnames within their family group and the Hutchinsons have consciously decided not to change her children's name in deference to their father's wishes.

Understandably, Mrs Dyson's youngest son does not yet comprehend the complexities of his kin network (see the Dyson's life history):

> He thinks of them as brothers . . . he dunnt understand about stepbrothers like . . . we don't talk to him about it . . . but he has said, 'How can Pamela be me Dad's daughter and Paul be your son', so it got all confused so I thought I'd leave it while later on when he can understand.

When asked about her son's understanding of divorce generally, Mrs Fox commented:

> The biggest problem'll be telling him who his actual father is.
> Q. He's had no contact, then, with his father?
> None at all, no . . . that's the biggest problem, not really . . . 'cos it'll hurt *me*, it's just how . . . trying to explain it to a . . . 'cos he really wants to know that before he goes into Juniors . . . they go up when they're nine and he really wants to know that he has another father that . . . and I shan't keep nowt back. . . . (   ) And when he asks . . . 'cos I think he will ask, 'cos he's inquisitive you know . . . and I think he'll understand especially wi' not having any contact with his father. . . .
>
> I mean, like . . . he's not got two men (   ) now I think that *does* complicate matters, like if his Dad had wanted anything to do wi' him and wanted to come and see him say once a week . . . and our Jonathan had called him Dad when he came to see him, then I'd never have let Martin be called 'Dad', it'd be 'Martin' all the time. . . . But I mean, he hasn't had no contact wi' his Dad, so Martin's the only Dad he's known really.

Mr and Mrs Dunwell have a foster child so there are three different sets of surnames in their family. Although she did not find this difficult, she found having a son in their new marriage,

> makes the family a bit more coherent somehow, I know that sounds stupid when you've three different surnames, but he's the one now that everybody's seen . . . from him growing inside me

> to being born so they . . . were *all* involved in that, all in exactly the same way, so I think it's probably a good pulling factor . . . tieing factor that.

Mrs Hutchinson described how,

> we were first going to call them [Hutchinson], I mean . . . it weren't for legal purposes and then they happened to mention to their Dad and he took us both to one side and said, 'I hope you don't mind, there's only two boys left with that surname,' which there are, all his brothers and sisters had girls, and well . . . they were a pretty big family and they all had girls, so obviously when they all get married, there just aren't going to be any Wallaces left, so he asked us both properly and when I thought about it, I couldn't really make me mind up, so I said, 'You tell t'lads what you've told me and see what they say' and t'lads came to me and said, 'We loved us grandad and we'd like to carry on his name,' 'cos they can remember him although he's dead now, and I said, 'Well, it's up to you what you are called,' and there's been nothing said about it since.

Parents' perceptions of their children's progress and happiness: their hopes for the future

We have no way of knowing whether the range and severity of child rearing difficulties described by the couples in our study are any greater than amongst a comparable group of first married couples but it is very clear that in their description and, more particularly, their *explanations* of problems, both past and present, earlier family events, divorce, lone parenthood and remarriage loom large. As we have suggested earlier in this and other chapters, new partnerships and remarriage present immediate solutions to some of the material and emotional problems of single parenthood, so that it is not surprising that many parents described how their children's health and general well-being had improved since they remarried. For example, minor health problems cleared up. Mrs Brown describes how her stepson Paul's speech had,

> come on marvellous in this last year (   ) in fact he used to go to speech therapy and I think he'd been from being about five, and when he first came I couldn't understand a word he was saying, but now . . . and he's been discharged and he hasn't got to go any more.

Mrs Baker felt that their children were now more secure:

They all like to take their turn in sitting at the side of us, they don't appear to do it now, (   ) they know they can have a turn *if* they want, they're not . . . pushing for love now. They know it's there and that's really basically it, they know it's there now, they're not looking for it, I think they've really got a sense of security now, a sense of belonging and I think that's basically love to them.

A number of parents referred to the way in which their own affection and security within their new partnership affected the children. Mr Smithson described how their children had seen their parents' unhappiness in their former marriages, so that,

. . . *now* I think . . . they're that happy, because we're happy obviously, I mean you know yourself if Mum and Dad are always fighting and arguing, it has a lot of effect on t'kids, but . . . we never go off like that (   ) 'cos I mean I might get home from work and we're in the kitchen and we're having a bit of a . . . snogging session in t'kitchen, you know . . . and all the kids'll come and look round the door and . . . 'Ooh, look at them . . .' and it's happiness, you know what I mean . . . it's, they like to see us going off like that rather than arguing.

Most parents described the inevitable problems of settling down together, as though such problems were now safely in the past. Dr Johnson is now able to talk to her son about his early feelings about his stepfather:

he didn't trust Derek, Derek barks at people [laughs] so he was a 'baddie' and obviously couldn't be trusted with his Mum. And he talks about it now, and says he didn't like Derek at first and 'I thought he was very fierce'.

Mrs Moseley described how her children and second husband have learnt to understand each other, so that she now views minor conflicts as predictable aspects of normal relationships between parents and children:

Q. Do you think your husband ever feels he's missed out from not knowing the children when they were small?
Yes, I do definitely . . . er, you see, he's taken a lot of adapting . . . everybody has their own personal little quirks . . . their own temperament . . . and, well, if you've grown up with a child . . . the child's grown up with you with those moods and you know what they're thinking, I mean, I know what mine are thinking before they even say it, and I think any mother does. But you see, Graham has not got that insight if you understand me . . . into what they are thinking . . . which, he's done very well really. And

again so have the kids with him, 'cos you know even adults have their quirks and their own particular ideas. (   )

These last three years they have . . . you know . . . really . . . come to terms with each other, and I don't think there's any bigger rift in what they say or do . . . like when he chastises them, than what it would be if it were their own father that were chastising them . . . not now, there was resentment at first, but I don't think now . . . I don't think there is now.

Even where she recognised problems had persisted, Mrs Pelham felt that they were not so much a consequence of her husband's relationship to his stepdaughter as his attitude towards children generally. Throughout her third interview she referred to various problems and conflicts which arose, she felt, because he was not a 'children's man':

you see to me there are two categories of people . . . you either like children or you tolerate children, and I think Michael is the sort of person that maybe tolerates children [laughs] and does not necessarily need children in his life, you know to make his life up.

They frequently disagree over his management of his stepdaughter, Vicky:

he says that I jump in on Vicky's behalf if I think his discipline is too strong with her I jump in and the thing gets escalated, whereas perhaps it wouldn't . . . I don't think I *do*. I just think it isn't any different . . . that's the point I'm trying to make, I don't think Michael's relationship with Vicky is any different than it would be if she was his daughter, you know . . . I don't think there's been any problems that there wouldn't have been if she were his own.

As they built up a picture of the improvements in their children's lives which had followed remarriage and how initial difficulties had been overcome, parents frequently referred to the comments and observations of others. Teachers' views were most often cited as they are the professional experts on children in daily contact and who were felt to have had the opportunity of observing any changes which may have taken place. Where their children's progress at school had improved, parents often replied that teachers saw this as a direct result of their new, settled family circumstances. Mrs Gilmour was relieved that her son,

has got a happy family life now. (   ) He's much better. He's happier at this school . . . when I saw his teacher . . . last July it was when I saw her and she says that he's a little behindhand but he was coming up, he wasn't going further back and he should

> catch up . . . he's better, more settled . . . now he's got a settled family life . . . he is better now.

Her husband accepts the evidence of his stepson's school report in a characteristically cautious way, placing much greater reliance on the observation of their next-door neighbours:

> His reports seem to be better now than, from what I can gather, beforehand, bearing in mind that I haven't seen the ones he had before . . . but the ones I have had from him seem to be quite favourable. (   )
>
> There's been a vast change in Derek over the past six months . . . in fact next door they were saying that the lad that come up earlier on, you know, December . . . January time, that there's no comparison between that and the lad he is now . . . totally come out of his shell and he's got a mind of his own now and he'll use it, which is . . . to my mind, how it should be.

Mrs Brown is also delighted by their children's progress,

> you can go to school and the teacher said she's never seen such contented children and Paul's maths . . . and Timothy's coming on great guns (   ) they're coming on great.

Mr Hutchinson described how the headteacher at his stepchildren's school had referred directly to their remarriage in a conversation with Mrs Hutchinson:

> The headmaster had a word with Susan and I weren't there and he said, 'I heard you got married and I'm going to tell you what, t'kids are happier, and more so t'little 'un,' . . . she were right sulky and that . . . and he said, 'She's different again at school and the same with her work, she's happier at that, in fact she's the first one in the school,' and they are . . . they're right keen.

Although we have presented a good deal of evidence which suggests that remarried parents frequently believed and tried to demonstrate that they transcended their earlier problems so that their children were now experiencing an 'ordinary', 'settled' family life, for some certain inescapable differences persisted, creating continued doubt and uncertainty. Mrs Turner is still not sure whether her stepchild has entirely got over losing his mother:

> It doesn't show in him now, at least I don't think it does and he's settled into the household quite well and everybody's been quite pleased with him, but I think until it actually takes effect, I don't think you know what reaction is going to come from . . . either side really, it's a big step.

For Mrs Vickers her stepsons' continued contact with their non-custodial mother in Newcastle seemed to exacerbate the endemic problems of adolescence. In her view problems have arisen,

> mainly because of the pressure from their mother, you know, not from . . . because of them. Most of the problems that I have experienced have been through . . . the pressure from up in Newcastle, and if it hadn't been for her, I don't think there'd be, you know . . . half the problems that there are.

A number of earlier quotations from the Hutchinsons show how delighted they are by the new life they have built for her children, but Mrs Hutchinson is still aware that,

> when their father comes and fetches them for a weekend, it seems to unsettle them for a while and then they say that they're not going next time, but when he comes they always go . . . I've never tried to stop them, but I think it's something that children who aren't stepchildren . . . they never go through, perhaps they go and stay with their grandparents, but it's not like going to stay with a parent that they don't live with.

Mrs Baker observed how their children have to

> lead a split life . . . the children they've got to be very tactful, so in a sense it teaches *them* a little bit about life, because they've got to learn what to say . . . it's very difficult . . . they go to one house and they . . . that parent doesn't really want them to talk about the other parent. ( )
>
> They've got to learn not to say *too* much and not to give too much away, because I don't want my personal life discussing with my ex-husband and neither does he so the children have got to learn to be a bit diplomatic.

Some parents believed that stepchildren grew up more quickly as a result of such experiences. Mr Heathcote, a stepchild himself, felt that stepchildren had,

> a more . . . I was going to say, savage upbringing, but I don't mean savage in the sense of being brutal and that sort of thing, but they grow up, they're made more independent.

Dr Johnson commented on her husband's children of his first marriage to whom she is part-time stepmother:

> The four that are from a broken home have moved about a lot geographically, and I think they've been exposed very young to their parents being in a rocky state . . . ( ) they're quite protective and they grow up much quicker.

Where parents had themselves come to terms with those aspects of their family life and relationship which prevented them from behaving as a completely 'ordinary' family they were more likely to talk about these as potential advantages rather than as hindrances to their passing as an unbroken family. Despite the acrimony surrounding his early remarriage, Mrs Kennedy had taken great pains to ensure that her husband and stepchildren did not lose touch with his first wife's family so that the children now have,

> . . . a wider . . . a larger family . . . they've got my side as well and I've kept the whole family together (   ) I don't think they've lost out on anything, in fact I think possibly they've gained.

Mr Dunwell made a similar point. Because his stepchildren experience family relationships with more people,

> . . . they get ideas from different sources and that must be enriching in itself, er . . . because I suppose if you . . . you're brought up in a family and you've just got those particular parents . . . ideas to listen to and interpret yourself then you're going to be channelled down a very narrow set of ideas whereas stepchildren have got two sets of values . . . perhaps to compare and decide between themselves, rather than just being guided by one set.

If Mrs Baker felt, as her earlier comments showed, that stepchildren had to learn to be tactful, she did not believe that it did them,

> . . . any harm at all, because, let's face it, children can be very cruel, and it teaches them . . . to think of other people's feelings that little bit. (   ) All of a sudden they have to start thinking of other people's feelings.

When the couples in our study considered their children's development and described their hopes for the future their preoccupations mirrored those of parents generally. If they differed on the relative importance of success at school, getting a good job or having a happy family life, such differences are more easily explained in terms of community and class differences than their particular family history or structure. However, some parents' answers to questions about their children's attitude towards sex, marriage and parenthood show their careful awareness of the way divorce and remarriage may have affected their children. They did this by recounting particular conversations from which they tried to draw conclusions about their children's feelings. Mrs Bingham is worried that what has happened has made her daughter, Catherine,

> . . . a little bit hard. I've heard her say once or twice that she's not getting married and I've thought, 'Ooh is she just going to live with somebody and not marry them, is she going to be one of these that's going to flit round from man to man and just live with them?' and that has worried me.

Mrs Heathcote's son, Raymond,

> . . . did pass one comment to me mother that er . . . he won't get married or get divorced and this sort of thing . . . and be unfortunate like his Dad.

Mrs Thornleigh described her middle son:

> He's a very, very loyal person and obviously they've had sex lessons and lessons on marriage and that at school . . . I mean he's only fifteen, but judging from what he's come home and said when they've had these lessons, he's a very big believer in marriage and children, one of the old school.

Dr Johnson is more optimistic, stressing how her stepdaughter's knowledge of her earlier difficult experiences encourages her to ask for advice:

> I think they've probably got a very balanced attitude (   ) you don't have to be married, if you do get married it doesn't always work out and it's bad at the time, but it's not total disaster, you know . . . you do come out of it the other side. (   ) They talk to us about it. . . . Certainly the eldest, Alice, will come with relationship problems and say, 'So much has happened to you, this must have, what do I do?' and is quite willing to accept advice, and she knows she can't shock us.

When we asked about giving such advice to their children, the responses varied; where guilt and uncertainty persisted, parents seemed unwilling to offer their children much guidance. Others, like Dr Johnson, argued that their experience of surviving, even transcending, marital disasters gave their advice and conclusions some credibility. The pitfalls of early marriage were mentioned frequently. Mrs Dunwell hopes her three girls realise that,

> you can make mistakes, therefore, if you give it more time you stand more chance of getting a sensible decision. And I keep on about marrying early, and don't always marry . . . when they used to talk about marriage, it was . . . just to have a home and cook and clean and look after children and . . . I tried to explain to them all along that this isn't necessarily going to be what they want . . . what they want to do or ought to.

Many parents talked about suggesting living together rather than immediate marriage. With some uncertainty Mr Fox admitted,

> I wouldn't put him off marriage but well . . . probably it's the wrong advice, but I would say, 'Right, if you like that person and she likes you, and if you can get a house or a flat, live with each other for so long and see how you go on (   ) it's no use getting married and then finding out that it's no good at all because . . . it's very . . . expensive.'

Women who had themselves cohabited before their remarriage and, like Mrs Bingham, quoted above, were anxious to differentiate between 'stable' relationships and promiscuity. Mrs Moseley described how she had tried to put across her views to her children when she was talking to them about the breakdown of her first marriage and why she now wanted to remarry. She told them she found it impossible to continue to have sex with her husband when there was no longer any love between them:

> and I think they realise that to . . . now, to have sex with somebody, it's got to be somebody you really respect and *love*, before you can even contemplate going into a relationship like that (   ) it's only fair for them to understand that . . . and I think it's . . . it gives them a better idea of the relationship they should look for . . . not . . . just a fly-by-night, you know, a once a week thing and things like that. (   )
>
> It's discussed at school . . . but I think it's the *reason* for sex that's lacking at school . . . they obviously teach them about the birds and the bees, but they don't give them any insight into any lasting relationship about it.

We still know very little about attitudes towards cohabitation but it would seem from our data that when remarried parents 'come out' in favour of trial marriage they share the concern of all parents that their children will eventually form lasting partnerships and establish a secure basis for their future family life.

However, because of their earlier experiences of marriage breakdown they know only too well that legal marriage itself does not necessarily mean 'happiness ever after' and are, thus, anxious that their children find a better way through avoiding early, hasty marriages based on an ideology of romantic love at variance with the mutuality of interests and shared everyday experiences on which, for the most part, their own second marriages were based.

Chapter 6

The private troubles and public issues of stepfamilies: problems and interrelationships

> Nowadays men [and women] often feel that their private lives are a series of traps. They sense that within their everyday worlds they cannot overcome their troubles, and in this feeling they are often quite correct: what ordinary men [and women] are directly aware of and what they try to do are bounded by the private orbits in which they live; their visions and their powers are limited to the close up scenes of job, family and neighbourhood; in other milieux they move vicariously and remain spectators. (Mills, 1967, p. 3)

> And I came to this conclusion last week: When I got married to Martin . . . I was going to imagine that I had never been married before and I was going to start afresh, and it hasn't been like that. It would appear that our marriage, on both sides, has taken over from where our last ones ended and it's very frightening. It'll only be love that'll pull us through, because we do both love each other but it's on such few occasions that we seem to be able to express this love. You know, we've still so many complications and ties with administration . . . bureaucracy . . . all those solicitors and tax people and courts and court orders and different things, we can't get things tied up and finished yet. (Mrs Graham)

The Grahams' experiences, summarised very powerfully in comments taken from Mrs Graham's third interview, bear ample testimony to the propositions about the interrelationship of private troubles and public issues found in Mills's classic essay, *The Sociological Imagination* (1967). Formerly a teaching text for us, this work has become much more immediately relevant as we have wrestled with some of the broader theoretical problems raised by our research data. An adequate understanding and appreciation of the material we obtained depended on detailed examination of individual cases in which we tried to locate comments, opinions and recounted incidents in terms of the individual and couple's earlier history and present circumstances. At the same time as our knowledge of individual families grew, we became increasingly aware of common elements within their accounts and ideologies. Whilst on the one hand, we were able to isolate issues and problems endemic to the remarried with children, we also became increasingly aware of the dangers of reification, of using the category 'stepfamily' in a way which suggested that every aspect of domestic life within such families was determined by their particular family history and structure. If it is true that to a greater or lesser extent all stepfamilies experience common and distinctive problems arising from their particular past inheritance, it is also important to recognise the extent to which the families in our study differed *from one another* as a direct result of persistent economic and social inequalities within society. Consequently, we found, for example, that a more satisfactory understanding of the experiences of the poorest families in our study was to be derived from comparing their accounts with data on unbroken families in similar economic circumstances than from attempting to explain their problems entirely in terms of the deviant family status which they shared with more affluent stepfamilies, with very different views and experiences of family life.

The declared object of our investigation was 'the stepfamily' so that we have had to guard against a tendency to explain issues and problems of family life revealed to us in terms of stepfamily structures and experiences which should more properly be understood in terms of the particular structural constraints which shape the domestic life of all family groups in industrial societies. Thus, in some important respects at least, any examination of the interrelationships between the private troubles and public issues of remarried couples with children involves consideration of ways in which an individual's family and personal life are shaped and controlled by public structures.

Mills argued that public discussion of many social problems, experienced by individuals as private troubles, is frequently couched in psychiatric terms, which he viewed as 'a pathetic attempt to avoid the large issues and problems of modern society' (Mills, 1967, p. 12).

Such an analysis 'arbitrarily divorces the individual life from the larger institutions within which that life is enacted, and which on occasion bear upon it more grievously than do the intimate environments of childhood' (ibid.). This suggestion is echoed in Lasch's stimulating and controversial analysis of contemporary American society *The Culture of Narcissism*, in which, using a variety of examples, he suggests that, 'Bureaucracy transforms collective grievances into personal problems amenable to therapeutic intervention' (Lasch, 1980, p. 43). His analysis is developed from an earlier work, referred to in chapter 1 in which he suggests that the family can no longer act as a 'haven in a heartless world' (Lasch, 1977). Although family life is widely held to be our chief source of personal and emotional gratification, it is itself under siege because of the invasion of a therapeutic expertise based on what he terms 'the cult of intimacy'. Thus: 'Our society, far from fostering private life at the expense of public life, has made deep and lasting friendships, love affairs, and marriages increasingly difficult to achieve' (ibid., p. 69). These therapeutic ideologies have transformed family and personal relationships into an area of professional expertise. Such ideologies now provide explanations of social problems and individual suffering which 'intensify the disease they pretend to cure' and thus, obscure 'the social origins of the suffering . . . that is painfully but falsely experienced as purely personal and private' (ibid., p. 7). Although there are a number of problems about Lasch's argument, his bold and, in some respects, over-simplified analysis has helped us to focus more sharply on the vexed issues which surround the location and transmission of the dominant ideologies shaping family life to which other writers, from a variety of theoretical perspectives, have referred usually in more cautious, tentative terms (see for example Bott, 1971; Busfield and Paddon, 1977; Leonard, 1980; Zaretsky, 1976; Oakley, 1974). Each of these accounts raises important problems, first about the means by which official public moralities of family and personal life are transmitted to individuals and, second, about the ways in which aspects of their personal lives are shaped by public rules, institutions and 'officials' of various kinds. Voysey's analysis of the experiences of families with a handicapped child, considered briefly in chapter 1, was an important source of inspiration to us, directing our attention as it did both to matters of ideology, for example official moralities of 'good parenting' and the 'ideal family', as well as to the manner in which basic aspects of their 'private' domestic life were largely determined by the policies and practices of various welfare institutions.

Like Voysey we have tried to examine why our respondents told us what they did and, in particular, to consider how they made sense of any personal troubles which followed from divorce and remarriage. We also wished to locate some of the principal sources of the imagery of family life they drew upon in their accounts and explanations. As we suggested in chapter 5, we found that couples differed significantly in the degree to which they wished, or were able, to perceive themselves as an 'ordinary family'. For our sample, the wish and the ability to be an ordinary family appeared distinct but related characteristics. The *wish* to reconstitute an ordinary family life for oneself and one's child through remarriage appears to have two elements. First, in so far as parents share the diffuse but widely held belief that a nuclear family group is the natural, good, and wholesome environment in which to bring up children, this will strengthen their desire to recreate such a group by their own efforts. In a number of significant ways those whom Lasch terms 'the therapeutic elite' foster such beliefs both by their public utterances and their daily practices. For example, it is evident that those who determine the placement of children, whether in disputed custody cases, or as do social workers when children are to be adopted, fostered or removed from their natural parents, favour family arrangements which conform to the norm of the nuclear family (Wilson, 1977). In addition the desirability and naturalness of the conventional family is powerfully communicated through advertising directed at individuals in their family roles as domestic consumers in which, against a background of affluent domestic comfort, every need of two immaculately dressed, attractive children, a boy and a girl, is met by their young, equally attractive parents. Such images powerfully confirm beliefs that to do the best by one's children involves the creation and maintenance of a family unit conventional in both its structure and standards of consumption.

In addition to providing the best possible social and emotional environment for their children, for some parents their wish to be seen as an ordinary family springs from their concern for the respectability, reputation and good-standing of their family. It is difficult to delineate this concern with respectability very closely. As we suggested in chapter 1, nineteenth-century bourgeois family ideologies laid great stress on the public display of family standing and respectability through appropriate standards of dress and domestic consumption as well as the public maintenance of absolute standards of moral probity. Contemporary evidence of the continued importance of personal and family respectability is more easily found in novels and from journalism than in the findings of social researchers, although Klein (1965) cites a number of community studies which illustrate the continued importance of respectability within some working- and lower middle-class communities. The maintenance of respectability appears to matter more to some than to others and, in part at least, such differences are linked with class. In our own study it soon became clear to us that conformity to the nuclear family norm was much more important to some couples than others. If, as Ball argues, respectability is an aspect of social differentiation (Ball, 1970), some couples, assured in their social position, can 'afford' to ignore pervasive public moralities which stressed the normality and desirability of conventional family life. Consequently, in their accounts and comments, they tended to stress the advantages of their unusual circumstances, referring both to the social and demographic trends which made them part of an ever-growing minority and to conventional 'therapeutic' orthodoxies. In the typology of images of family life which we have developed and present below, we designate such responses as typical of 'progressive' stepfamilies (category 3). Although most of the couples whom we placed in this category were middle-class, the Hutchinsons are an exception and their presence illustrates the danger of over-simplifying the relationship between ideology and class position.

Images and goals of family life

From the variety of subjects and issues discussed in their interviews, we shall now attempt to classify the couples in our study according to the images of family life which they called up to describe and explain family matters. Like Busfield and Paddon, we found that individuals tended to adopt elements of more than one perspective (Busfield and Paddon, 1977, p. 163). In addition, despite Berger and Kellner's faith in the nurturing force of the shared conversation of the married pair (Berger and Kellner, 1977, p. 30) husbands and wives did not always share the same perspectives, especially if, for example, their experiences of the long-term consequences of divorce differed greatly. In some cases one partner's account was tinged by a feeling of continuing failure and conflict not shared by their spouse.

When we attempted to draw up such a typology we realised that an important factor affecting couples' imagery of their family life was their age, or more particularly stage in the family life cycle when they divorced and remarried. When this had happened relatively early or late, their images and goals of family life were more clearly distinguishable from those couples for whom the pursuit of an 'ordinary' family life was an important, if unrealisable goal.

1 *'Not really a stepfamily'*

When any children involved in the divorce and new partnership are still very young, the remarried couple are able to think of themselves as 'just an ordinary family' quite quickly. The subsequent children of their new partnership confirm this so that for some couples our questions seemed somewhat irrelevant, raising topics which had never, apparently, been issues for them. This is clearly illustrated by David Clark's field notes on the Snows, dictated immediately after their their interview:

> A family who don't perhaps see their situation as one involving a conscious effort to weld themselves together into some kind of nuclear family . . . things fall into place, rather than their having to be carefully fitted into place . . . is perhaps to do with the fact that Susan, their only stepchild was a young child when the couple began living together . . . Mr Snow takes [the interviews] very lightly and is difficult to pin down in any serious way and on any topic whatsoever, but in a sense, the shortness, glibness and gloss of the interview perhaps reflect the fact that for them, life is relatively unproblematic, in terms of steprelations, contact with earlier spouses and so on and indeed having moved . . . and had a child of their own, things seem to approximate far more to the normal family situation than some of the families in the study.

2 *'Looking forward to the departure of their children'*

Remarrying couples with one or more sets of children who are already teenagers held and transmitted distinctive images of family life perhaps shared, as Nicholson suggests, by the majority of parents as their children pass through adolescence:

> If you are at all doubtful about the impact teenage children have on their parents, consider first one statistic from the results of [our] survey. When we arranged all the answers to the 'item in which people were asked to list the things they worried about', we found that the concern expressed about children by people of 36 and 45 was the largest single worry of either sex at any age. (Nicholson, 1980, p. 356)

For the newly remarried couples in this age group whom we studied there were inevitable additional strains as the presence and demands of their teenage children and stepchildren allowed them few opportunities to talk and enjoy each other's company without interruptions. In a number of cases their children's problems were largely explained in terms of their own earlier marriage breakdown about which they still felt some sense of guilt and uncertainty. The Walkers' eventual decision to compel their adult children to leave home illustrates the strength of their need to reduce their family problems in order to focus on their own relationship. For such couples, of course, additional children of the new marriage are probably impossible and certainly undesirable.

3 *The 'progressive' stepfamily*

Some couples, although at the famiily-building stage of the life cycle, do not articulate images of the conventional family in their attempts to reconstitute family life together. Their imagery of family life is pluralistic; they are aware of a diversity of patterns in family and domestic life and depict themselves as making choices and responding to constraints in a way which would exploit the advantages of their circumstances for their children, asserting, as Voysey noted, an ideology of 'the positive value of differentness' (Voysey, 1975, p. 201). In general there were few outstanding sources of conflict with ex-partners and financial worries were rare. Where such difficulties persisted they were faced, resolved and controlled. Decisions about having children of the new marriage are reviewed in this light.

4 *The largely successful conscious pursuit of an ordinary family life together*

In their efforts to reconstitute an ordinary family life for their children parents consciously attempt to adopt as full and normal a parental role as possible. Thus, stepfathers try to become full 'social' fathers to their stepchildren, transferring allegiances, wholly or in part, from any non-custodial children of an earlier marriage. The inevitable problems which attend the conscious pursuit of ordinary family life in the face of family structures which may deny such normality are, in the early stages, solved or successfully ignored. Any children of the new marriage symbolise the 'normality' of their new partnership.

5 *The conscious pursuit of an ordinary family life frustrated*

Other couples who attempt to reconstitute an ordinary family life for themselves find their efforts frustrated at every turn. Continued contact, intervention by, and, on occasion, conflict with the children's non-custodial parent undermine the stepparent's attempts to be a full 'social' parent and disrupt the autonomy of the family's daily domestic routine. Financial problems and disputes over property, custody or access provide continuing reminders of the past and render the whole family vulnerable to the public scrutiny of outsiders, including, if family privacy cannot be maintained, neighbours and kin. For most of the couples in our study

Table 6.1 *A typology of stepfamilies*

1 '*Not really a stepfamily*'
The stepchildren of the family were young at the time of divorce and remarriage; within a short time they were able to think of themselves as an 'ordinary' family.
Children of new marriage confirm this,
Browning
Elliott
Prior
Snow
Worthing

2 '*Looking forward to the departure of the children*'
Older couples with teenage children await departure of dependent children so that they can enjoy their new partnership more fully.
Too old for children in new marriage.
Dyson
Hammond
Moseley
Shannon
Vickers
Walker

3 *The 'progressive' stepfamily*
Prototype 'new' stepfamily in which conflicts with ex-partners have been resolved. They stress the advantages of their circumstances.
Few barriers to additional children of new marriage
Dunwell
Harper
Heathcote
Hutchinson
Kennedy
Johnson
Parker

4 *The successful conscious pursuit of an 'ordinary' family life together*
Stepparent becomes full 'social' parent transferring allegiance to stepchildren. Their initial problems are solved or successfully ignored.
Children of new marriage symbolise 'normality' of their family life.
Baker
Farmer
Gilmour
Pelham
Roberts
Smithson
Thompson
Thornleigh
Turner
Wickham

5 *The conscious pursuit of 'ordinary' family life frustrated*
The legacy of their past marriage(s) frustrates their attempts to build an ordinary family life together.
Children of new marriage are unlikely because of continuing problems.
Brown
Chapman
Fox
Graham
Hobson
Hurst
Morgan
Parkes
Spencer-Deam
Stanley

who had additional children, their decision to do so symbolised their sense of 'settling down'. Conversely, for those whose pursuit of an ordinary family life had been frustrated in some way, further childbearing was unlikely.

We have categorised the study families within this typology in Table 6.1, but it should be emphasised that some couples were difficult to place, either because of a lack of evidence, if, for example, they had dropped out of the study or if their comments seemed to bridge more than one category. The names in italics indicate those families whose accounts seemed to us to illustrate the values and experiences embodied in their category most clearly.

The close scrutiny of our informants' accounts for evidence of the ways in which their goals in relation to family and personal life were shaped by, and their achievements measured against, the ideal of recreating an 'ordinary' family life together helped us to locate some of the factors affecting their exposure and vulnerability to conventional public moralities of family life articulated by 'moral guardians' (Rex, 1974) and 'therapeutic experts' (Lasch, 1980). Their observations and experiences also raise questions, largely beyond the scope of this book, about the challenge posed to such norms by changing patterns of divorce, remarriage and domestic life generally.

Remarriage and conformity to conventional family norms

The pervasiveness of the nuclear family norm is based on its taken-for-granted quality. It is so much part of the 'natural order' of things that, as we suggested in chapter 1, it is rarely possible to locate distinct, clearly articulated ideologies of the family except in situations when either an individual's family life or the family as an institution appears threatened. As Plummer suggests:

> Every member of society . . . belong[s] to a family. It is one of the central statuses ascribed to individuals. Furthermore it is closely linked to the 'natural' tendency of members to seek and sustain couple relationships . . . whether these phenomena are seen as instincts or institutions, they come to be taken for granted; their original man-made nature is lost. (Plummer, 1975, p. 119)

At a very general level, therefore, norms exist which define family life as being a natural and central element of human existence. For most people this means a household and set of kinship obligations which are based on the nuclear family, but dominant ideologies stressing the normality and desirability of the nuclear family are undermined in part both by widespread deviance from such norms and the public articulation of alternative, sometimes opposing ideologies, which criticise and offer alternatives to typical family structures and patterns of relationships. For a variety of reasons, including the prevalence of divorce and remarriage, significant proportions of the population do not live in nuclear family households typical of their stage in the family life cycle and as we demonstrate below, our respondents were very much aware of this. Everyone in the study knew someone else who was divorced and many stressed how common divorce was in their neighbourhood, amongst their friends and colleagues, and even within their own families. However, as Mead has argued, widespread deviance does not necessarily result in the modification of prevalent norms. Discrepancies between ideals and practice persist, so that the ideal of a society in which 'the union of a male and female institutes a new social unit, and the identity and the care of the children depend upon the maintenance of that social unit' (Mead, 1970, p. 113) remains markedly at variance with the continued rise in divorce and remarriage, creating, as Mead suggests, peculiar contradictions and uncertainties for children who believe that their 'whole security depends on that single set of parents, who, more often than not, are arguing furiously in the next room over some detail of their lives.' Consequently, 'A desperate demand upon the permanence and all-satisfyingness of monogamous marriage is set up in the cradle' (ibid.).

The hegemony of ideologies which underpin the nuclear family is also threatened by the political theories and practices of a variety of interest or pressure groups hostile to the familialism of dominant ideologies. Criticism of the family by radical psychiatrists such as Laing; the demands made by the gay liberation movement for recognition of a form of sexuality which must inevitably threaten the family's place in the taken-for-granted order of things (Plummer, 1975), and personal growth movements of the kind described by Lasch, have all played their part. More significantly the public debate of the many issues raised by the women's movement over the last ten years or so has been accompanied by changes in both public policy and private practice in relation to the family. If the family itself continues to be taken for granted, there is undoubtedly much more personal questioning and discussion within families about its nature, significance and everyday organisation, so that, whilst relatively few people belong to, or articulate the rhetoric of groups which either criticise or defend the family, personal questioning and consideration of such issues is now more widespread. Such discussion will inevitably be influenced in one way or another by media presentation of the issues in which minority or alternative views, buttressed by a variety of 'expertise', receive considerable attention. Consequently, although Mills contended that individuals are

> seldom aware of the intricate connections between the pattern of their own lives and the course of world history, ordinary men [and women] do not usually know what this connection means for the kinds of men [and women] they are becoming and for the kinds of history-making in which they might take part (Mills, 1967, p. 4)

we found amongst our own informants considerable evidence of their ability to relate personal circumstances to a broader canvas of historical and social change which thereby undermined to some extent their unquestioning commitment to the nuclear family norm. Some of our informants had become increasingly aware of the prevalence of divorce because so many of their own friends were divorced. As Mr Thompson put it:

> . . . most of me friends have been divorced, I think, at one time or the other . . . er . . . it seems to be the . . . er . . . a middle-class disease at the moment.

Others commented on the number of their children's friends and fellow-pupils who came from broken homes. When Mr Turner went to talk to his son's teacher he was surprised to be told:

> . . . not to think that in any way was his situation unique, because there were so many children like him at school although . . . I would have thought that he was the only one (   ) but there were quite a few.

Mr Vickers recounted how his boys, then away at private school, accepted what had happened, because they,

> keep coming and telling us about other boys that are in the same position.

Mr Heathcote frequently finds himself talking about divorce in the course of his job:

> I come across a lot of people who are going through the throes of divorce, being separated, selling their houses, etc., or buying a new one.

As a result he is able to make connections between his observations about marriage breakdown generally and his personal experience:

> It's the sort of thing that I came across on a regular . . . very regular . . . basis and, er, it's not always the man's fault . . . it's normally a combination of both. I think it's a failure of . . . um

> . . . men and women to communicate . . . a failure on a woman's part that she doesn't become interested in what her husband's . . . hobbies are or activities are and . . . failure of the man . . . to appreciate how a woman thinks . . . and I think the outcome of me first marriage dis . . . being dissolved was, er, that I don't think I'll ever understand how a woman thinks anymore.

Mrs Baker is still an active member of a club for the divorced and separated and, from her experiences, generalises about divorce, drawing an analogy from the world of work:

> . . . it sounds very clinical to refer to . . . [but] . . . some men now are having to take two careers and having to rehabilitate and learn a new trade, well this is, um . . . what the marriage, half of the marriages are going through . . . well, at least a third, I don't know the percentage of them, but it is like, er, starting all over and learning again,

Thus, Mrs Baker is aware of marriage both as an individual relationship and as a social institution affecting everyone in very similar ways.

An awareness that they belong to an increasingly large minority whose private problems have common public origins often insulates individuals from unquestioning acceptance of professional definitions and explanations of their problem, and thus slavish adherence to the nuclear family norm. For example, Mr Heathcote and Mr Dunwell show very clearly how membership of a circle of divorced friends makes them feel that their experiences are quite normal. After Mr Heathcote had enumerated his various friends and acquaintances who had been divorced he commented:

> . . . it's going off so often these days that people just take it as normal. I mean fifteen years ago if someone got divorced it was . . . oh . . . terrible, these days it's um . . . seems to be accepted . . . part of life (   ) there's no longer any stigma about it . . . there used to be . . . in people's minds anyway . . . they used to think 'Oh, she's been divorced' or 'He's been divorced' this sort of thing, almost like a leper if you like, but these days it's so prevalent that er . . . people couldn't . . . you know . . . it becomes accepted.

Mr Dunwell's comments show his appreciation of the complications and diversity of marital relationships:

> Q. You said that some of your friends have been divorced, have you any idea how many exactly?
> Yes, it was almost a complete circle . . . my ex-wife and er . . . Jenny's ex-husband being on the open ends of the loop . . .

> ( ) Er, when I think about it, there's not been all that many divorces, there's been one or two reconciliations ( ) one divorce definitely and a remarriage, and one couple who . . . they looked like splitting up, but they never did . . . actually they'd have probably been better off if they had done. Yes, and there's another couple that split up and now . . . they seem to have a relationship of sorts, quite an amicable relationship which seems to be a much freer sort of relationship than they had before . . . they actually lived apart for some considerable time.

Mr Heathcote's observation that 'there's no longer any stigma' attached to divorce is not shared by all our informants. We have already described how some of the study couples tried to pass as 'ordinary' families by obscuring details of the past from neighbours, schools and so on. The families who were most preoccupied with rendering an appearance of conformity to dominant family norms were often found in category 5 of our typology. It is significant that their outstanding conflicts with ex-partners, as well as the legacy of earlier disputes, meant that they still had frequent contacts with solicitors, social workers and doctors and their accounts frequently bear testimony to the ways in which the ideologies and rhetoric of such experts have shaped their understanding of what has happened to them.

During the almost inevitable period of personal upheaval which accompanies marriage breakdown, divorce and remarriage, most people will consult or find themselves in contact with members of the legal, medical or welfare professions. The majority of our sample described such encounters in a way which suggested that they either used, ignored, tolerated, rejected or grumbled about their professional advisers largely according to their own preferences and values. If they understood little of the legal processes, ritual and jargon surrounding their divorce proceedings, they tolerated the necessary appointments with solicitors and footed the bill in order to obtain what they wanted. The treatment and advice of doctors was followed, if it worked and seemed sensible, or ignored it if it did not. Social workers were designated either useful or to be tolerated according to circumstances. Thus most of our sample seemed able to manage their encounters with professionals in a way which suggested that they would be resistant to those elements of professional ideology which did not accord with their own understanding of the problem or trouble under discussion. There were, however, a minority of our sample who perceived the professionals they encountered as moral guardians and who appeared much more directly vulnerable to the advice, definitions and interpretations of their troubles imposed by professionals. This was demonstrated where they described their slavish adherence to any advice which was offered and where they saw their professional adviser as directly instrumental in taking decisions *for them.* In addition they frequently employed the rhetoric and logic of therapeutic ideologies in their own accounts of past events. In our own sample, this minority included mothers who had experienced particularly damaging and violent first marriages and some of the custodian fathers. The events and circumstances of the first marriage or its breakdown had deprived them of either material or interpersonal resources, or both, so that for a time as a result of illness, poverty and the like they designated themselves, or were officially defined, as inadequate parents. As a result their private lives became peculiarly exposed to the public scrutiny of professionals so that in their efforts to make sense of what was happening to them they became increasingly susceptible to the explanations based on therapeutic ideologies, which thus strengthened their desire to recreate a normal, healthy family life which approximated as closely as possible to the nuclear family norm and which would allow them a greater measure of the privacy it is believed is normally enjoyed by 'ordinary' families.

The personal and public contradictions of remarriage

Although such unquestioning acceptance of expert definitions and prescriptions and an intense desire to conform to conventional family norms represent an extreme response to the problems and complications of remarriage, even those in our sample who espoused a generally optimistic and progressive view of their situation were sometimes affected by its inherent contradictions. In particular they were aware of a legacy of the past from which, despite the rhetoric of contemporary divorce arrangements, there could be no 'clean break'. Two interrelated themes punctuated their accounts when they described how the past still affected them. Some retained a strong sense of personal guilt about the break-up of their first marriage and most seemed anxious in one way or another about the potential long-term effects of their divorce and remarriage on their children.

Whilst current divorce arrangements formally allow married partners to give 'dead' marriages a 'decent burial' in order to render them free to enter new partnerships, some divorcees find that their attempts to do so are constantly undermined by feelings of personal guilt, which seem to be prolonged or intensified by more public evaluations of their failed marriages. Legal and religious institutions both retain an influence over such evaluations which goes way beyond their direct contact with specific individuals. Although most of our informants were divorced after the provisions of the Divorce Reform Act 1969 were brought into force in 1971, they frequently employed the rhetoric of guilt and innocence in their accounts of marriage breakdown. Furthermore, as Eekelaar has suggested, the doctrine of matrimonial offence continues to play an important part in contemporary divorce legislation. He argues that such a doctrine:

> is capricious because it seeks to single out forms of conduct which justify one spouse treating marriage as ended. Hence it represents an evaluation either by society (as where it singles out specific 'offences' like sodomy) or by a judge (in the case of generalised offences like cruelty) as to the limits of toleration within the marital partnership. Yet this judgement is bound to vary from spouse to spouse, judge to judge and society to society. (Eekelaar, 1978, p. 131)

Although none of our informants showed any awareness of the legal debates about the administration of divorce, it is evident that their accounts of their individual, personal experiences are frequently shaped by half-understood legal categories and doctrines transmitted through newspaper accounts of contested divorces or disputed custody cases in which common-sense notions of blame and guilt are confirmed and underlined. By the same token even those in our own sample who had no direct contact with the church were aware of certain church attitudes towards divorce because of recent public discussions within the Roman Catholic and Anglican churches about the remarriage of divorcees in church. Mrs Moseley believed that the usual practice was to allow the 'innocent' but not the 'guilty' parties a church ceremony:

> everybody's entitled to their own opinion about religion I suppose . . . the only disappointment that I did have was er . . . regards church . . . you see, . . . I don't see why one party in church should be allowed to marry in church and the other party not, 'cos there's never any smoke without fire and invariably I think that it takes two to make a bargain and it also takes two to, er, break it up. There are usually faults on both sides, so I don't see why one party should, er, be allowed to marry in church and the other side not . . . I think that is, er, something which, er, churches ought to put in line with themselves . . . try and sort out about remarrying again.

In the regular public debates of such issues taking place in synods and annual gatherings of the main churches it is evident that traditional orthodoxies prevail, powerfully articulated and defended by those members of the ruling class whom Rex designates as 'moral guardians' who also, he suggests, continue to exert a strong influence over the legal profession and legal institutions (Rex, 1974). The continuing influence of the churches in matters of divorce reform in Britain demonstrates the extent to which the majority of senior members of the clerical and legal professions share a commitment to uphold and transmit public moralities of marriage and the family in which divorce and remarriage are still condemned and designated as matters of personal and public regret. As a result even where the public pronouncements of a single powerful individual may go unnoticed, legal and church policy and practice continue to sustain a moral climate in which, we would imagine, a measure of personal guilt is experienced by all those whose marital unhappiness eventually leads to a divorce. In addition, whilst remarriage may help to assuage such feelings by giving individuals the opportunity to demonstrate that they can 'make a fresh start' and that it is possible for them to be married successfully, albeit to a different partner, such remarriages are undermined when the implicit message of either religious or legal institutions suggests that they are in some way 'second-class'.

For remarried parents and their partners children are a constant and lasting reminder of a part of their earlier biography not shared directly with their present partner. The anxiety experienced by all parents about how their children will 'turn out' has an extra edge because of fears about the as yet unseen consequences of the past events to which they were exposed because of their own parents' frailties and personal needs. Even when divorced parents are able to designate themselves as the 'innocent' partner, they may still feel guilty because of their failure to adhere to fundamental tenets of conventional family moralities; a life-long partnership has been broken and dependent children rendered vulnerable to the inevitably distressing and damaging consequences of a 'broken home'. In addition the non-custodial parent appears to desert his children, leaving his parental tasks partially completed. In their studies the Newsons found that, 'parents of every social station and every level of adequacy have in common the basic knowledge that, because they have produced this child from their own bodies, society requires them to see the job through and judges them accordingly' (Newson and Newson, 1976, p. 437).

Much of the material in chapter 5 illustrates the ambiguities and potential complications of post-divorce relationships and the institutional pressures upon both custodian and non-custodial parents to recreate a normal life for their children by 'replacing' a missing parent and/or 'giving way' to a new stepparent who now lives with the children of a former marriage. Amongst our own informants strongly-held ideologies of conventional family life tended to deter non-custodial parents from remaining in contact with their children after divorce, so that couples in category 3 were generally better equipped to develop relationships and patterns of contact with ex-partners which would survive future changes as children grew up and parents formed new partnerships. By contrast some of the couples in category 5 who had tried hardest to recreate a normal family life found that continuing conflict with ex-partners over custody and access arrangements prevented them from realising this goal. Although the numbers involved are very small, it is worth considering some of the characteristics which differentiate these two groups. Certainly the more obviously middle-class informants in category 3 were able to draw upon expert ideologies of child care and development as well as beliefs about the importance of personal change and growth in adult life in order to make sense of the past as well as to deal with current and anticipated problems. Sometimes such problems were couched in formal terms and were part of the 'expert' advice they had sought or received. They also referred to specific pieces of journalism or radio and TV programmes which had dealt with such problems. Their familiarity with popularised versions of such expertise was also apparent in their observations generally so that their comments often echoed the 'expert' perspectives on remarriage we considered in chapter 1. For all but the Hutchinsons in this category their class position not only brought them into working or social networks which included members of the personal service professions but also gave them a sufficiently assured social standing to render concern with conventional 'respectability' unnecessary. In addition their relative affluence had also helped them to cope with the inevitable reduction in their standard of living which followed divorce, so that they were able to reconstruct a new life together whose emotional and material security were closely interrelated.

Whilst the class membership and financial circumstances of the couples in category 5 varied greatly, they tended to be much more concerned about respectability and their good standing at work, within their neighbourhood and amongst their family and friends. Not only did they portray their own family as being under greater public scrutiny generally but many of them talked at length about their continuing contacts with public officials of various kinds. Many of the 'private troubles' which had brought them to the attention of officialdom were either material in origin or else brought considerable financial problems in their train. Although they asserted that divorce and remarriage offered the opportunity of putting the past behind them and making a fresh start, they sometimes implied that their continuing emotional, financial and legal problems were an inevitable and well-deserved consequence of personal failure which they must bear in isolation. Although this group were more likely to view their problems in highly personal terms, on occasion they showed that they were very much aware of the broader social context of their problems, as the quotation from Mrs Graham at the beginning of this chapter shows very clearly. For us, as well as perhaps for them, hope lies in being able to isolate some of the 'traps' to which Mills referred, looking beyond the 'close-up scenes of job, family and neighbourhood'. For them, as for other remarried couples, 'making a go of it' involves recognising the 'historical changes' and, on occasion, challenging the institutional contradictions which bear most heavily upon remarried parents and their children.

Appendix 1

Life histories

Unless otherwise stated, the couples came into the study after replying to a registry office letter. The life histories are written as for 1978, the mid-point of the study.

The Bakers

Harry Baker (34; divorced) *Janice Baker* (31; divorced)

Mr and Mrs Baker were married early in 1978 and have four children: Alan (12) and Ian (10) by Mr Baker's first marriage; Patricia (9) and Michael (6) by Mrs Baker's first marriage. Mr Baker is a foreman in a metal-pressing factory and Mrs Baker works part-time as a hairdresser. They live in their own terraced house in the city.

Harry Baker, an only child, was born in Sheffield in 1944. His father, who died four years ago, was a steel worker and later a salesman; his mother has worked in a variety of jobs connected with cutlery and light engineering. He left school at fifteen and began working in the grocery trade, then three years later, attracted by the higher wages, he took a job as a fitter's mate and then a labourer in a gas works. At about the age of twenty-three he was made redundant. He took a light engineering job and he has worked there ever since. He met his first wife at his local Methodist church. After they had known each other for about a year she became pregnant and they were married in 1965. Their first son, Alan, was born while they were living with his parents. Shortly afterwards they moved to a rented maisonette nearby. Their second son, Ian, was born two years later. According to Mr Baker their marriage problems began around the time when the children had started school and his wife had taken a job. From this period onwards she began to spend increasing amounts of time outside the home, socially and through her work. Arguments developed over this and their lives became more and more separate. They discussed the possibility of separation but at that time Mr Baker felt it better that they stay together for the sake of the boys – something he now believes to be wrong, since 'one happy parent is better than two unhappy parents'. They finally decided to split up in 1975; his wife left and moved into a flat and he stayed behind with the boys. As a single parent he had a number of practical and emotional problems to cope with, but found that after about six months he had begun to resolve these; he started going out in the evenings and meeting people. Towards the end of 1976 he met Janice, later to become his second wife, at a club for the divorced and separated. Three months later, in March 1977, they started living together.

Janice Baker was born in a mining village near Sheffield in 1947. She has one older brother. The family lived in a tied pit cottage and she recalls a family life which was at times quite stormy; her father, who was frequently absent from work due to his fear of going down the mine, was prone to nervous outbursts of temper in the home. She met her first husband, a sixteen-year-old apprentice plumber, when she was fifteen and training to be a hairdresser. Shortly afterwards her father left the mine and took a caretaking job, whereupon the family moved to Sheffield. The couple were married in 1967, when she was almost twenty, and moved into a small old house which they bought from her husband's brother. Their daughter, Patricia, was born the following year, followed by Michael three years after that. By this time her husband had joined the prison service and the family had moved to Birmingham. Shortly after the move, but unknown to her, her husband had been going out with other women. Then in 1976, after nine years of marriage, she discovered that her husband was having an affair. The decision was made to separate and after six months she moved back to Sheffield where, with considerable practical and financial assistance from her first husband, she bought the house in which she now lives. She then heard a radio announcement concerning a club for the divorced and separated in Sheffield and decided to go along; on the second or third occasion she met Mr Baker. At the time she was waiting for her divorce to be finalised, and would not agree to living together until the divorce on grounds of her husband's adultery was complete. They then began living together, and the decision to remarry came later, delayed by the finalising of Mr Baker's own divorce in 1978; they were married later that year.

The Barratts

Bruce Barratt (41; divorced) *Susan Barratt* (32; divorced)

Mr and Mrs Barratt were married in 1977 after living together for over five years; they have two children, Linda (11) by Mrs Barratt's first marriage and a child of their own, Thomas (2). When they first came into the study Mr Barratt worked as a council labourer and, along with his wife, also worked in the evenings in a pub; in the summer of 1978 they became resident managers of a social club in North Derbyshire.

Bruce Barratt was born in Sheffield in 1937 and was the youngest child in a family of thirteen. He describes his upbringing as a 'rough' one, in which all the children were forced to take part-time jobs in order to make ends meet. Each of his elder brothers joined the army and he too spent three years in the forces on national service. He remembers his army career with affection, but on leaving in 1957 found himself rather 'footloose'. He took a job as a labourer with the local council and enjoyed the bachelor life, buying a car and having numerous girlfriends. He met his first wife at a dance and they were married in 1965, when he was twenty-eight. For a while the couple lived with Mr Barratt's mother and then moved into a rented flat before buying their own home. At first they enjoyed going out together and had a full life but after a while his wife developed different leisure interests to him and they spent less and less time with one another; the sexual side of their relationship, which he had never found satisfactory, also deteriorated. He began going out occasionally with other women and around 1970 met Susan; he decided to separate from his wife and after a period living alone he went to live with Susan. In 1976 they had a son of their own and the following year he and his wife were divorced; he remarried later that year.

Susan Barratt was born in Sheffield in 1946 and has one younger and one older sister. Her father, a labourer in a steel works, remarried in 1975 after the death of her mother three years earlier. She recalls a happy family life but feels that her mother was too indulgent of her three daughters and that in her own case this has had a lasting effect. On leaving school at the age of fifteen she took a job in the offices of a local steelworks before moving to a chemist's shop. Whilst working there she met her first husband, an engineer, and they courted for three years before she became pregnant. They married when she was twenty. At first they lived with her husband's parents, then with her parents, and when their daughter, Linda, was about one year old they bought a small terraced house of their own in the east end of the city. Then quite suddenly, and to her complete surprise, her husband, who played in a pop group in his spare time, took a job abroad and left with another woman. She later discovered that he had been having affairs from the very beginning of their marriage. After a while he returned and she attempted a reconciliation; he then got into trouble with the law and was sent to prison for theft, during which time she visited him fairly regularly. On his release he took a job in the south of England but she refused to go with him and pressed ahead with divorce proceedings, which she had already initiated whilst he was in gaol. These were finalised, on grounds of desertion, in 1973. Sometime earlier she and Mr Barratt had met and begun living together. Nevertheless she had no intention of remarrying until, after the birth of their son. Thomas, and following initial pressure from Mr Barratt, she agreed and they were married in 1977.

The Binghams

James Bingham (31; divorced) *Sarah Bingham* (34; divorced)

Mr and Mrs Bingham were married in 1978, after living together for eighteen months. They have one daughter, Catherine (14), by Mrs Bingham's first marriage. Mrs Bingham also had two stepchildren in her previous marriage, Paul (21) and Sharon (18) who are living with their father. Mr Bingham has three children by his first marriage, Jackie (12), Peter (9) and Martin (8), all of whom are living with their mother. Mr Bingham is a foreman in a paper works and Mrs Bingham is a nurse. The family live in their own semi-detached house in an area to the north-west of Sheffield.

James Bingham was born near Barnsley in 1947. His father was a miner and he has a sister and a brother, both younger than himself. He passed the eleven plus and attended grammar school up to the age of sixteen, when he left to train as a surveyor. When he was seventeen his girlfriend became pregnant and they were married in 1965. He then took a job as a coalface worker in a colliery in order to earn more money. He and his wife lived at first with her parents and then in a house which belonged to his parents, before eventually getting a council house of their own. Two years after their daughter, Jackie, was born they had a son Peter. Soon after that his wife became pregnant again, with Martin; it was during this pregnancy that she left him and returned to her parents. Eighteen months later they were divorced on the grounds of his mental cruelty. His wife was awarded custody of the children and he was granted reasonable access. For several years he saw them regularly but this gradually tailed off; he believes now that it may be better to wait until the children are old enough to contact him. Consequently, at the time of the study he had not seen them for more than eighteen months. Looking back he feels that his divorce was the 'best thing' for he and his wife, although at the time he had not wanted to separate; he believes that the marriage failed largely because of his lack of maturity. For six months after the separation he lived alone and was looked after to some extent by his mother. Just before the divorce was finalised, he went to live in London, to 'try and start a new life' but after a while he returned to South Yorkshire where he began his present job. During the next few years he lived at first with his grandmother and then with his parents. In the summer of 1976, whilst on holiday in Blackpool, he met Sarah, who at that time was still living with her husband.

Sarah Bingham was born near Manchester in 1944 and is the youngest of five sisters in a Catholic family. Her father, who is now retired, was a platelayer. She attended a Catholic school in Buxton up to the age of fifteen when she took a job in a sewing factory. Shortly afterwards, and against her parents' wishes, she was engaged to a boy from Lancashire, with whom she subsequently went to live in his home town. Four months later she met her first husband, who, five years her senior, was recently widowed and had two small children. After about three months they discussed marriage plans but knew that it would be necessary to wait 'a decent amount of time' because of his bereavement. She soon became pregnant and they married in 1962, when she was eighteen. At first they lived with her parents but accommodation was cramped; after the baby was born there were occasional rows over the children. At first he worked as a lorry driver but after about three years started his own business as a market stall-holder. They both worked hard at this and it became a considerable success, enabling them to buy their own house. The marriage, however, began to go 'through a rough patch'. Her husband began going out with other women and on one occasion she left him. She began taking sedatives and even attempted suicide. But after a few years things did begin to improve. Then, whilst visiting her parents, who had retired to Morecambe, she met Mr Bingham; after their first meeting she remembers not wanting to go home. Two weeks later they met in Sheffield and a few weeks after that she decided to leave her husband and take her daughter, Catherine, with her. The circumstances of the separation were fraught with indecision and she was very unsure about giving up the security of her home and family. Nevertheless she went ahead and then stayed at first with friends before buying a house in the city. Early in 1978 her husband divorced her on grounds of adultery and she and Mr Bingham were married shortly afterwards, by which time they had moved into their present home.

The Browns

Michael Brown (34; divorced) *Jean Brown* (24; divorced)

Mr and Mrs Brown were married in 1978 after living together for eighteen months. They have two children, Paul (7) by Mr Brown's first marriage and Timothy (5) by Mrs Brown's first marriage. A transport manager with a haulage firm, Mr Brown has two other children by his previous marriage, Douglas (10) and Mary (9), both of whom are currently living with their mother. The Browns live in their own new semi-detached house on a housing estate to the south of Sheffield.

Michael Brown was born in Sheffield in 1944 and lived at first in the east end of the city before moving out to an area near to his present home. His father worked in a steel rolling mill and he has a younger brother and a younger sister. When he was fifteen he took a job as a newsboy with a local paper. Before long, however, he was moved into the composing room where he became an apprentice linotype operator. He was about seventeen when he met his first wife and they were married three years later in 1966, when she was nineteen. They immediately bought their own house and, some eighteen months later, had their first child, Douglas. About this time Mr Brown completed his apprenticeship and was transferred to work on a newspaper near Barnsley. The following year they had a daughter, Mary, and for a while his wife took a job as a nightclub croupier. Shortly afterwards they moved again, buying an off-licence in Rotherham, which his wife ran during the day and he at night. During this period they had their third child, Paul. Subsequently they bought a mobile shop before his wife lost interest in the business and in 1975 they sold up and moved back to Sheffield. Mr Brown then took his present job. Later that year his wife attempted suicide; he subsequently discovered that this had been precipitated by the break-up of an affair she had been having. At the time, however, he believed the cause to be that he was spending too much time at work. Then the following year he learned that his wife was having an affair with another man; he confronted them both but the relationship continued. In August 1976 he left her and returned to live with his parents. In the autumn of that year he was introduced to Jean, who at that time was living alone with her son. In January of 1977 they began living together and shortly afterwards were joined by his sons, Paul and Douglas. After a few months, however, Douglas returned to live with his mother. Mr Brown's divorce was finalised towards the end of 1977.

Jean Brown was born in Lewisham in 1954 and lived there up to the age of six, when her parents moved to the Barnsley area. She has three brothers, two older and one younger than herself. Her father, who is now a registered invalid, did a variety of jobs, including book-binding and paint-spraying. When she was about twelve her parents moved to Sheffield, where they took employment as steward and stewardess of a Working Men's Club. At fifteen she left school and took a job in a small factory before going to work in a department store. She met her first husband, a mechanic who was six years older than herself, when she was sixteen and they were engaged to be married about nine months later. Her parents strongly disapproved of her fiancé and eventually she decided to leave home to go to live with his family. About five months later she discovered that she was pregnant and they were married in August 1972. Their son, Timothy was born early the following year. For three years they continued to live with his parents in very cramped conditions. After a while her husband started going out in the evenings. Eventually they obtained a privately rented house in a nearby village, but shortly after moving there she discovered that her husband was having an affair. Within a short space of time they had separated. She continued to live in the house with her son, whose behaviour was by that time beginning to cause her considerable difficulties. In March 1977 she was divorced on the grounds of her husband's adultery. Towards the end of 1976, however, she met Mr Brown and soon afterwards they began living together. About one year later they bought a new house of their own on a nearby estate, before marrying in the summer of 1978. In December of that year Mr Brown obtained custody of his oldest son, Douglas, who came to live with them on a permanent basis.

The Brownings

Adrian Browning (30; divorced) *Lesley Browning* (24; divorced)

Mr and Mrs Browning were married in 1977 after living together for almost a year. They have two children: Martin (5) by Mrs Browning's first marriage and a daughter of their own, Sarah (four months). Martin has a slight mental handicap. Mr Browning works as a centre lathe turner and the family live in a new council house on the north side of the city.

Adrian Browning was born in Sheffield in 1948 and has one sister. He met his first wife when he was twenty and they were married three years later, in 1971. They lived in various rented properties and for a time worked jointly as managers of a newsagent's shop, which they gave up when they began to have problems over non-payment of bills, which his wife had led him to believe had been settled. He found that they were also spending less and less time together socially; eventually he discovered that his wife was having an affair. By now they were living virtually separate lives and he began taking his meals at his parents' home. Towards the end of 1975 he met Lesley whilst waiting for a bus. In the New Year they began seeing each other regularly and he spent increasing amounts of time at her flat. In the autumn of 1976 he moved in permanently. His wife then suggested that they begin divorce proceedings which, to his annoyance, were finalised on the grounds of his adultery, in 1977. He and Lesley were then free to marry in August 1977.

Lesley Browning was born in Sheffield in 1954 and has two older sisters and an older brother. On leaving school at fifteen she had various factory jobs before meeting her first husband, who lived nearby, when she was seventeen. They had known each other for less than nine months, however, and had no plans to marry, when she became pregnant. They were married in 1972 when she was still seventeen. Until their baby boy, Martin, was three months old, they lived with her parents; her husband disliked this and returned to his own home on a number of occasions. He was frequently absent from work and whilst at home took to cruelly tormenting her. He showed little interest in Martin. After a while they returned to live with his parents and she took a part-time job. Their marriage deteriorated and her husband began drinking and gambling heavily, refusing to give her any money. In August 1974 she decided to leave and returned with Martin to her own parents' home. In 1975 her divorce was finalised on the grounds of technical desertion and shortly afterwards she obtained a council flat of her own. At about the same time she met Adrian and they began seeing each other regularly from the beginning of 1976. Despite Martin's difficulties, Adrian, who had no children in his own marriage, accepted him readily and Mrs Browning believes he has been largely responsible for her son's subsequent progress. They were married in 1977 and decided to have a child of their own immediately. Their daughter, Sarah, was born in February 1978, shortly before they moved from the flat to their present home.

The Chapmans

Raymond Chapman (34; widowed) *Angela Chapman* (36; divorced)

Mr and Mrs Chapman were married in 1978 after living together for about three months. They have six children: Jenny (14), Alex (13), Sally (9) and Pauline (5) are Mrs Chapman's children by her first marriage; Mr Chapman, who has been married twice before, has a son Derek (7) and a daughter Lesley (6) by his second marriage. Mr Chapman works as a loader for a haulage firm and the family live in a new council house in an area to the south of the city.

Raymond Chapman, a twin, was born in Sheffield in 1944. His family, which included one older and one younger sister, lived in the east end of Sheffield, where his father was a steelworker. At the age of fifteen he left school and took a job in a toolmaker's for a short while before going into the steelworks himself. When he was seventeen he joined the army and subsequently spent six years in Germany. In 1968 he left and met his first wife in Sheffield shortly afterwards. She was an unmarried mother with a small baby and they were married in June 1969. The marriage lasted just seven months. After the wedding they went to live in a small terraced house but within a few weeks they began having serious arguments. Both felt hopelessly incompatible from the start and they soon decided to separate. His wife took him to court for a divorce on grounds of mental cruelty but the case was dismissed; then shortly afterwards he met Patricia, who became pregnant, and he and his wife were then divorced on grounds of adultery. He and Patricia began living together and had two children, Derek and Lesley, before they were married in 1973. At first they were very happy together, though she was very possessive, but after a while her jealousy turned to depression. One day in 1975 she was found wandering the streets with the two children. Two days later she went missing again and when Mr Chapman returned to their home after reporting her disappearance to the police, he discovered her dead from an overdose of painkilling tablets. In the wake of the tragedy he was left to look after his children for two years until he met Angela through their mutual involvement in a local play scheme. Within a few months they had decided to get married. In March 1978 they moved into a new council house together and two months later they were married.

Angela Chapman was born in Sheffield in 1942 and has two older sisters and an older brother. She describes the family as a close-knit one, with the exception of her brother who is now a university professor in Switzerland, and whom she has not seen for many years. Her childhood, however, was complicated by nervous problems and she had a breakdown at the age of nine. Just after she left school at fifteen her mother died and for a few years, in addition to having various jobs, she looked after her father. About this time she met her first husband, a labourer, and, against the advice of her family, they were married in 1961, when she was eighteen. For three years they lived with her husband's aunt before their first daughter, Jenny, was born, when they bought a small terraced house of their own. The following year she had a son, Alex. When Alex was about two years old, however, she discovered that her husband had been having affairs with other women. They separated twice, but on each occasion they were reconciled and she became pregnant, first with Sally and then with Pauline. She later learned that her husband had also had a child by another woman. Meanwhile, she began to suffer badly with her nerves and the children were also being affected; Alex was placed on probation for stealing and Jenny ran away from home. Her husband spent longer and longer periods away and eventually, in 1977, she saw a solicitor and they obtained a formal separation. She and the children stayed with her two sisters until the courts authorised her to live in the family home. Later that year she was divorced on the grounds of her husband's unreasonable behaviour. By this time she had already met Mr Chapman and early the following year they started living together as a family and were married in May 1978.

Mr Deam and Mrs Spencer

Maurice Deam (24; previously unmarried) *Heather Spencer* (28; divorced)

Maurice Deam and Heather Spencer came into the study at the end of 1977 and were at that time intending to marry within the near future. They never did marry but instead separated the following year, shortly before the third interviews took place. Mrs Spencer has two children, Robert (7) and Emma (4) from her first marriage. Mr Deam, an electrical engineer, has not been married before. During the study period they lived with the children in a house in the city, which they had bought jointly.

Maurice Deam, the eldest of seven children, was born in South Wales in 1954. His father was in the army and when he was a small child the family moved to Shropshire, where he spent most of his childhood. He attended a Roman Catholic grammar school and left with seven CSEs. On leaving he took up an electrical apprenticeship and began attending evening classes, where he gained a succession of qualifications. It was after one such class that he met Heather Spencer in 1975.

Heather Spencer was born in Sheffield in 1950. Her parents run a private nursing home, though her father is frequently incapacitated with alcoholism. She has one elder brother. At fifteen she left school and had a succession of different office jobs. Her father's drinking problem made her want to leave home and when she was seventeen she took a job in a hotel. She soon found hotel work to her liking and progressed through a number of jobs. In 1968, she met her first husband, who was working as a relief manager in the same establishment as herself. They were engaged that year and then moved around taking jobs in a number of hotels in different parts of the country. In 1969 they were married. The following year they had a son, Robert. They continued to move about the country and spent some time in Sheffield itself. Whilst living near Manchester, her husband began having an affair with one of their friends, but this ended when they moved yet again. At the end of 1973 the family moved to Shropshire where they rented a bungalow. The following year they had a daughter, Emma. By now Mrs Spencer had begun to think of the possibility of separating from her husband and felt that as a couple they had 'really grown apart'. In 1975 she took a part-time job in a local pub, which was where she met Maurice. They began seeing each other regularly, but she made no decision about separation. Eventually, early in 1976 she decided to move back to her parents' home in Sheffield, taking the children with her. A few months later Maurice moved to Sheffield and in the autumn of 1976 they bought a house and began living together.

The Dunwells

Geoffrey Dunwell (36; divorced) *Jenny Dunwell* (31; divorced)

Mr and Mrs Dunwell, who were contacted via a letter passed on by a colleague, have been married for one year, though they lived together for two years prior to that, and have two children by Mrs Dunwell's first marriage, Rachel (8) and Amanda (6), as well as Lesley (11) who was fostered in that marriage. They also have a son of their own, Sam, born in 1978 during the period of the study. Mr Dunwell is an electrical engineer and the family live in a Victorian terraced house which they are currently modernising.

Geoffrey Dunwell, the eldest of two boys, was born in Sheffield in 1942. When he was nine the family moved from privately rented accommodation into a house on a large council estate. He passed the eleven plus and went to a local grammar school, taking O and A levels, after which he worked in Staffordshire for one year before returning to study for an electrical engineering degree at Sheffield University. Since graduating in 1963 he has been employed at British Rail, mainly on research work. In 1966 he met his first wife at a folk music festival and they were married two years later, when he was twenty-five. His parents, particularly his mother, were not happy about the marriage – especially the couple's desire to marry in a Registry Office rather than a church. For a while they lived in rented rooms before saving up enough money for the deposit on a modern detached bungalow. They lived there contentedly for about five years after which they bought an older house more centrally situated in Sheffield. Here they became very friendly with another couple, Jenny and Michael, who lived opposite. Before long it became apparent that he and Jenny had more in common with one another than they had with their respective spouses and a close attachment developed between them. During this time Jenny had already decided to leave her husband and move with her children into another house; Geoffrey and she made no plans together. Matters finally came to a head when, whilst on holiday, his wife discovered a letter from Jenny and insisted that he had to come to some immediate decision about the future.

Jenny Dunwell was born in Sheffield in 1947 of an English mother and an Austrian father. She has one younger brother and a large family of aunts and uncles living locally. After passing the eleven plus examination she attended a local grammar school for four years before the family moved to Nottingham. Whilst still at school she met her first husband and after leaving at seventeen, did a variety of jobs before getting married three years later; she was twenty and her husband twenty-three. Her family considered that she had made a 'successful match' to a man who would 'go places' and 'calm her down'. On marrying they moved to Sheffield, he to work in a bank and she to become a receptionist. Three years later they had their first daughter, Rachel. When Rachel was one year old they fostered Lesley, who was then aged four, and one year later they had their own second child, Amanda. During this time she took various part-time jobs and for a while they took in student lodgers. Meanwhile her husband decided to go to university to study law. She became increasingly aware of differences in their orientations to life – he became more and more involved in his career and in establishing contacts in the local business world, an exercise which she found particularly futile. The emotional and sexual side of their marriage also deteriorated. In about 1974 a decision was made that they should separate, though they continued to live together for some time before her husband bought her a small house in a neighbouring area. Shortly after she moved into the house with the children she was joined, suddenly and rather unexpectedly, by Mr Dunwell. She was divorced two years later and they married some time afterwards. Their son, Sam, was born in 1978.

The Dysons

Walter Dyson (53; divorced) *Elsie Dyson* (50; widowed)

Mr and Mrs Dyson were married in 1977, after living together for ten years. They have two children, Martin (18) by Mr Dyson's first marriage and a son of their own, Ivan (10). Mr Dyson also has five other children by his first marriage, Gordon (29), Sally (26), Pamela (24), Shirley (22) and Judith (19). Mrs Dyson has four other children, born illegitimately to a man with whom she lived after the break-up of her first marriage, Paul (26), Doris (24), Barry (23) and Simon (22). Since Mr and Mrs Dyson began living together in 1967, Gordon has married Doris, Paul has married Pamela and Barry has married Shirley. Sally and Judith are also married. Mr Dyson is a bar straightener in a steel works and Mrs Dyson works in a tool factory. The family live in a council maisonette near the city centre.

Walter Dyson was born in Sheffield in 1925 and has three sisters and two brothers. At the age of fourteen he left school and went to work in a steelworks, before being called up into the army when he was nineteen. After the war he began working for his present firm, where he has remained ever since. He met his first wife when he was twenty-three and after they had known each other about nine months she became pregnant. They were married soon afterwards, in 1949, in the face of opposition from his family, who did not attend the wedding. He and his wife lived at first with one of his aunts, but after their son, Gordon, was born they found rented rooms on their own. The first daughter, Sally, was born in 1952, followed by Pamela in 1954, Shirley in 1956 and Judith in 1959. About this time, however, his wife began going out with other men and in 1960 she gave birth to a son, Martin, of whom Mr Dyson was not the father. She then began spending less and less time at home and eventually, in 1963, she left him and the six children. He and Gordon remained together but the five younger children were taken into care. For the next four years he and Gordon lived in various flats and lodgings and the children stayed in homes and with foster parents; he visited them when he could. Then, by chance, in 1967, he met Elsie, whom he had known when they were children. They steadily grew close to one another and began living together in the flat, along with her three children out of care and they all lived together as one large family. They then had a son of their own, Ivan, who was born in 1968. Eventually, in 1977, after they had been together almost ten years, Mr Dyson was divorced and soon afterwards he and Elsie were married.

Elsie Dyson was born in Sheffield in 1928. Her father, a miner, was killed at work when she was two years old. She has three sisters and two brothers, although five other brothers and sisters died at an early age. Her own life has been dogged by illness and she has spent long periods in hospital. She met her first husband, a soldier of eighteen, when she was sixteen and they were married two weeks later by special licence. Five years later they had a son, Alan, after she had almost given up hope of having any children. From the start however her husband was jealous of the baby and frequently grew angry with him, especially after Alan became ill with meningitis. Alan died when he was six months old and from then onwards she 'turned against' her husband. Their problems were made worse by his heavy drinking and refusal to work regularly; he also used to beat her. Before long they separated and, although they were reunited on a number of occasions, it was never for long. She then returned to live with her mother and after a while she met another man, Mr Brown, to whom she became pregnant and had a son, Paul, in 1952. She continued to live with her mother and received maintenance from Mr Brown, though she never saw him. She then had to go into hospital for almost a year, during which time her sister looked after Paul. On her return she was visited by Mr Brown and after a while they began living together, at first with her mother and then in a council house on their own. She had three more children: Doris, in 1954, Barry in 1955 and Simon in 1956. She continued to spend long periods in hospital and due to her ill health, her youngest child, Simon, went to live with one of her sisters, with whom he has remained ever since. In 1960, quite suddenly, Mr Brown was killed in an accident. She was left alone with the children and for the next few years life was a very hard financial struggle. In 1964 her first husband, whom she had never divorced, was killed in a fishing accident. A few years later she met Mr Dyson and they began living together. At first they had problems finding suitable accommodation, but eventually obtained a large council house where they and all nine children were able to be together. She and Mr Dyson then had a son of their own, Ivan, born in 1968. Eventually, all of the children, with the exception of the two youngest boys were married, and in 1977, following Mr Dyson's divorce, she and he were themselves able to remarry.

The Elliots

Raymond Elliot (43; previously unmarried) *Maureen Elliot* (43; divorced)

Mr and Mrs Elliot have been married for nine years and have a daughter, Jean (11) by Mrs Elliot's first marriage who was adopted by Mr Elliot in 1969. They also have four children of their own: Martin (8), Adrian (7), Anita (5) and Barbara (3). Mrs Elliot has an illegitimate son, Donald (24) and daughter, Janet (23), both of whom live with their father. The Elliots live in a new council house on the north side of Sheffield; Mr Elliot is a bus driver and his wife works as a part-time cleaner.

Mr Elliot comes from a large working-class family of six children and was born in the centre of Sheffield; he left school at fifteen and worked as an apprentice in a steelworks before entering the army at eighteen. On completing national service he remained in the forces for another four years. Subsequently he has had a variety of jobs, mainly connected with transport.

Mrs Elliot was born in a village on the south-east edge of Sheffield; her father was a miner and her mother a midwife. Her parents separated during her own childhood and with her mother and younger sister she moved many times and lived in various parts of the city. On leaving school she went into domestic service in London, returning to Sheffield when she was about eighteen. She then courted and became pregnant by a West Indian, of whom her mother disapproved, and had a son, Donald. After a second child, Janet, was born, the relationship came to an end but the children stayed with her. Mrs Elliot continued to live with her mother and worked as an etcher in a local cutlery firm. At this time her daughter spent a short period in care. In 1960 she met and married her first husband and had a son, John, the following year. Soon after she and her husband separated; several months later they were reconciled, however, and had a daughter, Jean. A few years later they split up again.

In fact Mr and Mrs Elliot had been at the same school for a short time as teenagers. They were therefore already acquainted when they met up again through Mr Elliot's milk delivery round. They married in 1969, soon after Mrs Elliot's divorce was finalised.

The Farmers

Trevor Farmer (30; previously unmarried) *Pauline Farmer* (34; divorced)

Mr and Mrs Farmer have been married for four years and have three sons by Mrs Farmer's first marriage: Michael (15), Jason (11) and Alan (8). During the period of study Mrs Farmer's oldest child, Maureen (17) became pregnant and left home to get married. Mr Farmer was unemployed for part of the study period but in 1979 took a job as a roof insulator. His wife works for the local authority as a night nurse. The family, who came into the study via a letter passed on by Jason's school, live on a large council estate on the north side of the city.

Trevor Farmer was born near Rotherham in 1947 in a small mining village, where he lived up to the age of six before moving to another village near Barnsley. His father worked as a council rent-collector and later as a brewery stocktaker; for most of his childhood his parents also worked as stewards in local Working Men's Clubs. He has one younger brother and a younger sister; another brother committed suicide during the study period. His father died in 1974 and his mother was subsequently remarried. On leaving school at fifteen he took a job as a stocktaker in a steelworks and stayed there for five years. Later he did a variety of manual and non-manual jobs. As a single man he 'always had plenty of money' and was able to buy his own house in the city, go away on foreign holidays and follow his favourite football team. When he was twenty-five he met Mrs Farmer, who worked in his local garage; they began going out together and eventually he was living at her home most of the time.

Pauline Farmer was born in Sheffield in 1944 and has three older brothers and an older sister. Her father, a steelworker, died when she was twelve. Some four years later her mother remarried. From the age of fourteen she courted a boy four years older than herself and in 1961, against her mother's wishes, but with the approval of her stepfather, they were married. At first they lived with his parents but this soon proved unsatisfactory and they moved in with a married sister. Soon after, she became pregnant and shortly before the baby was born they began renting a one-bedroomed flat on their own. Towards the end of 1961 she gave birth to a daughter, Maureen. Her husband began to leave her for short spells, returning unexpectedly and then just as unexpectedly going away again. In 1963 they had a son, Michael. Meanwhile, her husband's departures became more frequent and he began to lose and change jobs erratically; his drinking also increased. In 1967 she became pregnant again with Jason and also discovered that her husband was having an affair with a woman who was expecting his child. She then told him that, were he to leave again, it would be the end of the marriage. Shortly afterwards he did leave and she began separation proceedings; on his return, however, he persuaded her to drop these and resolved to reform his behaviour. For about a year things went well before he started drinking heavily and going out with other women again. The period which followed, Mrs Farmer recalls, was one of acute financial hardship, during which she relied heavily upon the support of her mother. In 1971 she became pregnant with Alan and very soon afterwards obtained a separation. The following year she was divorced on the grounds of her husband's adultery. After the final break with her husband, life improved considerably and when her stepfather died her mother came to live with her. This made it possible for her to take a job at a garage, where she later met Mr Farmer; a regular income also allowed her to learn to drive and buy a car. Just under a year after they had met she and Mr Farmer were married, in 1974.

The Foxes

Martin Fox (33; divorced) *Ann Fox* (25; divorced)

Mr and Mrs Fox were married in 1977 after living together for over a year. They have one child, Jonathon (4) fathered by another man after Mrs Fox separated from her first husband. Mr Fox also has a daughter, Diane (9) by his first marriage, who lives with her mother. Mr Fox is a steelworker and Mrs Fox works part-time as a barmaid. They live in a council house on an estate to the north-east of Sheffield.

Martin Fox was born near Doncaster in 1945 and was adopted at an early age under circumstances which he still does not fully understand. During childhood he saw his mother occasionally and has a sister in his adoptive family. Leaving school at fifteen he took a job in a local steelworks and at the age of nineteen met his first wife at a dance. She was five years younger than himself. Their courtship was a fairly stormy one and against his parents' wishes, they were engaged and married in 1968. The following year they had a daughter, Diane, but from an early stage in the marriage there were serious arguments between them. His wife began going out alone in the evenings, later, he discovered, with other men. Their relationship grew worse and on two occasions she left him. Eventually they separated permanently and in 1972 they were divorced. For some time afterwards he felt very depressed, but eventually began going out again in the evenings with friends. He then met an unmarried woman slightly younger than himself and for about a year they lived together, but had no intention of marrying. Then he met Ann at his local pub, where she was working as a barmaid. He began seeing her regularly and in 1975 they started living together. They were married in 1977.

Ann Fox was born on the north-east side of Sheffield in 1953 and has one sister. When she was fifteen her father, a steelworker, retired and she left school to provide money for the household. Towards the end of 1970 she began courting her first husband, whom she had already known for a year. In 1972 they were married and obtained a council house of their own. The house was pleasantly decorated and she remembers being pleased with it, but from the period that they first lived there they began to have problems in the marriage. Her husband, a labourer, started taking time off work and became increasingly violent towards her. She found it necessary to take various tranquillisers and before long was in fear for her physical safety; she received regular beatings. In 1973 she left her husband, returned to her parents and started divorce proceedings. During the early period of separation she was afraid of any further contact with her husband until, after several months, he moved to Scarborough, which allowed her greater freedom of movement. She then began going out with a man who was awaiting divorce, to whom she became pregnant. The man then returned to his wife, however, and refused to have any more contact with her or Jonathon, who was born in 1974. He has nevertheless continued to pay maintenance for the child. For the next eighteen months she remained with her parents before obtaining a council house. She then took a part-time job as a barmaid, which was how she met Martin. They began living together soon after and married when her divorce was finalised on grounds of cruelty.

The Gilmours

Alex Gilmour (33; divorced) *Janet Gilmour* (33; divorced)

Mr and Mrs Gilmour were married in 1978 after living together for almost a year and have two children, Derek (8) by Mrs Gilmour's first marriage and a daughter of their own, Alice, born in June 1979. Mr Gilmour's daughter by his first marriage, Frances (8) is currently living with her mother who has herself remarried. Mr Gilmour is the manager of a large retailing warehouse in Sheffield and the family live in a rented cottage on a farm to the north-west of the city.

Alex Gilmour, an only child, was born in Scotland in 1945; his father was in the navy. When he was twelve the family moved to Sheffield, where his father took a job as a hospital engineer. He recalls being brought up strictly on 'navy discipline'. He left school at the age of sixteen and started an apprenticeship with the local electricity board; relations with his parents, especially his father, deteriorated and at eighteen he decided to leave home to go to live in a flat. About this time he began courting his first wife and in 1966, aged twenty-one, and in the face of some opposition from his parents, they were married. The following year they moved into a new house of their own and shortly afterwards he took a job as 'troubleshooter' with a large catering organisation. Their daughter,

Frances, was born in 1969 but for about a year afterwards his wife suffered with post-natal depression. In 1970 he began working for a Sheffield export company before moving on to a large furniture firm. Increasing pressure was placed on him in this job, which necessitated long, irregular hours as well as working at home; his wife particularly disliked the incursions which his work made into their leisure time. In 1976 he suffered a minor breakdown and was given a less responsible position. By this time, however, things were going badly in the marriage and 'work was having to take precedence'. He and his wife discussed separation, but agreed to stay together for the sake of their daughter. Mr Gilmour then took up his present job, which involved more regular hours, but by now his wife had begun to immerse herself in committee work for local organisations. Meanwhile a close relationship began to develop between Mr Gilmour and Janet, a friend he and his wife had known for some time.

Janet Gilmour was born in Sheffield in 1945 and has two older brothers. Her father, who is now retired, was a sheep-shearer. They were and still are a 'close family'. At the age of fifteen she left school and took an office job in a local factory, where she stayed for almost nine years. When she was seventeen she met her first husband at a dance; he was eight years older than her and worked as a self-employed window cleaner. They courted for four years before getting married in 1966, when they started buying a small terraced house of their own. Things went well until she gave up work to have a baby in 1969 and they began to have financial problems. When their son, Derek, was six months old her husband suddenly deserted her, taking with him some money belonging to another member of the family. Nothing has been seen or heard of him since. For two years she lived alone, before moving in with her parents and unmarried brother. During the following years she led a quiet, home-centred life, which she feels was rather lonely at times. Her relationship with Mr Gilmour did not begin to develop until towards the end of 1976. The following year Mr Gilmour decided to leave his wife and he and Janet moved out of their village and began living together. Derek went with them, but Mr Gilmour's daughter stayed with her mother. Mr Gilmour was divorced later in 1977 on grounds of adultery, and Janet finally obtained her divorce, for desertion, early in 1978. They were married soon afterwards and had a daughter of their own, Alice, in June 1979.

The Grahams

Martin Graham (34; divorced) *Jennifer Graham* (36; divorced)

Mr and Mrs Graham were married in 1978 and have three children by Mrs Graham's first marriage, Diana (13), Sandra (10) and Michèle (8). Mr Graham also has a stepson, Peter (12) and a son, David (8) by his first marriage, both of whom live with their mother. Mr Graham is a self-employed mechanic and Mrs Graham, who is expecting a child in August 1979, works part-time as a telephonist. They live in their own semi-detached house in a quiet suburb on the south side of the city.

Martin Graham, whose father is a machinist, was born in Sheffield in 1944 and has an older sister and a younger brother. Throughout his childhood the family moved around to various parts of the city, though his father has worked for the same firm all his life. On leaving school at fifteen he took a job, first in a chartered accountant's office and then in a grocery store, before working for two years for a joinery firm. He then began working as a mechanic and was employed at various garages before setting up his own business in 1978. He met his first wife when he was twenty-four years old and was at first unaware that she already had a small baby. After about two years they were engaged to be married but this was later broken off. Shortly afterwards, however, his fiancée discovered that she was pregnant and they were married in 1970. They then went to live in a small house which belonged to his sister. From the start he found it difficult to settle down and soon began to believe that he would either settle or the marriage would break up. After their son, David, was born it became increasingly apparent that he and his wife had little in common. Within a few years he had fallen into a regular routine of going out alone each evening to the pub. He met Jennifer at work and offered to do some vehicle repairs for her in his spare time. In 1976 he decided to separate from his wife and returned to live with his parents. In 1977 he was divorced on grounds of adultery, by which time he and Jennifer had decided to get married. Eventually, after certain delays over the divorce and house purchase, they were married in 1978.

Jennifer Graham was born in London in 1942 and has two younger brothers. Her parents have their own newsagent's business. On passing the eleven plus she and the family moved to Surrey, where she attended grammar school up to the age of seventeen, taking O levels. She then took a job with a travel agent, but after two months began to suffer with anorexia nervosa. She then had a variety of secretarial jobs which, because of her illness, she had difficulty in keeping. Eventually, after undergoing various forms of psychiatric treatment, it was a boyfriend who helped her back to health; nevertheless she has continued to suffer with the complaint. She then took a job as a hotel receptionist in Liverpool, where at the age of twenty-one, she met her first husband. They were married in 1965. Shortly afterwards her husband took a teaching post in a college in Leicestershire and they also began a small catering business which they ran in their spare time. During the first year of the marriage she had a miscarriage and then gave birth to their first daughter, Diana, in 1967. Two years later Sandra was born and in 1971 she had Michèle. They began to experience numerous problems. In 1970 she discovered that her husband had been having an affair with a student, then the catering business went bankrupt and they were forced to sell their house. Her husband changed jobs and they moved to Lincolnshire; Mrs Graham believes that the marriage should have broken up at that point, instead of which it continued for another four years. Meanwhile they moved to Sheffield and bought another house. The situation became increasingly intolerable, however, and her husband took to coming home in the early hours and beating her; the girls' mental state also began to suffer. Eventually, in January 1974, she and her husband separated. The relief for both she and the children was enormous. Less than a year later she met Martin and they began seeing each other regularly. In 1976 she was divorced and she and Martin decided to get married. Numerous legal and financial problems beset them, however, mainly over Martin purchasing her ex-husband's share of the house. During the delay she became pregnant and had to have an abortion. Eventually, in 1978, they were married. Shortly afterwards Mr Graham set up his own garage business and they decided to have a child of their own.

The Hammonds

Stanley Hammond (44; divorced) *Jean Hammond* (56; divorced)

Mr and Mrs Hammond were married in 1977 after living together for some seven years. They have four children, Kenneth (18) and Katherine (17) by Mr Hammond's first marriage and Geoffrey (17) and Susan (14) by Mrs Hammond's first marriage. Mr Hammond also has a married daughter, June (20), and Mrs Hammond has seven other married children, Tina (36), Alice (30), Lesley (28), Raymond (26), Paul (23), Barry (21) and Jennifer (19). Mr Hammond is a long-distance lorry driver and his wife works part-time as a barmaid; the family live on a council estate on the south side of the city.

Stanley Hammond was born in the east end of Sheffield in 1934 and has one brother, four years younger than himself. When he was eight years old his mother died, followed by his father four years later; from then onwards he and his brother were brought up by a maiden aunt. At the age of fifteen he left school and took his first job in a garage before moving on to a wireworks soon afterwards, where he stayed for sixteen years before taking his present job. Whilst working there he met his first wife, a fellow employee; in 1954, after knowing each other for two years, they were married. From the outset they lived with his maiden aunt. In 1958 they had their first child, Jane, followed by Kenneth and Katherine in successive years. Then suddenly, early in 1968, he returned from work to find a note from his wife stating that she had found another man and was leaving. In fact she had left with the man for a town in the south of England where he was working. Mr Hammond was able to trace them there a few days later, when his wife agreed to return with him to Sheffield. The affair with the man continued, however, and in August of 1968 Mr Hammond insisted that his wife leave him and the children. He was divorced in 1977 on the grounds of adultery. Shortly after the separation his aunt, who continued to live with them, retired and was able to look after the children for him. It was about one year later that he first met his second wife, Jean, who at the time was working in a cafe which he visited before work each day. They began seeing each other occasionally in the evenings before she separated from her husband and moved into a rented house on her own. Mr Hammond spent increasing amounts of time there and after a while they obtained a council house in the city; they were then joined by Barry, Geoffrey and Susan, three of Mrs Hammond's children, though his own children remained with his aunt. She died in 1977 and they were then able to move into her larger council house, along with Kenneth and Katherine. They were married later that year.

Jean Hammond, who has one older brother (and another who is now dead) was born in Sheffield in 1922. At the age of seventeen her mother died and two years later, whilst in the forces, she met her first husband, whom she married within three weeks by special licence. Her first baby, Tina, was born nine months later. For the next four and a half years her husband was stationed abroad with the army. When he returned they had their second child, Alice. The remaining seven children came at roughly two-year intervals after that. The marriage was, however, beset with problems. Her husband, a labourer, was ill for long periods, drank heavily and was often unemployed. They began to lead increasingly separate lives socially. Then in 1970, about one year after meeting Mr Hammond, she finally separated from her husband. At first Paul, Barry and

Jennifer stayed with their father whilst Geoffrey and Susan lived for a time with their elder sister, Lesley. In 1972 she was divorced after two years' separation. A few months later her first husband, after numerous attempts over a long period of time, committed suicide. Later that year she and Mr Hammond were married.

Mr and Mrs Hammond, who were contacted through a Registry Office letter, were interviewed only once, in November 1977. Subsequently, despite considerable efforts by David Clark, they persistently failed to keep appointments and expressed no desire to continue with the series of interviews.

The Harpers

Geoffrey Harper (31; divorced) *Mary Harper* (32; divorced)

Mr and Mrs Harper were married in 1977, after living together for one year. They have three children, Paul (11) by Mrs Harper's first marriage and Mandy (11) and Nigel (7) by Mr Harper's first marriage. Mr Harper is a local authority engineer and his wife is a teacher. The family live in their own terraced house near the centre of the city.

Geoffrey Harper, whose father is a retired mechanic, was born in Sheffield in 1947. He has two older brothers and an older sister. At the age of fifteen he left school without any qualifications and took a job first as an apprentice mechanic and then as an apprentice bricklayer. In the years that followed he gained a variety of qualifications through evening classes and day release courses. He then took a job with the local public works department. At twenty he was married to a girl whom he had known for three years; she was pregnant at the time. At first they lived in a flat owned by his brother, where their daughter Mandy was born. For a while they also lived with his parents before moving to a house of their own. He continued attending college, gaining qualifications, but became concerned about their marriage. The birth of their son, Nigel, 'brought something back into the marriage that was going'. However various problems developed, some financial and some associated with his wife's 'compulsive lying'. He then discovered that she was having an affair with another man. He made various attempts at reconciliation but these proved unsuccessful and eventually his wife left, taking the children. He then brought the children back to live with him and applied for custody. For a time his retired parents lived with him and helped with the children. He then met Mary at a local sports club and they began to think about marriage. However, the situation was complicated by his wife's return. He tried to make the marriage work again, but believes that his wife had merely returned in order to frustrate his custody action. When he was finally awarded legal custody she left. A few months later he began divorce proceedings and he and Mary started living together. They were married a year later in 1977.

Mary Harper, who is the eldest of five children, was born in Sheffield in 1946. When she was five the family moved to a farm outside the city where she spent her childhood. She passed the eleven plus examination and went on to a Catholic grammar school. She left after taking O levels and her first job was as a laboratory technician. In her late teens she moved into a flat of her own. Whilst living there she met her first husband and they were married, within a few months, in 1966. She was pregnant when they married. They had a number of problems associated with her husband's attitude towards her Catholic beliefs, which were exacerbated when she wished to have their son, Paul, baptised. After a while she wanted to have another baby, but he was opposed to this. She eventually accepted this, as she did many of the other disagreements which arose between them. They then began their own second-hand car business. Through this involvement in the motor trade she met a lot of different men and eventually had an affair with one of them. She enjoyed the attention which was 'lavished' upon her by these men and had affairs with several more. Then in 1971 she began training to be a teacher. The business began to expand and her husband too had lovers of his own. She enjoyed the student life and their marriage continued with each of them 'doing their own thing'. In 1974, however, her husband began a serious relationship with another woman and after a strained and emotional period of indecision they separated. Two years later she was divorced. She found the early period of separation very difficult and suffered from acute depression and loss of confidence. She had a number of boyfriends and considered marriage with one of them. Having passed her final examinations she found a job as a teacher. She also took up sports and, as a result, met Geoffrey at her local club. They found they had much in common as a result of their similar legal and practical problems connected with separation and divorce. In 1976 they began living together and were married the following year.

The Heathcotes

Bruce Heathcote (38; divorced) *Jane Heathcote* (43; previously unmarried)

Mr and Mrs Heathcote were married in 1978 and have two children,

Raymond (11) and Sally (8) by Mr Heathcote's first marriage. Mr Heathcote is an estate agent and his wife, who formerly had her own furniture business in Cheshire, is currently working with him. The family live in their own detached house in a quiet suburb of the city.

Bruce Heathcote was born in Sheffield in 1944 and lived in a back-to-back house in the centre of the city. Born with club feet, he had a variety of manipulative operations throughout his childhood. Just before the end of the war his father was killed in action and when he was ten his mother remarried and later had a daughter. His stepfather, who died recently, was a park-keeper. As a schoolboy he sang in the Sheffield Cathedral Choir, passed the eleven plus and attended the local grammar school, where at first, he recalls, he was overawed by the size of the school and the social class differences within it. Although he had some difficulties at school he nevertheless took O levels before leaving. Thereupon he worked for two years with a firm of chartered accountants before taking a job in the City Treasury in 1958. He stayed there for nearly fourteen years. When he was seventeen he met his first wife at a local youth club and they married in 1963 after a long courtship. They moved immediately to their own brand new, semi-detached house, where, three years later, they had their first child, Raymond. Two years after that they moved out into a village to the east of Sheffield and in 1969 their daughter, Sally, was born. In order to make a little extra money he took a variety of part-time jobs, including selling life insurance. He enjoyed this enormously but eventually, he recalls, the work 'took priority over my wife and kids'. Towards the end of 1971 he left his job at the Town Hall and went into partnership as an insurance broker in Sheffield. Just over four months later the partnership collapsed. His family advised him to 'swallow his pride' and go back to the Town Hall. This he refused to do and undeterred he persuaded his bank manager to give him an overdraft and second mortgage so that he might go into selling insurance for himself. To supplement their income his wife took a job as a croupier in a casino. As a result their working hours became such that they rarely saw each other for more than a few hours each day. Looking back, it was the 'beginning of the end' and they 'gradually grew further and further apart'. After a while his wife admitted she had a boyfriend, a relationship which continued for some time before she left him and the children in April 1975. Meanwhile his business had flourished into an insurance brokerage and estate agency. His responsibility for the children presented him, therefore, with a number of practical difficulties and very soon he decided to go to live with his mother. A small house was bought for his wife to live in and during the summer, by taking her on holiday, he even made an attempt at reconciliation. This failed, however, and by the end of 1975 they were divorced on the grounds of his wife's adultery; he was awarded custody of the children. The following year, 1976, he took the children on holiday to Ibiza and whilst they were there he met Jane. A whirlwind holiday romance ensued, which, to their mutual surprise, continued after their return to England. They were married early in 1978.

Jane Heathcote, an only child, was born in Stoke-on-Trent in 1935. Her childhood, she recalls, was a difficult one, principally because of the frequent rows between her parents. Her father worked as a self-employed joiner and as her mother is Catholic she attended convent school up to the age of seventeen. She then took a job as a designer with a wallpaper firm and later went to work in interior design, becoming manager of a design centre in Manchester where she worked for some ten years. Eventually, early in the 1970s the company was involved in a takeover bid and, fearful for her future, she decided to leave and set up her own business. With outside backing she then opened up a kitchen shop in Cheshire and at the same time bought a bungalow, moving away from her parents to live alone. Three years after that she bought a country cottage. During her twenties she recalls having 'loads of boyfriends' and was, in fact, engaged on two occasions. When she was twenty-seven she began a long relationship with a married man, with whom she later went into business. The relationship finally ended when she met Mr Heathcote.

The Hobsons

Graham Hobson (50; divorced) *Patricia Hobson* (34; divorced)

Mr and Mrs Hobson were married in 1978 after living together for three years. They have three children by Mrs Hobson's first marriage, Stephen (8), Paula (7) and Jason (5). Mr Hobson has a daughter, Julie, by his first marriage who is married and lives in Sheffield. Mr Hobson works as a relief caretaker and the family live on a council estate about one mile to the south of the city centre.

Graham Hobson was born in 1948 in Bradford; his father worked as a mechanic and he has one older sister. When he was eleven his parents separated. At first he lived with his mother, then with an aunt and finally with his father. He passed the eleven plus and went to grammar school but at the age of sixteen he left both school and father and cycled to Sheffield to live with his married sister. At first he took a job as an office boy in a wireworks and then joined a YMCA scheme, 'British Boys for British Farms'. For eight weeks he trained in Lancashire before being sent to a farm in North

Yorkshire. He enjoyed the work and it was there that he met his first wife, when he was twenty. Three years later they were married and returned to Sheffield where he worked as a gardener in a home for mentally handicapped children. He stayed there for fifteen years, for part of which they lived in a flat on the site, later moving to a council house. When they had been married about three years they had a daughter, Julie: the marriage itself, however, 'just trudged along'. Some years later he left the gardening job and worked as a postman. This he recalls, was when 'the marriage really did start to go downhill'. He worked long hours, began drinking and gambling, and his wife worked in the evenings at a local club. The sexual side of the marriage also deteriorated and in 1970 he was placed on probation for two years after being found guilty of an act of indecent exposure. He found his probation officer enormously helpful, but soon afterwards he and his wife separated; his daughter continued to live with him. Because of the conviction he had to resign from his job with the post office. He then worked in a paper mill and in a wireworks before taking his present job as a relief caretaker. It was after his separation that he first met Patricia, who was working in a local pub. She was still living with her husband, although the marriage was going through serious difficulties. He struck up a friendship with her and after visiting her flat and seeing the problems she was having there, invited her to come with the children to live with him. She did so on the day after Mr Hobson's daughter was married in 1975. In 1977 he was divorced after two years' separation; the following year, despite difficult financial circumstances, he and Patricia were married.

Patricia Hobson was born in Sheffield in 1944 and is the youngest of nine surviving children in a family of sixteen. Her mother, who is now looked after by her only unmarried daughter, was forty-seven years old when Patricia was born. Her father, a lathe-maker, died before she left school, after being ill for seven years. She left school at fourteen and worked with her sister as a packer in a food factory, where she stayed for seven years. At eighteen she met her first husband and was married the same year, thinking, incorrectly, that she was pregnant. At first they lived with her mother-in-law but after about six months moved into a high-rise flat. She then had two miscarriages in succession and had almost given up hope of having any children when Stephen was born in 1970, followed by Paula the following year and Jason in 1973. During this time her husband began acting increasingly violently towards her and the children; she also received very little money from him for housekeeping. To supplement their income she took a job washing glasses in a nearby pub and it was there that she met Mr Hobson. Eventually she decided to go to live with him, but shortly afterwards her husband removed Stephen whilst he was out playing; the boy stayed with him at the flat until custody of all three children was awarded to their mother. She was divorced in 1978 after two years' separation and remarried immediately afterwards.

The Hursts

Alan Hurst (37; divorced) *Carole Hurst* (37; divorced)

Mr and Mrs Hurst were married in 1977, after living together for four months. They have seven children, Katherine (14), Sally (12), Lesley (10) and Michael (5) by Mr Hurst's first marriage, and Diane (14), Maurice (12) and Ivan (10) by Mrs Hurst's first marriage. Mr Hurst is a machinist in a tool-making factory and his wife, who has been married twice before, is a part-time cleaner. The family live on a large council estate on the south side of the city. They came into the study in October 1977 and in June of 1978 Sally returned to live with her mother, followed by her sister Lesley in November of the same year.

Alan Hurst was born in Sheffield in 1941 and has one older brother. For long periods his father suffered from mental health problems and was frequently in hospital. His mother was also ill for a long time. When he was fourteen his parents were divorced and from then up to the time of his first marriage he lived in various lodgings and with other relations. At his brother's wedding he met a girl to whom he was later engaged and for two years he lived with her grandmother before the engagement was broken off. He then returned to live with his mother and began working as a bus conductor; this was how he met his first wife, a passenger, some nine months later. After a courtship lasting six months they were married in 1963; he was aged twenty-two and she was one year older. Their first daughter, Katherine, was born in 1964, followed by Sally in 1966 and Lesley in 1968. Michael was not born until 1973. In the early stages of the marriage they lived in a bedsitter and with Mr Hurst's father before obtaining their present council home. In 1969, however, he discovered that his wife had been going out with other men and a number of serious arguments ensued. She in turn accused him, falsely at first, of unfaithfulness and eventually he did go out for several months with another woman. The situation continued for a number of years until finally he threatened his wife with divorce. She ignored the threat and in 1975 he left and went to live with his mother. Through daily visits to the children he discovered that his wife had been leaving them alone at night for long periods. He took them to live with him, until eventually his wife left the house and they were able to return there together. He and his wife then obtained a formal separation and he was awarded custody of the children. In 1977 he was divorced on grounds of her adultery. Later that year, whilst paying an electricity bill, he met Carole. They saw one another regularly and within a few months began living together; in December 1977 they were married.

Carole Hurst was born in Sheffield in 1941 and has two older sisters and a younger brother. At the age of six she fell from a children's slide and fractured her skull, which resulted in one year's absence from school. Her father, a steelworker, died when she was eleven. At fifteen she left school and took a job in a laundry and at the age of eighteen met her first husband at a dance. They were married six months later, in 1963, and went to live in a council house before their first child, Diane, was born the following year. Their first son, Mark, was born in 1966 followed by Ivan in 1968. At first she and her husband, who worked on public transport, were very happy together until, shortly after Ivan was born, she discovered that he was having an affair with another woman. They separated soon afterwards and she went to live with her mother, taking the children with her. The following year they were divorced on grounds of his adultery. She then lived in council houses in various parts of the city, finding life a financial and emotional struggle. She was introduced by a mutual friend to a single man, a salesman. They were married in 1972. From the outset her husband only worked sporadically and took to beating both herself and the children, whom he found very difficult to cope with. She eventually reported his behaviour to the NSPCC; as a result the children were placed in care and her husband was sent to prison for eight months. On his return in 1974 the family were reunited but before long the violence started again and once more the children were taken into care. Shortly afterwards she left him, obtained a council maisonette, and was subsequently reunited with the children. She was divorced in 1976. She met a divorced man at the end of 1975 and about a year later she became pregnant. The man had no desire to remarry, but in early 1977 she had a miscarriage. In July of 1977 she met Mr Hurst and in the September she and the children moved into his house. She and Mr Hurst were married later that year.

The Hutchinsons

Roger Hutchinson (41; divorced) *Susan Hutchinson* (29; divorced)

Mr and Mrs Hutchinson were married in 1978, after living together for several months. They have four children by Mrs Hutchinson's first marriage, Nicholas (11), Robert (9), Nina (8) and Patricia (7). Mr Hutchinson, a labourer who was unemployed for most of the study, has two children by his first marriage, Patrick (15) and Katherine (13), both of whom live with their mother. The Hutchinsons live on a council estate on the northern edge of Sheffield.

Roger Hutchinson was born in 1937 near to the place where he now lives and has both an older brother and an older sister. His father, now retired, was a miner, and having little interest in school, he too went into the pits at the age of fifteen. In his early twenties he was engaged to a German girl for a short time but this was later broken off and he was twenty-six when he met his first wife, who was seven years younger than himself. Whilst they were engaged she became pregnant. Influenced by her parents they broke off the engagement for a while, but were eventually married in 1963, before their son, Patrick, was born. For a while they lived with his parents-in-law before renting a cottage of their own. The following year they had a son, Keith, who died at an early age, the victim of a 'cot death'. In 1965 they had a daughter, Katherine, and soon afterwards moved to a new council house, which involved them in bigger financial commitments. His wife then started work and obtained a well-paid job with the post office; she began spending her money independently. One day in 1972 he returned from work and his wife announced that she intended leaving him; she had, in fact, already arranged to move with the children to another house. When she had gone he found himself left with considerable rent arrears and an empty bank account, as his wife had drawn out all their savings. There were also outstanding gas and electricity bills. Living alone he began to worry and neglect himself; he was also sleeping badly. One day he collapsed at work. Shortly afterwards a friend offered him a caravan to live in. After a while the man, who was a subcontractor, employed him as an odd-job man on a site in Wales. For the next few years he took casual jobs in various parts of the country. He tried to see his children whilst on weekend visits but found that he missed them badly. He then returned to the Sheffield area where, homeless, he slept rough in graveyards and derelict buildings. On a few occasions he was picked up by the police. He was helped by a social worker, who found him a small flat; he then obtained a job, his divorce was finalised and he began to 'get back on his feet'. In 1977 he met Susan, whose mother and ex-husband he had known for some time. They quickly grew very attached to one another and he got on well with her children. They were married in 1978 after living together for several months.

Susan Hutchinson was born on the north side of Sheffield in 1949; her father is a labourer and she has one older sister, two younger brothers and four younger sisters, including twins. Until she was three years old her family lived with grandparents before moving into a separate house where they enjoyed a period of relative affluence and were, she recalls, the first family in the street to have a television. Though intelligent she had no wish to pass the eleven plus, having seen the effects which this had had on her sister, who for a while came to look down on her parents. Nevertheless, she enjoyed secondary school, leaving at fifteen to take a shorthand and typing course at technical college, before obtaining a job as an office junior. At the end of 1965 she met her first husband. The following year she became pregnant and they were married immediately. She was aged sixteen and her husband nineteen. They lived at first, and unsuccessfully, with both sets of parents before getting a council house a few months prior to the birth of their first child, Nicholas, early in 1967. Her husband enjoyed looking after the baby and eventually ceased working in order to devote himself to it full-time. He was never in permanent employment again during their marriage. In 1968 they had another son, Robert, followed by a daughter, Nina, in 1969. By now her husband had started drinking heavily and had taken to beating her. Life became a terrible financial struggle, made worse by her husband's refusal to claim social security. He then had an affair with a neighbour's daughter, who became pregnant and had an abortion. In 1971 Mrs Hutchinson had her fourth child, Patricia, and not long afterwards she and her husband were legally separated, but for some time continued to live together in the same house. He was eventually taken to prison for non-payment of maintenance. She and the children then moved to another council house on their own. But early in 1974, after a casual affair at a party, she became pregnant. She did not know who the father was and was unable to look after the baby herself; consequently, when she was born, the baby, Sandra, went to live with Mrs Hutchinson's younger sister, with whom she has remained ever since. Mrs Hutchinson was divorced in 1974 on the grounds of her husband's cruelty and at about the same time she began living with an unmarried man aged twenty-two. She was not interested in marriage and after a while began to see the adverse effects which the relationship was having on her children. After about a year she and the man separated. She was then introduced by her mother to Roger, a figure who appears to have enjoyed something of a popular reputation in the area. They immediately found that they had much in common. In 1977 they began living together and were married the following year.

The Johnsons

Derek Johnson (44; divorced) *Lilian Johnson* (33; divorced)

Mr and Dr Johnson have been married for seven years and lived together for one before that. They have two children, Michael (12) by Dr Johnson's first marriage and a daughter of their own, Jessica (5). Mr Johnson has three children by his first marriage, Alice (21), a nurse living in Sheffield who lived with the family for a while after her father remarried, along with Catherine (19) and Peter (17) who live with their mother in London. Mr Johnson is a sales manager with a large organisation and his wife is a general practitioner. For most of the study period they lived in their own Victorian semi-detached house near the centre of the city, before in late 1978, going to work for a three-year period in Nigeria.

Derek Johnson, whose father was a printer, was born in London, of young parents (both under twenty) in 1934 and has one younger sister. As evacuees during the war they were moved to various parts of the country and he suffered, he recalls, from a badly interrupted education. However he passed the eleven plus and attended grammar school, going on to take the newly introduced A level examinations before taking a temporary job in a garage prior to national service. It was whilst working there that he met his first wife. They courted for the next two years and were married when he came out of the army, aged just twenty-one. He then took a job in the organisation and methods department of a large company and their first child, Alice, was born in 1957, whilst he and his wife were living with his parents-in-law. They then rented a house of their own and had a second child, Catherine, in 1959 followed by Peter in 1961. In 1960 he had obtained a job in Coventry, a city which he disliked intensely, and after only two years the family moved back to London. In 1964 at about the same time as the death of his father the marriage 'started to come apart at the seams'. He believes that the problems stemmed from the fact that the relationship with his wife was no longer a 'challenge'. In 1965 he began working for a computer firm which posted him to Birmingham for a short period of six weeks; this eventually extended to three years, which provided him and his wife with an opportunity to separate 'without appearing to do so'. He began seeing less of his wife, staying in Birmingham at weekends, but he was able to keep up fairly regular contact with the children. At this time he had a number of relationships with other women in Birmingham before, in 1968, moving with his firm to Sheffield. The following year his wife asked him for a divorce, which he had not thought seriously about before, and this was finalised within a few months on the grounds of his adultery.

Early in 1970, whilst still in Sheffield, he was introduced to Lilian; they began living together soon after and the next year they were married in an Anglican church in Sheffield, with both of their former spouses present among the guests. Since they were married his work has continually involved travelling away from the city, commuting to Leeds, Staffordshire and London. In 1973 he and his wife had a daughter, Jessica, and the following year moved into their present home.

Lilian Johnson, an illegitimate child, was born in Kent in 1945. The first nine months of her life were spent in a home before she was adopted by a couple living in Wembley who subsequently also had a son of their own. Her mother emigrated to Canada and she never had any contact with her. Though her parents were not Roman Catholic she attended a convent school up to the age of nine, when the family moved to Kent. At about thirteen she 'got very religious' and was confirmed into the Church of England. Her parents' marriage at that time, however, she describes as 'very rocky' and, as the elder child, she was often brought into the problems they had. After re-sitting A levels she realised a long-standing ambition and obtained a place at Sheffield University to study medicine. It was there, at the start of the second year, that she became pregnant to a fellow student, a Greek Cypriot. Unsuccessfully they sought an abortion and were eventually married in 1966. Meanwhile, she was concerned to keep up with her course work and make arrangements for the baby. She struggled through her examinations taking re-sits just one month after their son, Michael, was born. In the marriage too there were problems, with rows over the baby in whom her husband had little interest. She soon realised that the marriage could not possibly work out and so in 1968, after two years together, she and her husband separated. After completing her finals the following year she broke down physically and mentally under the strain and was forced to find foster parents for Michael whilst she completed her pre-registration work. It was at this time that she met Derek, with whom she began living soon after. She was divorced in 1971 and remarried later that year, taking Michael to live with her once again. In 1972 they were joined by Alice, her husband's fourteen-year-old daughter by the first marriage, who was having trouble with her own mother. Dr Johnson and Alice also experienced numerous difficulties, which she believes her husband tried little to alleviate. In 1973 they had a daughter, Jessica and two years later Alice began training as a nurse in Sheffield and moved into her own accommodation, leaving them once again as a family of four.

The Kennedys

Barry Kennedy (45; widowed) *Ann Kennedy* (28; previously unmarried)

Mr and Mrs Kennedy have been married for seven years and have four children by Mr Kennedy's first marriage, Brian (18), a craft apprentice who now lives in London, Edward (16), Victor (13) and Katherine (8) as well as their own daughter Angela (4). Mr Kennedy is a senior civil servant and they live in a large detached Victorian house on the south side of the city.

Barry Kennedy was born in Richmond in 1935 and has one sister, who is two years older. As a child he lived in various places in the home counties and at seven was sent to a boarding school in Cornwall. He later went to public schools in North Wales and Dorset. When he was thirteen his mother died after a long illness; his father became 'something of a recluse' for several years but subsequently remarried in the late 1950s. At eighteen Mr Kennedy entered the army for national service and was posted to Germany and the Far East before going to Cambridge to read Classics. On graduating he worked first for an electronics company in London and then for a large chemical concern in Manchester. Later he moved to Sheffield and worked in computing for a few years before taking up his present post in 1971.

He met his first wife in 1958 and they married six months later. Soon afterwards she became pregnant and their first son, Brian, was born the following year. Edward followed fifteen months later and Victor some three years after that. Their daughter, Katherine, was born in 1969. For some years Mr Kennedy's first wife had suffered from severe headaches and after lengthy tests migraine was diagnosed; in 1971 in sudden and tragic circumstances she died of a brain haemorrhage. Mr Kennedy was left to cope with four children and a large house.

Ann Kennedy, whose parents were Czechoslovakian refugees, was born in a refugee camp in Lincolnshire. She has one older sister. At the age of four she moved to Sheffield to live with an aunt, as her parents had separated. Her father moved to the south of England but four years later he took a laboratory job in a Sheffield steelworks and her parents were reconciled, though they are now retired and once again living separately. She failed the eleven plus and was sent to a private day school in the city. At sixteen she moved to a technical school where she took O and A levels. She decided to go into the theatre but found it difficult to obtain a place at drama school. In 1969 she was offered a theatre studentship in Sheffield, where she worked for nine months before going to work in an

Edinburgh theatre for almost a year. She returned to live with her parents and auditioned once again for drama school and in the meantime took a part-time job looking after a two-year-old girl, the youngest of four children. The children's mother was Mr Kennedy's first wife. Two months later she died suddenly and Mr Kennedy, who had, until that time, never met his daughter's part-time nanny, contacted her as he was in desperate need of help with the children.

Despite the circumstances and an eighteen-year age difference, a close relationship quickly developed between the two, which was matched by the children's affection for their nanny. Within two months Mr Kennedy proposed to her and she accepted; they were married the same autumn amid much parental and familial opposition. The Kennedys entered the study after a talk given on the research project at a local college. A member of the audience was a friend of Mrs Kennedy and, following a reference to the problems of contacting stepfamilies, was able to introduce her to us. Mr and Mrs Kennedy readily agreed to take part in the study.

The Morgans

Brian Morgan (36; divorced) *Mary Morgan* (33; divorced)

Mr and Mrs Morgan have been married for five years. They have three children, Kathy (11), Deborah (10) and Ian (8) by a relationship which Mrs Morgan had after her first marriage ended, as well as a son of their own, Keith (3). In addition Mrs Morgan's thirteen-year-old sister, Evelyn, has lived with them since her mother disappeared in 1976. Mr Morgan's son Alan (9) by his first marriage lives with his mother. Mr Morgan is a lorry driver and the family live in a council house on the north-west side of the city. Mr and Mrs Morgan withdrew from the study after the first interview.

Brian Morgan, who has one older sister, was born in Sheffield in 1942, near to where he currently lives. His father, who is now dead, was a chargehand in a local steelworks and his mother worked in riding stables. At the age of fifteen he left school and took a job in a steel-rolling mill, where he worked up to the age of twenty-one when he became a lorry driver. He met his first wife in 1959 and they were eventually married in 1966, when he was twenty-four. Their engagement he describes as 'on and off' and there were regular separations and reconciliations. On getting married they went to live in rented accommodation and after three years had a son, Alan. Shortly afterwards they began to have serious arguments and his wife objected both to his job which often entailed being away from home at night and to his preoccupation at weekends with his hobby of restoring old cars. Eventually his wife started seeing another man for 'driving lessons' and then he too began an extra-marital relationship, which lasted for three years. In 1969 he and his wife were separated and after a failed attempt at reconciliation, were divorced in 1971 on the grounds of his adultery. After the separation he lived for various periods, alone, with another woman and also with his mother. In the autumn of 1973 he met Mary and they were married soon afterwards.

Mary Morgan was born in the centre of Sheffield in 1944 and is the second oldest of nine children. She recalls a 'rough' up-bringing and 'couldn't wait to get away from home'. As a teenager she had numerous family responsibilities thrust upon her. Her father, who was a salesman, is now dead and her mother's whereabouts are not known to her. On leaving school she took a job as a nanny with a family in Sheffield and at the age of nineteen met her first husband, a soldier. They were married two years later in 1966. The marriage lasted just two weeks; her husband left for a posting in Aden and they were never reunited. In 1971 they were divorced. Soon after the separation, however, she met another man with whom she lived for seven years and to whom she had three children, Kathy, Deborah and Ian. Their relationship was on the point of breaking up when, in 1973, she met Mr Morgan. They were married in the same year and had a son of their own, Keith, in 1975. The following year Mrs Morgan's mother disappeared and her younger sister, Evelyn, then came to live with them.

The Moseleys

Graham Moseley (40; divorced) *Marian Moseley* (44; divorced)

Mr and Mrs Moseley were married in 1977, after living together for two years. They have four children by Mrs Moseley's second marriage, William (17), Karen (16), Tina (14) and Leslie (12). Mrs Moseley also has two sons by her first marriage, Martin (25) who is married and Graham (24) who lives alone. Mr Moseley is a bus driver and his wife drives a garage delivery van. They live in a council house on a large estate in the city.

Graham Moseley was born on the southern outskirts of Sheffield in 1938 and has one younger sister. His father, now retired, was a miner and he recalls being 'brought up fairly strict Methodist'. At the age of fifteen he left school and became an apprentice mechanic before entering the army for two years of national service. He then returned to his former job; following a back injury he moved into the offices. He met his first wife at their local chapel when he was about fifteen. They knew each other for some time before deciding to marry but then had to wait for a house to become available. They were married in 1962, when he was twenty-four. At first his wife wanted to have children but she became increasingly involved with her job at the Coal Board and they did not start a family. In 1970 they moved into a new bungalow of their own; he too began to get involved in his job, working long hours at night and at weekends. His wife objected to this. He started to suffer with migraine headaches; one day, after an attack, he had to come home from work in the afternoon and discovered his wife with another man. He subsequently learned that she had been having affairs for some time. During this period he became increasingly friendly with Marian, who was employed by the same firm. Her marriage was also going through difficulties. For some time he and his wife continued to live together, each leading separate lives; they discussed divorce, but she was reluctant to go ahead with it. After Marian and her husband had separated, however, he moved in with her and the children and at the same time took a job as a bus driver. A few months later his wife suggested that they begin divorce proceedings. These were finalised, on the grounds of his adultery, in 1977, and he and Marian were married later that year.

Marian Moseley was born in Sheffield in 1934 and up to the age of fourteen was looked after by her grandparents, who lived in a village in North Derbyshire. She has one brother four years younger than herself. At fourteen she left school and worked in a draper's shop for two years before becoming a window dresser in a large department store. During this period she met her first husband, who was a grocery boy, and they were married in 1953, when she was eighteen. Early the following year they had a son, Martin, and the next year they had Graham. Life was a financial struggle at the time and to supplement her husband's income she did a variety of cleaning jobs. They had frequent rows, however, which she attributes to their mutual lack of maturity. Eventually, in the face of strong opposition from her parents, she decided to leave her husband. Her father would not let her stay in his house and she was forced to find a bed-sitter, where, living alone, her physical and mental condition deteriorated badly. The children remained with their father and she began going out with another man, Geoff, who she subsequently started living with. From the start the relationship was far from equal and she soon found herself burdened with financial responsibilities, as he frequently took time off work. Shortly after they began living together she had a miscarriage and then contracted pneumonia. In 1959 her husband divorced her on grounds of adultery, keeping the children, and the following year she and Geoff were married. Their first son, William, was born in the summer of 1961 and they had a daughter, Karen, the next year, after which they managed to buy a small house of their own. Two years later they had another daughter, Tina, and at about the same time began buying a new house. After another two year interval they had a fourth child, Leslie. Shortly afterwards her husband was involved in an industrial accident and had to have a leg amputated. After a long period he returned to work and she then discovered that he was having an affair with a neighbour. They continued living together under very strained circumstances and eventually, when he received compensation for his accident, they moved into a bungalow. For a while her husband used the money to buy a succession of extravagant cars. They then bought a small grocery shop but this was not a success and before long they were in debt; eventually they were declared bankrupt. It was at this time that she first learned of her husband's unstable mental state. From the shop they moved to a council house; her husband refused to work for a time and their financial problems worsened. She took various jobs before they transferred to a council house in Sheffield. Her husband was then made redundant but refused to look for another job and retreated more and more into his own private world. As her problems at home grew worse she became increasingly friendly with Mr Moseley, who she had met through her work; his marriage was also in trouble. In 1975 she finally convinced her husband that it would be better if he left her and the children. At the time of the break-up she went away on holiday with a friend and Mr Moseley moved in to stay with the children; on her return they all began living together as a family. In 1977 she was divorced and soon after she and Mr Moseley were married.

The Parkers

Nicholas Parker (34; divorced); *Maureen Parker* (28; previously unmarried)

Dr and Mrs Parker have been married for seven years and have four children. Amy (16) and Emily (11) are respectively Dr Parker's stepdaughter and daughter by his first marriage, whilst Ben (3) and Lionel (6 months) are children of the present marriage. Dr Parker is a research psychologist and until the birth of her first child Mrs Parker was a social worker. The family live in their own semi-detached house in a suburb on the south-western edge of the city; they entered the study in October 1977, in response to a poster advertising a proposed discussion group for stepparents.

Nicholas Parker was born in Banbury in 1944, where his family been evacuated during the war. His father, a journalist, and mother, who has written a number of plays and novels, were separated when he was thirteen. He has a brother and a sister. On leaving school at the age of sixteen he took a course in shorthand and typing before going to work for a local newspaper in Folkestone. After about a year he moved to a newspaper in London. After another year, however, he became disillusioned with journalism and left to do a variety of odd jobs, saving up in the meantime in order to finance a trip to India. On returning in 1964 he worked in a bookshop and then with the Universities Central Council on Admissions. About this time he met Janet, later to become his first wife, and they began living together. Janet already had a daughter, Amy, aged three, by a previous marriage. He then began working for A levels, with a view to going on to university, and in the spring of the following year, 1966, he and Janet were married. He obtained a place at Cardiff University, where they moved, and in November had a daughter, Emily. He settled down to his studies in psychology and, enjoying his work, grew steadily happier although his wife found it difficult to adjust to the change in lifestyle. In 1967 she decided to return to London. Initially conceived as a temporary measure, this soon became a permanent arrangement. For the next two years he visited the children regularly and had them for weekends and holidays. Meanwhile, although this was not clear at the time, his wife's mental condition began to deteriorate and she was later diagnosed as schizophrenic. Then in 1969, after completing his finals, he met Maureen, an undergraduate at Bangor. Their relationship developed over the next two years, during which time he found that visits to the children became easier and more frequent. In October 1971 he was divorced after three years' separation and the following month he and Maureen were married. On completing his doctoral research in 1972 he obtained his present job and they moved to Sheffield.

Maureen Parker was born in Manchester in 1950 and is the eldest child in a Catholic family of six children; her father is a sales representative in a textile company. Up to the age of eleven she attended a Catholic preparatory school before passing the eleven plus and going on to grammar school. After taking A levels she went to university at Bangor to read English and Psychology. Although she was homesick at first she eventually began to enjoy herself socially; she did however suffer with certain emotional problems. At the end of her first year as a student she met Nicholas and over the next two years became increasingly involved with him and his children. On graduating in 1971 she and Nicholas were married and lived in Cardiff, where he continued his postgraduate studies and she went into social work. In 1971 they moved to Sheffield. During these early years, she recalls, the marriage was a stormy one; she and her partner had little self-control at times in a relationship which she describes as one of 'destructive honesty'. As a social worker she had a very heavy case-load and often found it difficult to avoid unburdening herself of this to her husband. Nicholas's first wife's mental state was becoming more unstable and it appeared increasingly likely that Amy and Emily might have to come to live with them. They did in fact, just three weeks after Maureen had given birth to a baby boy, Ben, in 1975. At first she found the responsibility of three children totally exhausting, but by dint of careful attention to routine she and Nicholas eventually managed to overcome many of the practical problems. They also found that their own relationship steadily got better and in 1978 they had another child of their own, Lionel.

The Parkes

Stephen Parkes (41; divorced) *Mavis Parkes* (41; divorced)

Mr and Mrs Parkes were married in 1977, after living together for six years. They have six children, by Mrs Parkes's first marriage, Alec (17), Diane (16), Tina (15), Geoffrey (13), Patricia (11), and Linda (10). Mrs Parkes's eldest daughter, Ann, who was living with the family when the study began, was married in June 1978. Mr Parkes has three children by his first marriage, Jackie (20), who is married, along with Melanie (14) and Alan (13) who live with their mother. Mr and Mrs Parkes both work at the same hospital, he as an engineer and she as an auxiliary. The family live in a council house in the east side of Sheffield.

Stephen Parkes was born in Sheffield in 1937 and has a brother and two sisters, one of whom is now living in Spain. At the age of fifteen he left school and had a variety of jobs in heavy engineering before entering the RAF for two years of national service. He describes these as 'the best years of my life' – a time when he was able to develop his wide interests in sport. Shortly before joining the forces he met his first wife and they courted whilst he was away. In 1957, aged twenty-one, he was married and he and his wife went to live near Rotherham. They had three children: Jackie in 1958, Melanie in 1964 and Alan the following year. Looking back Mr Parkes believes that he was 'never happy' in his first marriage; life was dull and unstimulating. In the early 1970s he met Mavis, who was working in a pub, and 'rightly or wrongly we started seeing each other'. After a while he decided to leave his wife. He and Mavis then made a number of unsuccessful attempts at living together, but, in poor accommodation and without their respective children, both found it very difficult. Eventually, in 1971, they settled in a small house and gradually Mavis's children came to live with them. Unfortunately his wife would not agree to a divorce and he had to wait for a five-year period of separation to elapse before it could be finalised; during this time she made it increasingly difficult for him to see their children. Eventually, in 1977, he and Mavis were able to marry.

Mavis Parkes was born in Sheffield in 1937; she is the second youngest girl in a family of eighteen. Her father, who is still alive, was a miner and later worked in engineering. Her mother, she recalls, was 'a big strong family woman' and the family was an extremely happy one, despite her father's strong domination. As the fifteenth child, though, she feels she may have been slightly neglected. At the age of sixteen she left home for a period of two years; she then returned to her parents and took a job as a bus conductress, which was how she met her first husband, a driver. They were married six months later, in 1955, when she was eighteen. At twenty-one she had her first baby, Ann, followed by Alec, two years later. Ann was delighted with her baby brother and after that she found that the children always welcomed each new arrival in the family. In the early 1960s her husband switched from bus driving to lorry driving, where he worked on 'tramping', picking up loads and delivering them from one part of the country to another; he was often away for two or three weeks at a time. They continued to have children, though she feels that throughout their marriage her husband 'never made any attempt to shoulder his responsibilities'. After her youngest child, Linda, was born she was sterilised. As Linda grew up her mother experienced a 'frightening' need to get out of the house; she was taking various tablets and was told by a friend – 'you've got to get out or you'll crack up'. She then found a job as part-time barmaid in a nearby pub, which was where she met Mr Parkes. This gave her the opportunity to leave her husband which she had been looking for. They separated in 1970 and for a short time the children, who had been left with their father, were taken into care before she and Mr Parkes found a house where they could all live. She was divorced in 1973 and has since maintained a good relationship with her first husband, who now lives in Wales. She and Mr Parkes were married in 1977.

The Pelhams

Michael Pelham (37; divorced) *Ann Pelham* (34; divorced)

Mr and Mrs Pelham were married in 1978, though they had lived together for eight years before that. They have one daughter, Vicky (12) by Mrs Pelham's first marriage and a child of their own, Robert (5). Jonathan (10), Mr Pelham's son by his first marriage, lives with his mother and Mark (10), Mrs Pelham's son by her first marriage, lives with his father. Mr Pelham is a self-employed jewellery dealer and the family live in a new detached house on a housing estate to the south of Sheffield.

Michael Pelham, an only child, was born in Retford in 1941. After the war his parents moved to Sheffield where he passed the eleven plus and attended grammar school. When he had taken O and A levels he went to work in his father's grocery shop. After four years, personality clashes between him and his father led him to take a job as a salesman with a jewellery firm. With the exception of a short period when he ran his own grocery store, he has worked as a salesman ever since and is now self-employed. Mr Pelham met his first wife in 1962 and they were married two years later, moving to Lancashire where he took a sales job with a confectionary company. After four years they had a son, Jonathan. Mr Pelham recalls the early years of their marriage as happy ones when they were both involved in establishing themselves materially and financially. Later they began to drift apart. Then in a period between jobs he began driving a taxi in the evenings and it was at the taxi firm that he met Ann, his second wife. They began going out together until their respective partners learned of the relationship; all four then met to discuss what should be done and it was decided that they should separate. Mr Pelham was divorced relatively quickly, in 1971, after admitting adultery, and Ann some time later, after two years' separation.

Ann Pelham, who has one younger brother, was born in Leeds in 1943. Her father, a policeman, was pensioned out of the force after being disabled during the war. When she was nine the family moved to Morecambe. Mrs Pelham recalls being very close to her mother as a child but states that she 'never had much of a relationship' with her father. Her parents argued frequently and were in fact separated for three years in the early 1970s. She passed the eleven plus and attended grammar school but left whilst in the fifth form as a result of pressure from her father who wanted her to get a job. Soon afterwards, however, she decided to leave home and took a secretarial course at college before obtaining a job as a secretary in a hospital. It was there that she met her first husband; she was eighteen at the time and they were married three years later. For a short while the couple lived in a flat before buying their own bungalow. Within five months of the wedding she became pregnant and their daughter Vicky was born in 1966. Two years after that they had a son, Mark. Looking back Mrs Pelham believes that she 'expected too much' of the marriage and that in marrying at an early age she became bored. After a while therefore she started going out with a woman friend in the evenings and also took a part-time job, where she met Mr Pelham. At first her husband wanted to try to 'patch up' the marriage but she had resolved to separate from him. When she found a job and began looking for a flat, however, the problems of coping with two children became increasingly apparent and her first husband suggested that Mark should go and live for a while with his grandparents. The arrangement was to have been a temporary one but soon became permanent with Mark's father later obtaining custody of him. To Mrs Pelham's considerable regret, her two children have lived with separate parents ever since. Soon afterwards Mr and Mrs Pelham and Vicky set up home together. Three years later they had a son, Robert, and at about the same time moved to Sheffield where they bought a grocery store. They worked hard at the business but it failed to prosper and Mr Pelham decided to go back to work as a jewellery salesman. This he did with considerable success; the shop was sold and the family moved house. In 1978, motivated largely by legal and financial considerations, they decided to marry after living together for eight years.

The Priors

Keith Prior (34; widowed) *Audrey Prior* (34; previously unmarried)

Mr and Mrs Prior have been married for twelve years. They have two children, Karen (18) and Tracey (15) by Mr Prior's first marriage, and one child of their own, Susan (11). Mr Prior is a bus driver and his wife works part-time in a school canteen. They live in their own large terraced house in a comfortable suburb of the city.

Mr Prior's father died when he was six weeks old; he and his elder brother were then supported by their mother, who had a grocery shop. He met his first wife at a youth club and when, in 1960, she became pregnant they were married; he was seventeen, she sixteen. A second daughter was born three years later. About this time he joined the army and spent several years stationed abroad, during which the marriage deteriorated. In 1965 his wife and children joined him in Cyprus in a final attempt to save the marriage. The attempt failed and plans were made for them to return to Britain, but his wife suddenly contracted a rare throat infection and died on the same day. Mr Prior left the army and returned to Sheffield. His mother looked after the children and he began drinking heavily. After about four months, he remembers, 'I just woke up one morning and thought, "You've got two kids to think about, you've lost your wife, stop feeling so bloody sorry for yourself and start thinking about your children".'

Mrs Prior was born in Darnall in 1945. She remembers a 'happy childhood', though as an only child, believes she was 'rather spoilt'. Leaving school at fifteen she took an office job and worked for various Sheffield firms before meeting Mr Prior in 1965. They first met in a pub about six months after Mr Prior's return to England and whilst they saw each other regularly, marriage plans had not been discussed when Mrs Prior found she was pregnant. Mr Prior's mother reacted strongly to the news but eventually agreed with their decision to marry and in fact they lived with her until the baby was born. They then bought a small house, before fortuitously inheriting their present home from Mr Prior's grandmother.

The Priors came into the study via a letter passed on to them by their local doctor (also a stepparent), and during the period 1977–9 were experiencing difficulties with their eldest daughter, who eventually became pregnant and left to get married.

The Roberts

Eric Roberts (36; divorced) *Mary Roberts* (41; divorced)

Mr and Mrs Roberts were married in 1978, after living together for nine months. They have three children, Jackie (17), Adrian (14) and Martin (11) by Mrs Roberts's first marriage. Mr Roberts's two daughters by his first marriage, Alison (8) and Annabelle (6), live with their mother in Cambridgeshire. Mr Roberts is a service manager with a machine tools firm and Mrs Roberts runs a general store in the village where they live, some eight miles to the south-west of the city.

Eric Roberts was born in the Barnsley area in 1943 and was adopted when he was three weeks old. His adoptive parents already had five daughters and subsequently had four sons of their own. The family lived in Sheffield but when he was about two years old they emigrated to Canada, returning several years later. He left school at fifteen and became an apprentice toolmaker, before deciding to join the RAF. He remained in the forces for nine years, four of which he spent in Singapore. In the late 1960s he became increasingly concerned about civilian job opportunities and decided to leave. He had also met a girl from Sheffield and they were engaged to be married. They were married in 1969 and he took a job with a local engineering firm; he made rapid progress, taking various management qualifications. However, he and his wife had problems from the outset. After only a few weeks she became pregnant, then caught German measles and had to have an abortion. Buying their own house was also a financial struggle. When their first daughter, Alison, was born Mr Roberts became very possessive towards her – 'I got it into my head . . . that my eldest girl is the only thing I know which belongs to me, flesh and blood.' Consequently, he believes, he tried to exclude his wife from the relationship with Alison. Then when their second daughter, Annabelle, was born two years later his wife accused him of neglecting her in favour of the older child and they began quarrelling regularly over the children. After a while he developed a friendship with a neighbour, Mary, and over a period of time, as part of a circle of friends, they grew closer to one another. Eventually he and his wife decided to obtain a legal separation; he was transferred to London by his firm and for nine months he spent only weekends at home. When he returned to Sheffield in 1975 he went to live with his father and he and his wife divorced in 1978. Meanwhile, a year earlier, he and Mary, who had by now separated from her husband, had decided to live with one another. In 1978 they were married.

Mary Roberts, an only child, was born in Sheffield in 1937. Her father was a steelworker and she had grandparents and a number of aunts living nearby. At the age of fifteen she left school and began working in the office of a local store, before moving on to an office job with an engineering firm. When she was seventeen she met her first husband at a youth club; they were engaged two years later and married in 1958. She says of the marriage – 'I was married to him for twenty years but I was only married to him about a month when I decided I'd made a mistake.' In 1961, they had a daughter, Jackie; when she was three Adrian was born and four years later they had Martin. Throughout this period she and her husband had regular arguments, which often resulted in him being violent towards her. She mentioned this to no one, however, until 1974 when she finally told her parents. At about this time she became increasingly friendly with Mr Roberts, a neighbour whom she had met socially. The arguments grew worse and in 1976 she and her husband separated. She began to think about opening a small business of her own, and after a difficult but finally successful search for suitable premises she and Mr Roberts began living together in June 1977. Her divorce was finalised early the following year and they were married soon afterwards.

The Smithsons

James Smithson (33; divorced) *Mary Smithson* (32; divorced)

Mr and Mrs Smithson were married in 1978, after living together for almost eighteen months. They have five children, Alice (12), and Lesley (7) by Mr Smithson's first marriage and Robert (11), Linda (9) and Martin (6) by Mrs Smithson's first marriage. Mr Smithson is transport manager at a fruit and vegetable warehouse and the family live in their own modern semi-detached house on the north side of Sheffield.

James Smithson was born in Sheffield in 1944 and has three brothers; another brother was drowned at the age of six. On leaving school he began an apprenticeship as a mechanic but left after a year to join the army. He met his first wife, a student nurse, whilst home on leave and they wanted to get married fairly soon afterwards. Her father objected to this however and they decided that the only means by which they would be able to marry was for her to get pregnant, which she subsequently did. To the opposition of both sets of parents they were married in 1965, when he was twenty-one. Their first daughter, Alice, was born the following year and the family lived in married quarters in Germany, where he had been posted. From the early days of their mariage his wife had little interest in the home or in housework and he found that many of the domestic tasks fell to him. She began suffering from migraine and stayed in bed for long periods; eventually, arrangements had to be made for him to take the baby into work with him. His wife continued to suffer intermittently with the same problem until, after about six years, he was posted to the Persian Gulf and she returned to England, to married quarters in Leicester. On his return, nine months later, they moved to Colchester. Their second daughter, Lesley, was born whilst they were living there and for a while they were joined by his wife's sister, who had separated from her husband. Shortly afterwards he bought himself out of the army and the family moved back to Sheffield, where he began working as a lorry driver and his wife took a job in a night club. However, their problems grew worse and after a while his wife disappeared for two days, before returning to announce that she was leaving him. Mr Smithson then took the children and returned to live with his parents; his mother looked after the girls but eventually she began to object to this and Alice and Lesley had to go back to their mother for a while. They then came back to Mr Smithson, after which he obtained legal custody. After about eighteen months he met a single woman, bought another house and they began living together. She got on very badly with the children and after two years together they separated. Luckily, promotion at work gave him greater freedom of movement during the day and he found that, with some outside help, he could cope with the children successfully. It was through his work that he met Mary, in 1976; a few months later she and her three children moved in with him. The following year his divorce was finalised after five years' separation and early in 1978 he and Mary were married.

Mary Smithson, whose father was a miner, was born in a village near Barnsley in 1946; she is the youngest of three children. On leaving school she worked at first in a clothing factory before taking a job as a bus conductress. It was at work that she met her first husband, a bus driver. At the age of nineteen she became pregnant and was married in 1967. She then had three children, Robert, Linda and Martin, in fairly quick succession. From the start of their marriage her husband was always violently possessive towards her, however, and she found that she was rarely able to get out or meet other people. In 1976 she had a miscarriage and during the spell in hospital which followed she thought deeply about her life and her marriage. Shortly afterwards she decided to leave her husband. She then took a part-time job in a supermarket and whilst at work she met Mr Smithson. Their relationship developed quickly – some of her friends, she recalls, suggested that she might be 'jumping out of the frying pan into the fire' – but she decided first to go back to her parents and then to go with the children to live with Mr Smithson and his two daughters. They found that all five children got on well together. In 1976 her husband divorced her on grounds of adultery, enabling her to remarry early in the following year.

The Snows

David Snow (27; divorced) Hazel Snow (33; divorced)

Mr and Mrs Snow were married in 1978 after living together for four years. They have a daughter, Susan (10) by Mrs Snow's first marriage and two children of their own, Rachel (1) and Leslie, who was born in January 1979. Mr Snow is a transport manager in a local bakery and the family live in their own semi-detached house in an area to the south of Sheffield.

David Snow was born near to his present home in 1951 and is the second oldest of eight children. His father, who is disabled by silicosis, worked in a variety of jobs connected with cement-making. As a boy he attended the local village school before passing the eleven plus and going on to grammar school. He confesses to having hated school and left at fifteen to be an apprentice vehicle mechanic with a local bakery. He progressed to garage foreman, transport foreman and then transport manager with the same firm. At the age of eighteen he began courting his first wife, whom he had already known for some time; they were married in 1973 when she was twenty-two and he twenty-three. During the period of their engagement he had already met Hazel, later to become his second wife and who was at the time still married to and living with her husband. They saw each other regularly and Hazel was opposed to him marrying. In fact the relationship with her continued after the wedding and they met regularly at the flat which he and his wife had bought. Within a year their relationship was discovered and he and his wife separated from one another. He then went to live with Hazel, who had by that time also separated from her husband. In 1976 he was divorced on grounds of adultery.

Hazel Snow was born in 1945 on the north side of Sheffield. Her father, who is now retired, was a miner and she has one younger brother. She recalls having a fairly strict upbringing and 'muddling through' her junior and secondary schools. On leaving she began training as a nursery nurse but left before qualifying. She then took a job as a telephonist, which she enjoyed and stayed at for four years. Meanwhile, whilst still at college she had met her first husband, a warehouseman. Looking back she believes she married him in order to get away from home. After their wedding, in 1966, the couple went to live in a new council house and the following year they had a daughter, Susan. When Susan was about four years old her mother began to get very depressed and went to her doctor for help; he advised her to go back to work and so she began working as a van driver. Relations with her husband steadily deteriorated and she found herself enjoying the attention of the men she met through her work, including Mr Snow. In 1974 her husband decided to leave her and Susan. Shortly afterwards Mr Snow separated from his wife and moved in with her. She was divorced in 1975, on the grounds of her husband's adultery.

In 1977 they had a daughter, and were married the following year. Then in the spring of 1978 they bought their own house in Mr Snow's home village. Their second child, Leslie, was born at the beginning of 1979.

The Stanleys

Leslie Stanley (42; divorced) *Valerie Stanley* (28; previously unmarried)

Mr and Mrs Stanley have been married for two years and lived together for almost five years before that. They have five children, Colin (16), Nicholas (12) and John (10) by Mr Stanley's first marriage, along with Jennifer (11), Mrs Stanley's illegitimate daughter, and a child of their own, Sally (1). Mr Stanley's oldest daughter by his first marriage, Julie (18), is currently living with her mother. The family were contacted following an article in a local newspaper, concerning a cat which they had found. When the study began they were living in a council house in a village some ten miles to the east of Sheffield. At this time Mr Stanley, a fitter and heavy goods vehicle driver, was unemployed. In 1978 however they moved to Coventry, his home town, where he found another job.

Leslie Stanley, an only child, was born in Coventry in 1936. He was evacuated during the Second World War and shortly afterwards his mother became seriously ill and he was sent to boarding school in Shropshire for two years. He went to a commercial school until he was fifteen, followed by one year at technical college. At sixteen he became an apprentice electrician and two years later joined the RAF on national service. He remained in the forces for twelve years, firstly as a radar mechanic and then working on transport. At the age of twenty-one, whilst home on leave in Coventry, he met his first wife and they were married two years later in 1959, when she was seventeen. They lived at first in married quarters, where their first child, Julie, was born in 1969, and the following year they were posted to Germany, where they had a son, Colin. Their second boy, Nicholas, was born during the last week of Mr Stanley's RAF service in 1966, by which time they had been posted to Sheffield and bought their own house in the area. Mr Stanley then took a variety of lorry- and coach-driving jobs. They had a fourth child, John, in 1968 and at about the same time took out a second mortgage in order to buy a coach of their own, which they ran as a business in their spare time. A number of arguments began to occur, 'mainly over money', and in the summer of 1971 his wife left him and the children and went away with a lover to a town in the south of England. He followed her there but was unable to persuade her to return and was left to look after the children himself. He also began divorce proceedings but these proved complex and lengthy and were not finalised until 1976. Looking after four children was difficult and he was forced to give up work; after several months he was introduced by a mutual friend to Valerie, a single woman, with a child of her own who was in need of a job. She came to live with him and the children as a housekeeper and nanny but within only a few weeks a sexual relationship had developed between them and they began living together with all five children as a family. They were married in 1976.

Valerie Stanley was born in a mining village on the east side of

Sheffield in 1950 and has one older sister and a younger brother. When she was eleven months old her parents separated and from then up to the age of five she and her sister lived with her father and his cohabitee (her mother had been pregnant with her younger son when she separated). In fact it was not until Valerie was eight years old that she met her mother again. At the age of five however her father separated from his cohabitee and she went to live for the next ten years with her grandparents. On leaving school at fifteen she took a job in Rotherham where she lived for a while with an aunt and uncle. One year later she became pregnant and since there was no likelihood of her marrying the father she was thrown out and had to move in with another aunt. After her daughter, Jennifer, was born in 1967, she lived in a mother and baby home before being introduced by a social worker to a couple in Barnsley with whom she lived for some time. From there she went to live with her own mother, who had had six more children after remarrying. She was soon thrown out by her stepfather, however, and lodged first with an unmarried mother and then with a couple and their small child in a caravan. When the sexual relationship which had developed between her and the man was discovered she tried to commit suicide and had to spend some time in hospital. She was eighteen and her daughter was taken into care. Her mother took her in for a short time but she was soon thrown out again. For a while she lived in a bed-sitter in Doncaster and then stayed with her sister before going to Lincoln with her lover from the caravan. There they both took jobs on public transport and she wanted to try to get her daughter out of care. He did not want to and before long they separated and she returned to her home village where she managed to find a small house to rent. When she was twenty-one she succeeded in getting her daughter back. It was then that she was introduced to Mr Stanley and they began living together in 1971. They were married in 1976 and shortly afterwards Julie, her husband's eldest daughter, returned after some problems, to live with her mother. In 1977 they had a daughter of their own, Sally.

The Shannons

Arthur Shannon (55; widowed) *Marjorie Shannon* (52; widowed)

Dr and Mrs Shannon have been married for eight years and have three children, Colin (20) and Geoffrey (18) by Dr Shannon's first marriage and Heather (20) by Mrs Shannon's first marriage. At the time of their entry into the study Colin and Heather were university students. Dr Shannon is a coal scientist and his wife works in a hospital laboratory; the family live in their own modern detached house in a quiet suburb on the south side of the city. They came into the study in 1977 after writing in reply to a newspaper item on the research project.

Arthur Shannon was born in London in 1923 and his parents, both primary school teachers, were active members of the Congregational church. He left school for Queen Mary College, London, and was evacuated immediately to Cambridge where he took a two-year wartime degree in Botany. His first job after graduation was as a soil scientist with an army operational research group; he spent two years working with this group in Germany during the late 1940s. Whilst there he met his first wife, a Welsh woman who worked for the YMCA. In the early 1950s he took a job with the Coal Board in Sheffield, where he obtained a PhD in Geology. He was married in 1955. Their first son, Colin, was born in 1957 and they had a second child, Geoffrey, two years later. Soon after he moved to Sheffield he became a regular attender at a local Free church. In 1969, whilst on holiday in Cornwall, in sudden and tragic circumstances, his wife was killed when she fell from a cliff while they were out walking. He was faced with the responsibility of looking after the two boys as well as the demands of his work. He had a succession of housekeepers, most of whom were not very successful. In 1970 he was introduced by a friend to Marjorie, a widow with a daughter. Their relationship developed very quickly and they decided to marry. As he puts it, 'We had a lot of interests in common, we seemed well-suited to each other and it just seemed that, in fact, I'd made a better match on the second occasion than I had on the first.'

Marjorie Shannon, the elder of two sisters, was born in Barnsley in 1926. Her father was a policeman. She won a scholarship to the local high school and took the School Certificate. To her regret, her full-time education finished at the age of sixteen, largely due to lack of finance. She very much wanted a 'good and interesting job'; marriage, at the time, was low on her list of priorities and she began working at the laboratory of a local dairy. Before long she moved on to a laboratory job in a hospital; she has been doing this kind of work ever since. She met her first husband at work just after the war and they were married in 1948, when she was twenty-two. For a brief spell she gave up work but soon returned and, at first, had no desire to have children. Meanwhile her husband started work in an insurance company. Their daughter, Heather, was born after they had been married for eight years; she gave up her job at this point. In 1965 her husband died suddenly from a coronary thrombosis. She then decided to go back to work but was surprised to find herself relatively isolated as a widow. Nevertheless she was quite content with life as a single parent and had no financial worries. Then, in 1970, she met Dr Shannon and they were married later that year.

The Thompsons

Barry Thompson (34; divorced) Sarah Thompson (32; divorced)

Mr and Mrs Thompson were married in 1977 after living together for over a year. They have one son, Jeremy (8) by Mrs Thompson's first marriage. Mr Thompson's daughter, Tracey (11) by his first marriage is currently living with her mother. Mr Thompson is a youth and community worker and Mrs Thompson is a clerical assistant. The family live in their own terraced house on the south-western side of the city.

Barry Thompson, the younger of two brothers, was born in Sheffield in 1944, one month after his father had been killed in action. About two years later his mother remarried and had two more children, a boy and a girl. For a time his stepfather had his own painting and decorating business, but this went bankrupt, forcing the family to move to a poorer area of the city. He failed the eleven plus and left school at fifteen to work in a butcher's shop but he only stayed there six months before joining the decorating firm for which his stepfather then worked. The firm allowed him to attend college on a day release basis, but in 1961, aged seventeen years and a half, he joined the RAF, attracted largely by the prospects of mountaineering and parachuting. The following year he was engaged to a girl from Sheffield whom he had met whilst at college. During the next two years he travelled extensively to Cyprus, Turkey and Singapore and the wedding, which had been arranged for 1964, had to be postponed as he had contracted a venereal disease. They were married in 1965 and he was actually recalled from honeymoon to Aden; on his return, six months later, he and his wife went to live in married quarters near Bath. After a further six months there – the longest period they ever spent together during the marriage, he was sent to Zambia, followed by periods in various other parts of the world. Their daughter Tracey was born in 1967, although his wife did not really want a baby. During his short breaks at home Mr Thompson found that he spent most of his time away from his wife, drinking and playing cards. His marriage and military career, in fact, came to an end at about the same time when in 1970, six months before he was due to leave the RAF, his wife left him and returned to Sheffield. For some time he hoped for a reconciliation, but this was never achieved. Whilst still in the RAF however he had been involved in a variety of youth work schemes and had also taken some O levels; when he left he decided to enrol in a youth and community work course at Liverpool. When he had completed this he began living with a female student from the same course, starting divorce proceedings which were finalised in 1975. He and the girl then left college and moved to London. About the same time he met Sarah at a folk club and after a few months he began living with her, along with her son Jeremy. They were married towards the end of the following year, 1977.

Sarah Thompson was born in Sheffield in 1946 and is the eldest of three sisters. She passed the eleven plus examination and attended a local grammar school, leaving at sixteen with three O levels to take a job as a window dresser. At the age of nineteen she was engaged to a man one year older than herself, who worked in local government. In 1967 they were married and went to live at first in a council flat. Later they bought a new house on an estate to the north of Sheffield where they lived for about four years; during this time they had a son, Jeremy, born in 1970. She gave up her job when the baby was born and found that her husband would frequently spend his evenings with his friends, leaving her at home. At the time, however, this did not trouble her unduly and, despite occasional feelings of dissatisfaction with the marriage, she never confronted her husband. Then, at the beginning of 1975, they moved to a large new bungalow near Rotherham; shortly afterwards her husband became increasingly moody and, she suspected, was worrying over financial matters. In order to give him time to sort things out she and Jeremy returned to her parents for a while. Two weeks later she arranged to meet her husband whereupon he informed her that he was having an affair with a woman whom he had met whilst away on business. After much discussion he decided, for the sake of their son, to try to make a success of the marriage and forget the other woman. They were reunited but he soon began seeing the woman again and she eventually moved from her home in the Midlands to Sheffield. In the summer of 1975 she and her husband finally separated and she returned with Jeremy to her parents. In November, after the sale of the bungalow had been completed and at about the same time that she first met Barry, she bought a small terraced house quite close to her parents' home. In 1976 she and Barry began living together and the following year, after her divorce was finalised, they were married. In 1978 they bought another, slightly larger, house nearby.

The Thornleighs

Keith Thornleigh (37; divorced) *Vera Thornleigh* (36; divorced)

Mr and Mrs Thornleigh were married in 1978, after having lived together for three years. They have three sons, Nigel (18), Nicholas (15) and Neil (14) from Mrs Thornleigh's first marriage. Mr Thornleigh's children, Alan (13), Jennifer (12) and Jacqueline (6) by his first marriage live with their mother. Mr Thornleigh is a lorry driver and his wife works as an import supervisor with a Sheffield firm. The family live in their own semi-detached house in an older suburb on the east side of Sheffield.

Keith Thornleigh was born in Sheffield in 1941 and spent part of his childhood in Scotland before returning to the city when he was fourteen. He has one older brother and a sister who died in childhood. On leaving school he took an apprenticeship in the steelworks where his father also worked, before going on the railway, where he stayed for twelve years. With the demise of steam his interest waned and he left to work as a lorry driver; nevertheless he was, and still is, a keen railway enthusiast. When he was seventeen he met his first wife at a wedding reception and they were married three years later in 1961. At first they lived with his mother before getting a house of their own. Financially life was a struggle; as an apprentice his earnings were low and they had considerable commitments. Their first child, Alan, was born in 1964, followed by Jennifer in 1966; then, in 1972, Jacqueline was born. For some time before this his wife had begun to find it difficult to meet people and became increasingly reliant upon her family, refusing to go out except to her mother's. Eventually he began to 'act like a single bloke again' and made a new set of friends. His wife seemed quite content with this but after a time he could not stand the atmosphere at home any longer. In 1975, whilst still living in the same house, they obtained a legal separation and some six months later he left and moved into lodgings on his own. Shortly afterwards, whilst at work, he met Vera, later to become his second wife, who was at the time still living with her husband. They began going out together. At first he saw his children regularly but then his former wife began to make this increasingly difficult and he subsequently saw them hardly at all. In 1975 he was divorced after two years' separation. Towards the end of 1974 Vera and her husband separated and early the following year they began living together.

Vera Thornleigh was born in Norfolk in 1942. Her father was in the RAF and the family, including her younger brother and sister, were posted to various stations. She passed the eleven plus and attended grammar school in Louth before moving to Sheffield where she took O levels and then went on to a secretarial course. Her first job was as a secretary with the Electricity Board. She describes her family life as being 'not very close' and attributes her early marriage to a desire to get away from home. When she was seventeen she met her first husband who worked in a local butcher's shop. Within a year she became pregnant and they were married. Their son, Nigel, was born in 1960. Shortly afterwards she went back to work in order to save for the deposit on a house. Then two years later she had her second son, Nicholas, and Neil was born just one year later. Family life at the time was dominated, she recalls, by 'work and children and housework'. When the youngest boy was around four years old she started working again part-time, but after some ten years of marriage she and her husband began to drift apart and she started to go out in the evenings with some women friends from work. As she now puts it, 'I'd got my own money 'cos I was working, I'd found my independence and that was the end, we just had nothing in common.' When her relationship with Keith was discovered her husband reacted violently and for a short period of time she left home, first to live with friends and then, briefly and unsuccessfully, to share a flat with Keith. After about a month she could stand it no longer and returned to her husband, sought Marriage Guidance and tried to re-establish their marriage. Their reconciliation failed and early in 1975 her husband left. Soon afterwards, following discussions with the boys, Keith moved in with them. Later the same year she was divorced on the grounds of adultery. Three years later, in 1978, after some indecision, they were married.

The Turners

Paul Turner (31; divorced) *Carol Turner* (29; divorced)

Mr and Mrs Turner married in 1977 and have one son, Trevor (9) by Mr Turner's first marriage and a child of their own, Geoffrey, born in July 1978. Mr Turner is a railway worker and until the birth of their son his wife worked in the civil service. They live in their own semi-detached house in an area to the north of Sheffield.

Paul Turner is the eldest of five children and was brought up in the area of Sheffield where he now lives. His father was a miner, who, he recalls, drank heavily and the family were often in financial difficulties – a problem which seriously affected the relationship between his parents. When he was fourteen the family were evicted from their home, the children went into care and his father and mother separated. He was sent to a children's home in West

Yorkshire but soon absconded to live with an aunt in Sheffield, where he stayed until he was twenty. During that time his mother, who had by now divorced, regained custody of his sister and three brothers. However, he moved to a town in Lancashire to work in a sports store, the kind of work he had been doing since leaving school at fifteen. He met his first wife in Lancashire. She had a small daughter, Linda, and at that time was awaiting a divorce. After about one year in Lancashire they moved back to Sheffield. Mr Turner took a job on the railway and they began living together. In 1969 they had a son, Trevor, and were married soon after. The marriage seemed, however, 'to go downhill from the start' and they had problems finding suitable accommodation. After three years of marriage they separated; both children stayed with their mother at first but after a few months she handed over responsibility for Trevor to Mr Turner, who has had custody of him ever since. By this time Mr Turner had gone to live with his mother and she subsequently looked after Trevor. After his separation he became a trainee manager in a Sheffield nightclub and was later made manager of a club in Harrogate; his mother continued to look after Trevor and he came home at weekends or when he was free. During this time he sought a reconciliation with his wife but they were never actually reunited and were eventually divorced in 1975 after two years' separation. Then, after a company takeover, Mr Turner found himself redundant and went back to his former railway job; it allowed him more time with his son which was important because he had become increasingly worried about his mother's desire and ability to look after Trevor all of the time. He also began to involve himself heavily in a variety of local organisations – drama groups, parent-teacher associations, etc., before meeting his second wife in a pub in Sheffield in 1976. The relationship developed quickly and within a year they were married.

Carol Turner was born in 1950 in a village in north Derbyshire. She has one older sister and an older brother. After leaving school at sixteen she took a secretarial course before obtaining her first job as a secretary in the Department of Employment. Subsequently she had a variety of jobs in the civil service, gaining steady promotion. At eighteen she met her first husband, an engineering worker, whom she married three years later, in 1970. They bought their own semi-detached house, spent a considerable amount of time and money modernising it and, at first, enjoyed a full social life. But after about two years they had begun having serious and protracted arguments; attempts at talking over the problem between themselves failed and eventually, in 1973, she returned to live with her parents. Two months later, however, an opportunity arose to share a flat with an old friend in Sheffield; she applied for a transfer and moved. In 1975 she was divorced after two years separation.

The Vickers

Alan Vickers (44; divorced) *Maureen Vickers* (46; divorced)

Mr and Mrs Vickers were married in 1977, after living together for two years. They have three children, Nigel (16) and Colin (11) by Mr Vickers's first marriage and Eileen (18) by Mrs Vickers's first marriage. Mr Vickers has been married twice before and Mrs Vickers also has a married daughter, Margaret (24) by her first marriage. Mr Vickers is director of his own interior decoration business and his wife is a teacher; they live in a modern detached house on the western edge of the city.

Alan Vickers, an only child, was born in Somerset in 1934. At the time his father was a greengrocer's assistant, but later began his own engineering firm. His mother was ill for long periods and died when he was thirteen, shortly after they had moved to Sheffield. He was sent to public school and his father married about three years later. From the outset he and his stepmother had problems, which became so bad that he stayed in hotels whilst on visits home during school vacations. On leaving school he went into national service and then joined his father's business. In 1957 he met his first wife and three years later they were married amidst great opposition from his father, who did not attend the wedding and who insisted that he leave the family business forthwith. Two years after their marriage in 1960 he and his wife had a son, Nigel, who was followed by Colin in 1967. His wife, who had not been in paid employment since they married, decided around this time to take in student lodgers and she eventually had an affair with one of them. He began divorce proceedings and the student left for South Africa. For two years Mr Vickers lived alone with the boys and had a succession of nannies, before complications set in over the divorce. Then for a while he and his wife were reconciled but after just over six months they were separated again. New divorce proceedings were started and after two years' separation they were divorced in 1973. The following year he met and married his second wife. Within three months of the wedding however, she announced that she was leaving, largely Mr Vickers believes, because she thought she was a 'glorified housekeeper', and found it difficult to cope with the children. The marriage, he feels, was 'a serious mistake that neither of us should have made'. Once again he began divorce proceedings. Whilst these were under way he met Maureen through an item placed in the personal column of the local newspaper. In 1975 they bought a house and began living together; he was divorced in 1977 and soon afterwards they were remarried.

Maureen Vickers, an only child, was born in the east end of Sheffield in 1932. Her father was a clerk of works. At the age of eleven she passed the scholarship and attended the local grammar school, where she passed School Certificate before going on to a one year secretarial course. When she was seventeen she met her first husband, who was in the navy. In 1951 they were married and during the next few years moved around to various naval bases. After only one year of marriage her husband had an affair with another woman, but when the woman in question emigrated they were reconciled. About the same time she became pregnant. After their first daughter, Margaret, was born they continued to move about, sometimes together, sometimes apart; whilst stationed abroad her husband had other affairs. She hoped that things might change when he decided to leave the navy. They returned to Sheffield and their second daughter, Eileen, was born there in 1960, but as the children were growing up the marriage went 'from bad to worse'; her husband began drinking heavily and they were often short of money. When Eileen was five Mrs Vickers took a job as an unqualified teacher. She saw less and less of her husband and eventually decided to go to teacher training college. After qualifying she took a permanent job; her husband's drinking increased and he spent little time at home. Eventually she told him to leave, which he did, only to return shortly afterwards. She grew more determined to separate from her husband and decided to buy herself a small house, but he persuaded her to let him live there too and they finally bought the house jointly. When their eldest daughter was married she and her husband finally decided to separate and she was able to buy his share of the house. In 1974 they were divorced on the grounds of his adultery. A little time later she met Mr Vickers through a personal column advertisement which she had placed. They decided to buy a new house, began living together, and were married in 1977.

The Walkers

Philip Walker (46; divorced) *Elizabeth Walker* (46; widowed)

Mr and Mrs Walker were married in 1977. They have one daughter Patricia (19) by Mr Walker's first marriage living with them as well as Mrs Walker's married daughter, Jackie (17) and her husband Dennis (18) and their six-month-old baby, Jason. In addition Mr

Walker has a son, Donald (16) and a daughter Carole (14) by his first marriage, both of whom are living with their mother. Mrs Walker also has two married sons, Alan (28) and Peter (26). Mr and Mrs Walker both work for the same engineering firm, where he is a production controller and she a machinist. They live in a council house about a mile from the city centre.

Philip Walker, whose father was a clerk, was born in Sheffield in 1932 and has two older sisters. He attended school in the city and worked in a steelworks for two years before entering the RAF on national service; at about this time his father retired and his family moved out to a village in the Peak District. Shortly after coming out of the RAF he met his first wife. Two years later, in 1954, they were married and began living in Sheffield, where he took a job with his present firm. Within a few years they bought their own house and in 1959 their first child, Patricia, was born, followed by Donald in 1962 and Carole in 1964. After the children were born he and his wife began to spend less and less time together socially and each would stay in the house to babysit whilst the other went out in the evenings. He became worried about the marriage but was unsure what to do about it. Then one day in 1973 he came home to find that his wife and children had left. He and his wife were then legally separated and at one point he made an unsuccessful attempt to gain custody of Patricia. Mr Walker quickly adjusted to life alone, indulging himself in his main hobby of fishing, making home improvements and going out regularly. He had no thought of remarrying. When the house was eventually sold he moved into a flat. He had already known Elizabeth, later to become his second wife, for some time through his work. When her husband died she invited him to come to live in her council house as a paying lodger; he applied for a sub-tenancy and moved in. As time went on he and Elizabeth became closer to one another and after his divorce in 1976 they decided to get married. At about the same time they were joined by his daughter, Patricia, who had been having problems in her relationship with her mother.

Elizabeth Walker was born in Sheffield in 1932 and has two older brothers and a younger sister. Her father, who died in 1976, worked for fifty years in a steel-rolling mill. She recalls a strict upbringing with 'a certain amount of tears and a certain amount of laughter'. At the age of fourteen she left school and two years later met her first husband, who was some eight years older than herself. Four months later they were engaged. At the time, she believes, marriage was the only means by which she could get away from home. Married in 1950, she had her first son, Alan, the following year and Peter two years after that. Their daughter, Jackie, was born in 1961. Shortly afterwards her husband, who was a general handyman in the building trade, became ill with bronchitis and then asthma. Each year his illness grew worse and he had long periods off work, which he disliked intensely. Financially, life became a struggle and in about 1965 she took a job with a local engineering firm. Meanwhile their two sons were married. Her husband's condition deteriorated steadily and he died in 1974. The following year her daughter Jackie became pregnant and was married, giving birth to a son, Jason, later that year. Jackie, her husband and the baby all continued to live with her. In 1977 she and Mr Walker, who had been living in her house as a lodger, were married. By this time they had also been joined by Mr Walker's daughter, Patricia. Before long they found that a strain was being placed on their marriage by the presence of their respective children. In the summer of 1977 therefore they asked all four to leave. Since then they have enjoyed the opportunity to be on their own for the first time.

The Wickhams

John Wickham (38; divorced) Ann Wickham (29; divorced)

Mr and Mrs Wickham have been married for one year and have four children, Jennifer (15), Lesley (14), Mark (10) and Liam (8) by Mrs Wickham's first marriage. Mr Wickham's three children by his first marriage, Brian, Michael and Julie, live with their mother, who has remarried. Mr Wickham works for a haulage firm and the family live in an old terraced council house in the centre of the city. Mr and Mrs Wickham withdrew from the study after the first interview.

John Wickham was born in Sheffield in 1940 and has three younger sisters and three younger brothers. He claims to have 'never hit if off' with his father and refers to his early childhood experiences in a 'rough school, rough neighbourhood'. At the age of fifteen he left school and took a job at a local bakery, after which he had a succession of unskilled jobs with various firms. He was nineteen when he met his first wife and they courted for three years before getting married in 1962. She was eighteen years old and pregnant at the time. For the first six months of the marriage they lived with his wife's parents before buying a small house of their own in which they had two more children. After they had been married some ten years his wife started having an affair with another man and the marriage broke up soon afterwards. He was then seriously injured in a car accident and was confined to a wheelchair for several months. On his recovery he returned to live with his mother and began to enjoy a full social life. Then in 1976, as a joke, his mother suggested that he reply to a personal column item in a local newspaper. He did this and as a result came into contact with Mrs Wickham.

Ann Wickham was born in Sheffield in 1945 and has one older sister and two younger brothers. Her father was a welder and for most of her childhood the family lived on a large council estate on the north side of the city. When she was fifteen she left school and took a job at a local food factory, which was where she met her first husband. They were the same age. When she was seventeen she became pregnant and her parents reluctantly allowed her to marry. The couple lived at first with her husband's widowed mother, where their first child, Jennifer, was born. The following year they had Lesley. Already, however, her husband had begun to absent himself for long periods and was unable to hold a job for long. After a while they moved into a privately rented house but he continued to disappear unexpectedly and then came back without explanation. He also began to drink heavily and as a result she developed nervous problems. He was then sent to prison for stealing a car and during his sentence she began living with another man. They were reunited upon his release, however, and she had two more children, Mark and Liam. He also spent another short spell in gaol. In 1974 they were separated again and were divorced in 1977. During the period of separation she had an illegitimate child who was immediately taken into care and then adopted. Living alone she became increasingly lonely and depressed and eventually decided to place an item in the personal column of a local newspaper. As a result she began seeing Mr Wickham regularly. They then started living together and were married when their respective divorces were finalised in 1977.

The Worthings

Ian Worthing (30; divorced) *Diane Worthing* (25; divorced)

Mr and Mrs Worthing were married in 1978 after living together for eighteen months. They have two children by Mrs Worthing's first marriage, Sarah (5) and Susan (3) and a son of their own, David, born in 1978. Mr Worthing is a policeman and the family live in their own semi-detached house in a suburb on the south side of the city.

Ian Worthing was born in Sheffield in 1949; his parents ran a small leather goods shop and he has one younger brother. He passed the thirteen plus examination and went to technical college but left school at sixteen without any qualifications to take a job as a trainee draughtsman. He stayed there for almost five years before joining the police force on his twenty-first birthday. He was sixteen when he met his first wife and they were married three years later. At first they rented a house near to his parents' home before they bought a house of their own in 1970. His wife continued to work and neither of them had any desire to have children. After a few years he went into plain-clothes CID work and it was then that the marriage began to deteriorate; he worked long hours and began drinking heavily with other policemen whilst off-duty. The police, he recalls, 'totally changed my personality' and he became 'totally committed to work . . . it just never entered my head to go home'. His wife began seeing another man and in 1976, after about a year, they separated. He returned to his mother's and then straightaway joined a ten-week police training course, during which he again drank very heavily. When he returned he met Diane, a new barmaid at his local pub. At the time she was still living with her husband but their marriage was in difficulties. They began going out together and a few months later Diane's husband left and they were able to see each other more regularly. His drinking decreased; by the end of the year they were virtually living together and the following spring, 1977, they bought their present house. Later that year he was divorced on the grounds of adultery. In February of 1978 they had a son, David, and shortly afterwards they were married.

Diane Worthing was born on a council estate in Sheffield in 1953 and comes from a large family of two brothers and three sisters, of which she is the second oldest. She failed the eleven plus and attended a local girls's secondary school, where she had a successful career, taking O levels and becoming head girl. However, she failed her A levels and took a clerical job with the regional hospital board. Within five months she became pregnant; she had known her boyfriend, who was one year older, from the age of fifteen. They were married towards the end of 1972 and had a daughter, Sarah, the following spring. Her husband was a painter and decorator and they lived at first with her married sister. After about a year they were able to buy their own small terraced house and she took a secretarial job at the university whilst her sister looked after Sarah during the day. In 1974 a failure in contraception resulted in her becoming pregnant again and when her second daughter, Susan, was born, she gave up her job. It was about this time, she recalls, that 'the rot really started to set in'. Her husband did very little around the house and had very little involvement with the children. Rows would occur, during which he became violent, and there were problems over money, which he managed very badly. Then in 1976 she took a job as a barmaid to supplement their income and it was here that she met Mr Worthing. Relations with her husband became worse and in the summer of that year she took the children away on holiday by herself. On her return the situation did not improve and a few months later he left and returned to live with his parents. She and Mr Worthing began spending more and more time together and eventually, early the following year, bought a house and began living together permanently as a family. She was divorced in 1977 on grounds of her adultery and was awarded custody of the children.

Appendix 2
Aides mémoires

As we saw in Chapter 3, there was not even an *aide mémoire* for the first interview, in which individual life histories were collected. For the second interview, sets of questions were tailored to fit the previous marital and parental experience of each of our respondents, whilst for the third, certain questions only applied to stepsibling families, or families with children of the remarriage.

Second interview

Previously married

Could we begin by going back to some of the things we talked about last time? If it's OK with you I'd like to ask a few more questions about your previous marriage(s). . . .

1 First of all, would you say there are any ways in which your previous marriage(s) differed from this one? – How about the ways in which you and your ex- shared out the household tasks, e.g. cooking the meals, doing the washing up, tidying the house, washing and ironing clothes, doing the shopping, decorating, gardening, car, . . . etc?
2 What about in your present marriage . . . ?
3 Do you tend to organise your finances differently now, when compared with your previous marriage(s)?
* For those with custody of child(ren) after divorce or bereavement:
  Has the fact that you had to look after the children/——— yourself after the separation/bereavement had any effect on the kind of things you do around the house in this marriage?

Previously unmarried

Could we begin by going back to some of the things we talked about last time? I'd like to talk a bit about the time when you were still single.

1 Before you were married did you have much experience of looking after yourself? Had you lived away from your parents? Would you say you'd been a particularly independent person?
2 What were your views on marriage at this time?
3 Do you feel that in not being married before, you've adjusted to this marriage in a different way to your husband/wife?
4 Did you feel any different about the marriage because he/she was not a bachelor/spinster?
5 How did you feel about the fact that you were, to some extent, inheriting a ready-made family?
6 How did your family feel about your marriage? What about your friends . . . ?

Previously married

1 When your first marriage finally ended, what kind of feelings were you left with? Would you say that the experience of marriage breakdown/bereavement had any effect on your health? – Did you experience any of the following symptoms?
   (a) Serious weight change (gain or loss)
   (b) Sleeping difficulties
   (c) Beginning to drink, or drinking more heavily
   (d) Difficulties with concentration
   (e) Difficulties with work
   (f) Tendency to weep/cry unexpectedly
   (g) Tendency to become excessively tired
   (h) Tendency to neglect yourself. What sort of ways?
2 For the divorced
   Is it possible to say when you suffered from these symptoms? Was it –
   (a) During the marriage troubles, before your separation
   (b) At separation or just after
   (c) When the final decision was made to divorce
   (d) At the time of the divorce hearing/proceedings or just after
   (e) At any other time
   How long did the symptoms last?
3 For the bereaved
   Is it possible for you to say when you suffered from these symptoms? Was it –

(a) Immediately before your husband/wife's death
(b) Immediately after he/she died
(c) During the weeks/months which followed
How long did the symptoms last?

4 Did you come into contact with any of the following during the period of your divorce/separation?
(a) Solicitor
(b) Social worker
(c) Probation officer
(d) Education welfare officer (schools)
(e) Marriage guidance counsellor
(f) Supplementary benefits/social security
(g) Hospital social workers
(h) Clergyman, priest, minister
Did you find these people particularly helpful or unhelpful?

5 Looking back on it now, how would you sum up the whole experience of divorce/bereavement? – Does it, for example, seem very much different to you now than it did at the time?

Divorced parents without custody

1 Now that you are divorced and remarried how often do you see ————/your children?
2 Are you happy with that arrangement?
3 What access arrangements were made at the time of the divorce?
Were these formal or informal?
4 Do you feel they are reasonable?
5 Do you foresee any change in these arrangements?
6 When do you see ————/the children?
7 Do you ever see him/her/them at any other time – by chance or occasionally?
What about special occasions like birthdays, Christmas . . .?
8 Whereabouts do you normally see them?
9 What kinds of things do you do together?
10 Would you say————/the children are/is happy with this?
11 Are you happy with it?
12 Would you say the visits have had any particular effect on ————/the children, either in the past or now?
13 Does ————/Do your children have any contact with your stepchildren/————?
14 Could you possibly give me some idea of the amount of maintenance you pay for ————/your children? (Also ex-wife, if she's not remarried.) Do you feel this is reasonable?

Divorced parents with custody

1 Now that you are divorced how often does ————/your children see his/her/their father/mother?
2 Are you happy with this arrangement?
3 What access arrangements were made at the time of your divorce? Were these formal or informal?
4 Do you feel they are reasonable?
5 Can you foresee any change in these arrangements in the future?
6 When do the children/————see his/her father/mother?
7 Do they/———— ever see him/her at any other time – casually or occasionally?
What about special occasions like birthdays, Christmas . . .?
8 Whereabouts do they usually see each other?
9 What kinds of things do they do together?
10 Would you say the children/———— are/is happy with this?
11 Are you happy with it?
12 Would you say that the visits have had any particular effect on the children/———— – either in the past or now?
13 Do the children/———— have any contact with your parents?
14 How do your parents feel about this? How do you feel about it?
15 What sort of contact do they have with their new grandparents?
16 Do you know if the children/———— have much contact with your ex-husband/wife's parents. Do you feel it's important they should keep in touch?

Divorced/widowed parents with children from previous marriage(s)

1 What effects would you say your divorce/bereavement had on ————/your children?
2 Where you ever concerned about ————'s/their health?
3 Would you say the divorce/bereavement had any impact on the way they/———— got on at school? Did any teachers mention anything about this to you?
4 Do you think the divorce/bereavement affected their relationship with their friends?
* For the widowed
Do the children have much contact with your former husband/wife's parents?
5 Generally speaking, how well would you say the children have adjusted to your remarriage?
6 Again in general terms, how well equipped would you say children are to deal with situations like divorce/bereavement?

7 About what sort of age do you feel they can best cope with that sort of situation?
8 Could you offer any advice to a father/mother currently going through the experiences you went through?

All divorced/widowed persons

Could I ask you a little bit more about the rest of your family?
1 Whereabouts/how far away do your parents live?
2 How regularly do you see them? Can you remember precisely when you saw them last?
3 Do you tend to see them just on special occasions, or are they likely to drop in at any time? Do you tend to drop in on them?
4 Have you any brothers or sisters living in Sheffield – or anywhere else?
5 Do you see much of them? Whereabouts? Socially?
6 Did you notice any changes in your relationship with the rest of your family after/during your divorce/bereavement?
7 Have any other members of your family been divorced?
8 Can you remember when you last saw your ex-/late husband/wife's parents? How do you get on with them? Where do you tend to see them?
9 Do you see much of your new parents-in-law?
10 What about your neighbours – What sort of people live around here?
11 How friendly would you say you are with them?
12 Do you see them here or in their homes fairly regularly – say every day/every few days/about once a week/less than once a week . . . ?
13 Do you tend to help each other with anything – like babysitting, taking the children/picking them up from school, shopping . . . etc.?
14 How do you feel about your neighbours in general – would you prefer to see more or less of them/know them better . . .?
15 Is any of this particularly different to the kind of relationship you had with your neighbours in your previous marriage?
16 Do you know if any of your neighbours have been divorced/remarried/bereaved?
17 How about other people – would you say you had a large or small circle of friends?
18 How, in the main, did you get to know them?
19 Where do you tend to see them most – in your/their home(s) – or do you tend to go out somewhere together?

20 Are you a member of any type of club or organisation?
21 Was your circle of friends altered much as a result of your divorce/bereavement?
22 Are any of your friends divorced/widowed/remarried?

All previously unmarried persons

Could I ask you a little bit more about the rest of your family?
1 Whereabouts/how far away do your parents live?
2 How regularly do you see them? Can you remember precisely when you saw them last?
3 Do you tend to see them just on special occasions, or are they likely to drop in at any time? Do you tend to drop in on them?
4 Have you any brothers or sisters living in Sheffield – or anywhere else?
5 Do you see much of them? Whereabouts? Socially?
6 Did you notice any changes in your relationship with the rest of your family after your marriage?

* *Where spouse divorced*
7 Have any other members of your family been divorced?
8 Can you remember when you last saw your husband/wife's parents? How do you get on with them? Where do you tend to see them?

All persons

1 How much does your/your husband's job affect your family life? Do you/does he bring work home?
2 When you're not working/doing jobs round the house – how do you spend your free time?
3 Are there any particular things you like to do as a family? Has this changed at all over time?
4 What do you usually do for holidays?

Third interview

General

1 How important is it to you that you are a parent?
How much would you say it means to you?
What is it about having children that gives you most pleasure?

Do you ever wish you didn't have children?

2 There's a tendency to think that stepchildren have more eventful childhoods than children from unbroken families. How far do you agree with that?
Positive aspects of their experience?

Discipline

1 Who normally deals with ———/the children when he/she/they do something wrong?
2 What sorts of things do you particularly *not* like your children to do?
3 Do you and your husband/wife have the same opinions on this? Were you aware of his/her opinions before your remarriage? (Also, influence of non-custodial parent – where contact frequent.)
4 How do you usually punish ———/the children when they've done something they shouldn't? – smacking, withdrawal of affection/privileges, sending to bed, etc.
Do you feel that being a step-parent creates special discipline problems for you? How about your husband/wife?
5 Do you have any particular views on pocket money – how much, how often, who gives it, do the children have to do jobs for it, etc.?
6 Do you ever sit down with your husband/wife specifically to talk about the children/child management/parenthood. Often?

Intimate life

1 Children seem to vary a lot in the amount of intimacy/closeness they enjoy with their parents – how about yours, e.g. very affectionate, kissing, cuddling?
Are there any differences in this respect between you and your husband/wife?
2 Do you think the fact that you/he/she are/is (a) stepparent(s) has anything to do with this?
How did you react when you first got together as a family and you were coming into regular day-to-day contact with ———/the children for the first time?
(For non stepparent)
How did your husband/wife react when you first got together as a family and he/she was coming into regular day-to-day contact with ———/the children for the first time?
3 Families differ a lot in their attitudes to things like nakedness/

nudity in the home – seeing each other in the bath and so on – do you have any particular feelings about that?
Parents often worry about what sort of attitudes their children will have when they grow up – to subjects like sex, love, marriage. Do you feel your divorce/remarriage will have affected the children's attitudes in any way?
(For non-custodial parents)
How about as far as ——— is/are concerned?

Relations with non-custodial parent

1 Do the children's contacts with their father/mother have very much effect upon your family routine?
2 Do(es) ———/the children receive pocket money/gifts from his/her/their father/mother?
3 What about Christmas, birthdays, etc., (do(es) ———/the children receive special gifts/visits? How do(es) he/she/they feel about seeing his/her/their father/mother at these times?
4 Do(es) ———/the children ever talk about going to live with their father/mother? How do you see the future developing in that respect?

Step-sibling families

1 All children quarrel at times, would you say yours do more than average?
What sorts of things set them off?
2 What was it like when the two sets of stepchildren first met/started to live together?
3 Does the fact that they are stepbrothers/sisters affect the way they get on together?

Families with own child(ren)

1 How much difference has ——— made to your family life?

Concluding questions

1 When you look at ———/the children would you say he/she/they are getting on generally?

2 How about school? – any particular problems/successes? – reasons for this?
3 What about his/her/their health – how would you describe it?
4 Do you think ———/the children has/have any particular worries or problems?
How did you find out about these? Could you tell? Did he/she/they mention it first?
5 Could you tell me about ———'s/the children's friends – do(es) he/she/they make friends easily? What sort?
Are you worried about any of this?
Are any of his/her/their friends in a similar (family) position to themselves?
6 How do you see the children's lives developing from there, what are your aspirations for them for the future?
How would you like to see your family life in ten years time?

Notes

Chapter 1 **The theory and practice of remarriage**

1 Although it is possible to make a clear distinction between marriage and cohabitation in legal terms, because many cohabiting couples consider themselves as married and try to 'pass' as married wherever possible, our comments on remarried couples and remarriage generally also apply to cohabiting couples unless otherwise stated.

Chapter 2 **A natural history of the research project**

1 In the early stages, when David Clark visited some of the couples and explained the problems involved in contacting them, several were quick to suggest an appeal on local radio.
2 Cf. George and Wilding, 1972, p. 9.
3 We should note here, and with hindsight deplore, our methodological sexism in writing in the first instance to the men, when we were primarily interested at that stage in their wives.
4 For simplicity, our reply slip did not include a 'no children' category.
5 At the end of the first month, dismayed by our response rate and concerned lest otherwise interested persons should have overlooked the letter, we sent out reminders to all who had not replied, stating that even a negative response would be useful to us. This yielded a further handful of 'no's, but no one willing to take part, or even hear a little more about the research. We therefore decided that the cost of reminders (which also included s.a.e.s) could not be justified and the practice was discontinued.
6 See below pp. 34–5.
7 Many of the couples felt that it would also be worthwhile to hold joint interviews. We agreed but constraints of time prevented this. Nevertheless *ad hoc* conversations between David Clark and the couples often took place over a cup of tea or coffee when the interviews had been completed and these frequently proved a valuable source of additional insights.

8 Mrs Worthing, for example, explained to David Clark before the third interview that as a result of taking part in the study and discussing the issues further, she and her husband had decided to stop trying to conceal from neighbours and friends that they had both been married before.

Chapter 3 **The private troubles of the remarried**

1 In the interview quotations in this and subsequent chapters the following conventions apply:

. . . indicates a pause in the narrative;
(   ) indicates an omission from the narrative;
[   ] indicates an inclusion in the narrative to make the meaning clearer.

Bibliography

Acker, J. (1973), 'Women and social stratification: a case of intellectual sexism', *American Journal of Sociology*, vol. 78, no. 4, pp. 1–24.

Anderson, M. (1971), *Family Structure in Nineteenth Century Lancashire*, London, Cambridge University Press.

Askham, J. (1975), *Fertility and Deprivation*, London, Cambridge University Press.

Baker, W., Barrington, Eekelaar, J., Gibson, C., and Raikes, S. (1977), *The Matrimonial Jurisdiction of Registrars*, Oxford, SSRC Centre for Socio-Legal Studies, Wolfson College, Oxford.

Ball, D. W. (1970), 'The problematics of respectability', in Douglas, J. D. (ed.), *Deviance and Respectability*, New York, Basic Books, pp. 326–72.

Banks, J. A. (1956), *Prosperity and Parenthood*, London, Routledge & Kegan Paul.

Banks, O. (1976), *The Sociology of Education* (3rd edn), London, Batsford.

Becker, H. (1970), 'The relevance of life histories', in Denzin, N. K. (ed.), *Sociological Methods*, London, Butterworths, pp. 419–28.

Bell, C., and Newby, H. (1977), *Doing Sociological Research*, London, Allen & Unwin.

Berger, P. L. (1963), *Invitation to Sociology*, Harmondsworth, Penguin.

Berger, P. L. and Luckmann, T. (1971), *The Social Construction of Reality*, Harmondsworth, Penguin.

Berger, P. L., Berger, B. and Kellner, H. (1974), *The Homeless Mind*, Harmondsworth, Penguin.

Berger, P. L. and Kellner, H. (1977), 'Marriage and the construction of reality' in Berger, P. L., *Facing up to Modernity*, Harmondsworth, Penguin, pp. 27–47.

Bernard, J. (1971), *Remarriage*, New York, Russell & Russell.

Bernard, J. (1973), *The Future of Marriage*, Harmondsworth, Penguin.

Bertram, G. (1970), 'Methods of surveying categories of people presenting special problems or needs', *International Social Security Review*, vol. 23, no. 2.

Bohannan and Erikson (1978), 'Stepfathers: a success story?', *Psychology Today*.
Bott, E. (1971), *Family and Social Network*, rev. edn, London, Tavistock.
Bowerman, C. E. and Irish, D. P. (1962), 'Some relations of stepchildren to their parents', *Marriage and Family Living*, Vol. 24, pp. 113–21.
Brittan, A. (1977), *The Privatised World*, London, Routledge & Kegan Paul.
Burchinall, L. G. (1964), 'Characteristics of adolescents from unbroken, broken, and reconstituted families', *J. Marr. and the Fam.*, vol. 126, pp. 44–50.
Burgoyne, J. L. and Clark, D. (1980), 'Why get married again', *New Society*, Vol. 152, no. 913, 3 April 1980, pp. 12–14.
Burgoyne, J. L. and Clark, D. (1981), 'Family reconstitution: remarried couples and their children', in Family Research Committee (eds), *Families in Britain*, London, Routledge & Kegan Paul, pp. 286–302.
Busfield, J. and Paddon, M. (1977), *Thinking About Children*, London, Cambridge University Press.
Campaign for Justice in Divorce (1979), *An Even Better Way Out*, Wokingham, Kingdale Press.
Chester, R. (1971), 'Health and marriage breakdown: experience of a sample of divorced women', *Brit. J. of Preventative and Social Medicine*, vol. 25, no. 4, pp. 231–5.
Chester, R. (1976), 'Official statistics and family sociology', *J. Marriage and the Family*, vol. 38, no. 1, pp. 117–26.
Chester, R. (1977), 'Report on step-parent survey', *Woman's Own*, 26 February 1977.
Denzin, N. K. (1972), *The Research Act in Sociology*, London, Butterworth.
Douglas, J. W. B. (1964), *All our Future*, London, Peter Davies.
Duberman, L. (1975), *The Reconstituted Family*, Chicago, Nelson-Hall Publishers.
Dunnell, K. (1979), *Family Formation 1976*, London, HMSO.
Eekelaar, J. (1978), *Family Law and Social Policy*, London, Weidenfeld & Nicolson.
Eekelaar, J. and Clive, E. (1977), *Custody After Divorce*, Oxford, SSRC Centre for Socio-Legal Studies, Wolfson College.
Ennew, J. (1979), 'Oral Testimony as Text', Paper presented to BSA/SSRC Conference on Methodology and Techniques of Sociology, Lancaster, 1979.
Epstein, J. E. (1975), *Divorce: the American Experience*, London, Jonathan Cape.
Family Research Committee (ed.) (1981), *Families in Britain*, London, Routledge & Kegan Paul.
Fast, I. and Cain, A. C. (1966), 'The step-parent role', *Amer. J. of Orthopsychiatry*, vol. 36, pp. 485–91.
Ferri, E. (1976), *Growing up in a One-Parent Family*, London, National Foundation for Educational Research.
Finer Committee (1974), *Report of the Committee on One-Parent Families*, Chairman Finer, London, Cmnd 5629, HMSO.

Fletcher, R. (1975), *Marriage and the Family in Britain* (rev. edn), Harmondsworth, Penguin.
Garnsey, E. (1978), 'Women's work and theories of class stratification', *Sociology*, vol. 12, no. 2, May 1978, pp. 223–43.
George, V. and Wilding, P. (1972), *Motherless Families*, London, Routledge & Kegan Paul.
Goffman, E. (1968a), *Asylums*, Harmondsworth, Penguin.
Goffman, E. (1968b), *Stigma*, Harmondsworth, Penguin.
Goldstein, J., Freud, A. and Solnit, A. J. (1973), *Beyond the Best Interests of the Child*, New York, Free Press.
Goldthorpe, J. H., and Lockwood, D., Bechhofer, F. and Platt, J. (1969), *The Affluent Worker in the Class Structure*, London, Cambridge University Press.
Goldthorpe, J. H. and Hope, K. (1972), 'Occupational grading and occupational prestige', in Hope, K. (ed.), *The Analysis of Social Mobility*, Oxford, Clarendon Press, pp. 1–25.
Goode, W. J. (1956), *After Divorce*, Chicago, Free Press.
Gorer, G. (1973), *Sex and Marriage in England Today*, London, Panther.
Group for the Advancement of Psychiatry (1973), *Joys and Sorrows of Parenthood*, New York, Scribner.
Halmos, P. 1965), *The Faith of the Counsellors*, London, Constable.
Halmos, P. (1970), *The Personal Service Society*, London, Constable.
Hansard (1978), 'House of Lords Debate on the Family', *House of Lords Weekly Hansard*, No. 1041, London, HMSO, pp. 15–122.
Hart, N. (1976), *When Marriage Ends*, London, Tavistock.
Hobsbawm, E. J. (1977), *The Age of Capital*, London, Abacus.
Home Office (1979), *Marriage Matters*, London, HMSO.
Houghton Report (1972), *Report of the Departmental Committee on the Adoption of Children*, London, Cmnd 5107, HMSO.
Klein, J. (1965), *Samples from English Cultures*, vols 1, 2, London, Routledge & Kegan Paul.
Lake, T. and Hills, A. (1979), *Affairs: the Anatomy of Extra-marital Relationships*, London, Open Books.
Langner, T. S. and Michael, S. T. (1963), *Life Stress and Mental Health*, New York, Free Press.
Lasch, C. (1977), *Haven in a Heartless World. the Family Besieged*, New York, Basic Books.
Lasch, C. (1980), *The Cult of Narcissism*, London, Abacus.
Laslett, P. (1977), *Family Life and Illicit Love in Earlier Generations*, London, Cambridge University Press.
Law Commission (1980), *The Financial Consequences of Divorce: the Basic Policy, A Discussion Paper*, London, Cmnd 8041, HMSO.
Leach, E. (1967), *A Runaway World? The Reith Lectures*, London, British Broadcasting Corporation.
Leete, R. (1979), *Changing Patterns of Family Function and Dissolution 1964–1976*, Series on Medical and Population Subjects, no. 39, London, HMSO.
Leonard, D. (1980), *Sex and Generation*, London, Tavistock.

Lockwood, D. (1975), 'Sources of variation in working-class images of society', in Bulmer, M. (ed.), *Working Class Images of Society*, London, Routledge & Kegan Paul, pp. 16–31.
McCann-Erikson (1977), *'You Don't know Me': a survey of youth in Britain*, London, McCann Erikson.
Maddox, B. (1975), *The Half Parent*, London, André Deutsch.
Marris, P. (1958), *Widows and their Families*, London, Routledge & Kegan Paul.
Marsden, D. (1969), *Mothers Alone: Poverty and the Fatherless Family*, London, Allen Lane.
Mayer, J. E., and Timms, N. (1970), *The Client Speaks*, London, Routledge & Kegan Paul.
Mead, M. (1970), 'Anomalies in American post-divorce relationships', in Bohannan, P. (ed.), *Divorce and After*, New York, Anchor Books, pp. 132–46.
Mills, C. W. (1967), *The Sociological Imagination*, London, Oxford University Press.
Morgan, D. H. J. (1975), *Social Theory and the Family*, London, Routledge & Kegan Paul.
Morgan, D. H. J. (1981), 'Berger and Kellner's construction of marriage', Occasional Paper Number 7, Dept of Sociology, University of Manchester.
Murch, M. (1980), *Justice and Welfare in Divorce*, London, Sweet & Maxwell.
Newson, J. and Newson, E. (1972), *Patterns of Infant Care in an Urban Community*, Harmondsworth, Penguin.
Newson, J. and Newson, E. (1976), *Seven Years Old in the Home Environment*, Harmondsworth, Penguin.
Nicholson, J. (1980), 'Is there really a mid-life crisis?', *New Society*, vol. 53, no. 927, 21 August 1980, pp. 355–7.
Nicholson, J. (1981), *The Seven Ages of Man*, Glasgow, Fontana.
Nye, I. (1957), 'Child adjustment in broken and in unhappy and unbroken homes', *Marriage and Family Living*, November 1957, pp. 356–61.
Oakley, A. (1974), *The Sociology of Housework*, London, Martin Robertson.
Oates, N. (1980), 'When she is older than he is', *Good Housekeeping*, June.
Office of Population Censuses and Surveys, *Social Trends 1977, Social Trends 1981*, London, HMSO.
Pahl, J. M. and Pahl, R. E. (1971), *Managers and their Wives*, London, Allen Lane, The Penguin Press.
Parsons, T. and Bales, R. F. (1955), *Family, Socialisation and the Interaction Process*, New York, Free Press.
Perry, J. B. and Pfuhl, E. H. (1963), 'Adjustment of children in "solo" and "remarriage" homes', *Marriage and Family Living*, May, pp. 221–3.
Pfleger, J. (1947), 'The "Wicked Stepmother" in a Child Guidance Clinic', *Smith College Studies in Social Work*, no. 17, pp. 125–6.
Plummer, K. (1975), *Sexual Stigma*, London, Routledge & Kegan Paul.
Podolsky, E. (1955), 'The emotional problems of the step-child', *Mental Hygiene*, vol. 39, pp. 49–53.

Rapoport, R. and Rapoport, R. (1975), *Leisure and the Family Life Cycle*, London, Routledge & Kegan Paul.
Rapoport, R., Rapoport, R. and Strelitz, Z. (1977), *Fathers, Mothers and Others*, London, Routledge & Kegan Paul.
Rauta, I. and Hunt, A. (1975), *Fifth Form Girls: their Hopes for the Future*, London, HMSO.
Reed, A. (1973), *The Challenge of a Second Marriage*, London, Ward Lock.
Rex, J. (1974), 'Capitalism, elites and the ruling class', in Stanworth, P. and Giddens, A. (eds), *Elites and Power in British Society*, London, Cambridge University Press, pp. 202–20.
Rooseveldt, R. and Lofas, J. (1976), *Living in Step*, New York, Stein & Day.
Rosenbaum, H. (1978), *Familie als Gegenstuktur zur Gesellschaft: kritik grundlegender theoretischer Ansätze der westdeutscher familiensoziologie*, vol. 2, Überarbeitete Auflage, Stuttgart, Enke Verlag.
Rosenburg, M. (1968), 'The broken family and the adolescent self-image', in Heiss, J. (ed.), *Family Roles and Interaction: an Anthology*, New York, Rand McNally, pp. 447–63.
Schlesinger, B. (1970), 'Remarriage and family re-organisation for divorced persons – a Canadian study, *J. Comp. Fam. Studs.*, pp. 102–17.
Schulman, G. L. (1972), 'Myths that intrude on the adaptation of the step-family', *Social Casework*, vol. 53, pp. 131–9.
Sennett, R. (1977), *The Fall of Public Man*, London, Cambridge University Press.
Simon, A. W. (1964), *Step-child in the Family: a View of Children in Re-marriage*, New York, Odyssey Press.
Smith, W. C. (1953), *The Step-child*, Chicago, University of Chicago Press.
Stacey, M. (1960), *Tradition and Change*, London, Oxford University Press.
Stacey, M. (1975), *Power, Persistence and Change*, London, Routledge & Kegan Paul.
Statham, D. (1978), *Radicals in Social Work*, London, Routledge & Kegan Paul.
Thomson, H. (1967), *The Successful Step-parent: a Practical Guide*, London, W. H. Allen.
Thornes, B. and Collard, J. (1979), *Who Divorces?*, London, Routledge & Kegan Paul.
Tufte, V. and Myerhoff, B. (1979), *Changing Images of the Family*, New Haven, Yale University Press.
Tybring, J. B. (1974), 'Remarriage: parenting someone else's children', *The Single Parent*, vol. XVII.
Visher, E. B. and Visher, J. S. (1979), *Stepfamilies*, New York, Brunner/Mazel.
Voysey, M. (1975), *A Constant Burden*, London, Routledge & Kegan Paul.
Walker, K. N., Rogers, J. and Messinger, L. (1977), 'Remarriage after divorce: a review', *Social Casework*, pp. 276–85.

Weiss, R. (1975), *Marital Separation*, New York, Basic Books.
Westergaard, J. and Resler, H. (1975), *Class in a Capitalist Society*, London, Heinemann Educational Books.
Wilson, E. (1977), *Women and the Welfare State*, London, Tavistock.
Wilson, K. L. *et al*. (1975), 'Step-fathers and step-children: an exploratory analysis from two national surveys', *J. Marr. and the Family*, vol. 37, pp. 526–35.
Wolff, S. (1973), *Children under Stress*, 2nd edn, Harmondsworth, Penguin.
Woolf, M. (1971), *Family Intentions*, London, HMSO.
Young, M. and Willmott, P. (1956), 'Social grading by manual workers', *Brit. J. Sociology*.
Young, M. and Wilmott, P. (1973), *The Symmetrical Family*, London, Routledge & Kegan Paul.
Zaretsky, E. (1976), *Capitalism, the Family and Personal Life*, London, Pluto Press.

Index